Wally Hammond

The Reasons Why

a biography by
David Foot

Robson Books

This edition published in 1998 by Robson Books Ltd
First published in Great Britain in 1996 by Robson Books Ltd, Bolsover House, 5-6 Clipstone Street, London W1P 8LE

British Library Cataloguing in Publication Data
A catalogue record for this title is available from the British Library

ISBN 1 86105 125 5

Set in Plantin by Pitfold Design, Hindhead, Surrey.
Printed and bound in Finland by W.S.O.Y.

To Julia, with love

This book is, overall, an affectionate portrait of someone who brought so much joy to the game yet appeared to find too little of it himself away from the crease.

A Photograph of Hammond

Alan Ross

Even at I/500th you can't freeze him,
Make his image quite static.
He remains more mobile than diagrammatic.

Take compass, protractor. However
You dismantle him, the parts
Remain true, suggest velocity.

Leonardo would have made him fly,
This batsman so revving with power
He seems airborne.

Like some prototype birdman
Straining at silk moorings, he conveys
Ambiguity, both imprisonment and release.

Never mind the earthbound heaviness
Of hip, of shoulders, his cover-drive
Evokes airiness, an effortless take-off.

A study in anatomy, circa 1930. Anonymous.
But there, nonchalantly stuffed
In his pocket, that blue handkerchief signs it.

Contents

Acknowledgements ix

PART I COMPLEXES AND ILLNESSES

All Those Questions 3

Concern at the Quayside 18

Tour Triumph – and Trauma 23

Bedside Whispers 36

PART II BOY AND MAN

Mystery of the School Holidays 59

Chasing Down the Wing 73

PART III THE CRICKETER

County Days Between the Wars 85

The Test Match Career: Bodyline and All 108

Technique of a Prince 123

PART IV RIVALRIES

The Spectre of Bradman 143

Charlie's Not My Darling 161

PART V THE WOMEN

Distractions of the Flesh 171

Contrasting Wives 186

PART VI GRADUAL DECLINE
Not a Bad War 203
One Tour Too Many 213
No Head For Business 228
Posthumous Charity 241
Redressing the Balance 259

Facts at a Glance 275

Bibliography 277

Index 279

Acknowledgements

This book has been in my head for a long time. Research, in effect, began some years ago. I talked to dozens of Wally Hammond's contemporaries and many of them are alas now dead. They were all unfailingly helpful – and honest in their appraisals.

I am grateful to all the players and officials who gave me their time and their opinions. They included Gubby Allen, David Allen, Leslie Ames, H J Hampden Alpass, Charles Barnett, Alec Bedser, A H (Podge) Brodhurst, Donald Carr, Sam Cook, Jack Crapp, Godfrey Evans, Ken and Tom Graveney, Roly Jenkins, Trevor Jones, George Lambert, Arthur Milton, Grahame Parker, Reg Sinfield, Andy Wilson, R E S Wyatt, John Warr and Graham Wiltshire.

Gloucestershire CCC kindly gave me access to their records; their diligent archivist, Bert Avery, was as good-natured as ever. I had interviews with numerous medical men, specialising in diverse parts of the body – from the head to the groin. I much appreciated their professional assistance and background knowledge. In particular, I thank Dr Malcolm Campbell, Dr Richard Bernard, Dr C J G Franklin, Dr John Bush, Dr Ken Smith, Dr Michael Apter and Mr Andrew Ball, a consultant urologist.

A cricket writer is wise to enlist a couple of wise, conscientious 'umpires' to keep an eye on his factual line and length. The admirably watchful David Smith, of Corsham, and Keith Ball, of Bristol, maybe aware of my natural fallibility when it comes to the game's sacrosanct statistics, have reassured me with their hovering presence.

Several years ago, HTV made a fascinating and under-praised documentary on Hammond. It so happened that I did the preliminary research for the programme. The producer, Derek Clark, generously let me see a transcript of the various interviews, including material that wasn't used. I am grateful to him and his programme consultant, Christopher Douglas, himself a cricket biographer, as well as an actor. My gratitude to the late Bert Williams, one-time trainer of Bristol Rovers and a father-figure to Wally, will be evident from the text.

A substantial number of the illustrations came from my own collection, some donated to me by the late George Baker, once my respected sports editor on an evening paper in Bristol. Others came from the Warwickshire County Records Office, and I thank the archivist. I also value those kindly lent me by Mr W L A Coleman.

Calls to distinguished writers like John Woodcock and E W Swanton were never in vain. I insatiably milked the memories of Bill Bowes on his boundary walks between innings and deadlines. Scyld Berry and David Frith were, as ever, helpful.

And there were so many others who assisted me with an elusive fact, a distant insight, a reminiscence. I list them in no more than alphabetical order – and thank them equally: Ken Brown, Mrs Jean Blowen, Mrs 'Peggy' Barnett, David Cardew, Eustace Crawley, Bill Curtis, Nico Craven, Mrs Betty Collins, David Cardew, Ralph Domican, Jim Gazzard, Miss E M Gough, Stephen Green (Lord's), Mrs Norah Guest, Mervin Harris, Eric Hill, Col. Bill Hooper, Mrs Iris Hutchings, Clement and Alec Maslin, E G Morgan-Fletcher, Bill Mountjoy, Mrs G Munday, Mick Pope, Ally Phillips, E C A Roberts, Cyril Savage, Mrs Margaret Sealey, Mrs Eileen Sims, Gerard Sullivan, Jimmy Thomas, Frank Twiselton, Mrs Yvonne Tyler, Michael Williams and Tex Woodward.

I am particularly grateful to Alan Ross for allowing me to include his poem, 'A Photograph of Hammond', from *Blindfold Games*, published by Collins/Harvill, 1988.

In conclusion, there was my family to lift the spirits when a few self-doubts were threatening to surface: Anne, Mark and Vivien, Julia and David . . . and six grandchildren.

PART I

COMPLEXES AND ILLNESSES

All Those Questions

It was never intended that this should be in any sense a conventional biography of Wally Hammond. There have already been two of these, contrasting in style and treatment, conscientiously researched and written, by Ronald Mason and Gerald Howat. Each contains a comprehensive account of the great cricketer's exceptional deeds at the wicket and his Test achievements; there are also intermittent insights into the uneven emotional contours of his life. Yet much has, it seems to me, always been left unexplained. What follows is more an attempt to interpret the paradoxes and the darker mental caverns which dogged and distracted him.

Hammond was, we all accept, a wonderful player. If only he could have been goaded somehow or other to shed his innate stubbornness and bowl more often, he could have been one of the greatest allrounders in the history of the game. Bob Wyatt was one of many perceptive judges who considered him capable of regularly taking more than a hundred wickets in a season; as it was, on the self-imposed paucity of evidence, Hammond had every reason to be mentioned in the same breath as Sobers as an allrounder. They even held almost exactly the same number of Test catches, mainly at slip. Such evaluations of his cricketing prowess are not my central interest here – though I, like many others, would like to know why he chose to station himself in the slips for endless overs while a succession of captains, not least Gloucestershire's normally persuasive Bev Lyon, looked yearningly and in vain in his direction. In the following pages I have tried to explore facets of his fundamentally withdrawn character and complicated psyche. Here surely is something of more absorbing interest. Why, for a person frequently surrounded by sycophants as well as genuine, doting admirers, was he for much of his career a solitary and even friendless figure?

Dozens of people I spoke to – some his confidants – said without a moment's prompting or any suggestion of what the lawyers call a leading question: 'He was famous and fêted. But he also struck us as a sad figure, unloved as well as worshipped . . . and a loner.' This opinion, expressed in different ways, was offered with no vindictive relish. Usually it was accompanied by a gentle shaking of the head, as if it was beyond the speaker's comprehension. 'Loner' was used most of all. The term is somewhat ambiguous, but it can often be interpreted as a euphemism for a deeply, if privately, unhappy person.

Why did so many of his dressing-room contemporaries fail to warm to him? Distance is inclined to soften sentiments of that kind, in the way we end up eulogising old rascals at their funerals. But a number of Hammond's team-mates continued to express reservations about him for years afterwards. Some still do today. In one or two cases I was shaken by the measure of disaffection.

Why, as a senior player and then a captain, was Wally so sparing in his praise and encouragement of young, emerging cricketers? That was embarrassingly apparent at both county and Test level. How often, when they needed it most, did he slap that ebullient cockney George Lambert or the blond, striving, inhibited Colin Scott on the back as they perspired in unison for Gloucestershire? It was hard to know what they needed more – a timely compliment or some seam back-up from Hammond himself.

Ask Alec Bedser about the absence of a few kindly words which would have elevated the spirit on his nervous debut as a Test bowler. Or ask, if you could – as I did before they died – some of the journeymen pros from the West Country. 'You'd have liked a bit of praise when you'd had a good day. Usually he was changed and gone before we had our boots off. Hardly ever stayed for a drink with us.'

And why was he so defensive in life? Journalists were inclined to have an unproductive time with him, the Australian press most of all, especially during that wretched and misconceived Antipodean tour of 1946-47. He had his favourites, but he never really knew how to handle reporters' questions. At times he took a patronising view of popular journalism, even though the writers were far less intrusive then. This was a period when they were still being encouraged by their sports editors to express their own views, and did not have to submerge their match reports in the often meaningless quotes and indiscretions of those in charge of teams.

In Bristol there were one or two cricket writers Hammond confided in. They had nice accents and carried social clout in the city. He could be brusque to some of the others, desperately in need of basic information for their evening papers. A former sports editor of mine, who had covered cricket at Nevil Road before and immediately after the war, told me: 'Wally could be very difficult. At times we were almost afraid of approaching him. We idolised him as a player – but did well to get anything at all from him off the field.'

I worked for a weekly paper in the West Country in 1946. I saw him seldom, and never professionally, but occasionally dared to slip a line or two about him into my greenhorn reports. Once I was rebuked for presumptuously referring to 'Wally' Hammond. 'The style on this paper is WALTER Hammond', I was told.

Len Hutton always called him Walter, but then Hutton always did things correctly in the social sense. Hammond's own books were 'by Walter R Hammond.' That appeared to take matters altogether too formally for my liking. To a nation of schoolboy devotees he was indisputably just 'Wally'.

Why was he a snob? The background was at first humble military; he was academically nondescript at grammar school and then went off to try his luck as an underpaid professional footballer for a season or two as he qualified for county cricket. His voice in those days was lightly touched by the Hampshire vowels he'd picked up while living in Southsea, and a little later by the soft burr of the Berkeley Vale, which he acquired when staying with school friend and future team-mate, Billy Neale on the farm during the holidays from school in Cirencester.

But as his cricketing genius began to flower he became

increasingly drawn to the outward trappings of middle-class country living. He began dressing well and bought his first car before he could realistically afford it. He liked going to expensive dances and finding partners who wore expensive and fashionable gowns despite the looming Depression. He went on to drink with wealthy businessmen. He paid homage, in conversation and print, to the game's lofty elite. His undisguised regard for Sir Pelham Warner (MCC President 1939–45) never lessened, though this may have been influenced by the paternal and kindly way he had been treated by 'Plum' in the 'black months' of 1926. Bev Lyon was an unspoken role-model: not so much because he was a rare visionary in terms of first-class cricket but because he drove a Rolls, gave the best parties and always had a stack of notes in his breast pocket. Wally wore a flamboyant trilby to be like him. He copied Lyon's trademark of the blue-silk handkerchief peeping out of the hip trouser pocket.

Why did he have to prove himself all the time socially? It was evident to those who knew him best. They noticed how successfully he discarded the gaucheness of his Cirencester Grammar School days, the studied refinement of his vowels. What a pity acquisition of these graces was not complemented by a less remote persona as he assumed power in the dressing rooms. There was rarely more than a cursory 'Good morning'. In moments of self-analysis, he acknowledged that he was incorrigibly moody. Team-mates used to say that on the occasional days when he arrived at the County Ground with cool smile and greeting he had had a productive night.

'See Wally?', his mischievous county colleague Charlie Parker would whisper. 'Must have dipped his wick last night.' It was possibly true. But one never really knew. Hammond's private life was not shared. He boasted about neither his cricket nor his conquests. Before, during and after his first marriage, he drove away from the ground on his own at the end of the day's play for what were assumed to be clandestine meetings. Speculation was rife among the players; hardly ever was there confirmation of a specific liaison.

It was Parker, the county's socialist philosopher, who one day turned to Tom Goddard and said: 'Wally's a deep bugger.'

Goddard had known Hammond well since the early 1920s. There was a sort of constant, pragmatic friendship between them. They used to room and share a lift to the ground together; one or two of the pros rather resented the unlikely mateyness and wondered at times whether dressing-room politics were at work.

It's unlikely. Big Tom, a taciturn Gloucester man whose most assertive moments came when, in cathedral-style bass, he appealed for LBW, was out of Wally's class and aspirations when it came to the parties and the evenings of cut-glass grandeur. Goddard was happy for a pint of draught and then home to the carpet shop in Barton Street, to tell his wife of his half dozen wickets. Some of the players used to say, no doubt unfairly, that Hammond used Tom to pick up undercurrents and apprehensions from the dressing room.

In the language of pulp fiction, Hammond had a dark side. It manifested itself in the brooding eyes, the self-induced solitude, the uncommunicative nature. His life, touched by genius on the cricket field, was elsewhere strewn with failure: in business, in human relationships, in the relative obscurity of his later years in South Africa. His last abortive appearance for Gloucestershire, ill advised and monumentally embarrassing, remained hurtful to him. He cocooned himself in a state of unyielding privacy. He chose not to tell his friends what he did in his spare time. Nor did he have anything revealing, or even very interesting, to say about himself in his books. Some of them were well written: but not by himself. His first, *Cricket My Destiny*, published in 1946, was the best-selling book of its kind at that time. But do 'ghosts' have to give themselves away so easily? Here, in his follow-up, *Cricket My World*, is purportedly Hammond's description of Learie Constantine's confrontation with Bedser in a war-time match at Lord's, the Dominions against England:

'Bedser was the man to act the tempting Mephistopheles – and Bedser it was who dangled the ball in the air in front of the West Indian's flashing bat that sometimes seems to smile, too . . . .'

And so on. I've no wish to take a condescending view of medieval mythology as taught at Cirencester, but I can't see even a gullible public believing that Hammond would want to introduce devil-trading into an uncomplicated cricket match. Maybe Cardus: but I'm not so sure he was too adept in the classics either!

Myths and remembered rumours surfaced as I talked to friends, players and dozens of acquaintances during the preparation for this book. 'You know his real trouble, don't you?' some of my informants would confide: 'It was drink.' They would say it with an air of finality. It is true to say that I was told this, by varied contacts, 20 or 30 times.

There were the occasions when, it was said, he had had to be driven home from official banquets; the roistering with his first wife's wealthy father on trips to Yorkshire; the episodes of almost constant inebriation during the war years; the near-fatal car crash that could be put down to heavy drinking. 'Just look at his fleshy, dissolute appearance after the war. Booze was more of a distraction than women', was the verdict of many.

It was a verdict that gained strength. But in truth I can find little evidence to support it. The fact is that Wally Hammond could drink most people under the table. If he drank excessively a few times during the war, who would wish to blame him? If he was known to put away the strong West Country ales into the small hours, with the farmers, at the Prince of Wales on the A38 – they used to call the pub 'The Kicker' – he staggered back to Billy Neale's farm with no greater difficulty or less good humour than the rest of them.

He was certainly a big drinker. Long before he was 20, probably before he'd left school, he was gulping down farmhouse cider, made even more potent after six pounds of raw beef had been dropped into the barrels. There may have been only fleeting signs of the romantic in him, but he loved being one of the countrymen, faces flushed, rough cotton sleeves rolled up, sitting in the corner of the fireplace and taking audacious, big sips from a two-handled china mug. The Neales playfully encouraged him – and came to admire his capacity.

When he first worked in a car showroom in Bristol, in the winter months, he regularly went out for a Saturday lunchtime drink. As a former works colleague remarked, 'Wally would sink five pints on average. No trouble at all, I never once saw him the worst for drink'. His fellow county cricketers said the same.

He was a democratic drinker. At a cocktail party, he liked his gin. At the family homes in Failand and in Knole Park, at Almondsbury, near Bristol, there were always empty whisky bottles in the rubbish bin. They may not all have been emptied by him alone. This was a childless and thirsty home. During his years in South Africa he gravitated more to wine. What is certain is that strong drink had nothing to do with his road accident there. Nor, as far as I know, was he ever belligerent, indiscreet or in any other way obnoxious as a result of his drinking.

E M Wellings was an outspoken cricket writer, not always popular by any means with the players. He used to watch them on tour at close quarters and some of his more trenchant opinions about their cricket, and occasionally their behaviour, could anger them. He recalled one party at Victor Harbour, an Australian surfing beach not far from Adelaide. It clearly surprised him that Hammond was 'the life and soul of the party'. This suggests that someone who wasn't gregarious by nature could still be, if he chose, an affable companion in the evening. Wellings wrote: 'He was a steady whisky drinker but it seemed to have little effect on him'.

We can clearly reject now any lingering notion that Hammond had a long-standing alcohol problem which affected his judgment and accounted for his moods. We must look deeper than that. At the same time we must attempt to balance our reservations about his withdrawn personality and misanthropic moments with a sympathetic understanding of what seems unquestionably to have been an unfulfilled life. Maybe he never recovered from the rootlessness of his youth, the loss of a father in the war, the elusive search for a domestic rock – not helped by a restless libido – social confusion and an inability to equate fame with friendship.

His real friends remained unwaveringly loyal to him. Les Ames, the great Kent and England wicket-keeper/batsman, was the staunchest of companions. He appeared to worship Wally. Ames was a good and gentle man, and his choice of friends should not be discounted. Bill Edrich defended Hammond – though, the cynic might say, so he should have. Edrich kept his England place at the behest of his captain, whatever the statistics and suspect form might have suggested. Godfrey Evans, Ames' successor behind the stumps for Kent and England, was another to extol his virtues and do his best to restore a tattered reputation. Denis Compton was less generous.

Within the county side, Wally had few intimates. He liked, envied and aped Bev Lyon, and only wished he was half as articulate. Tom Goddard was as close as any of the pros got. Charlie Barnett was a friend at first, until they fell out – and seldom traded a mutual term of warmth again.

We can safely omit the name of the New Zealander Charlie Dacre from any 'inner circle' of Hammond confidants. Here was another man with some kind of mountain of complexes resting on his sturdy shoulders. He was the son of a harbourmaster, strong in the forearms and in his language. His first visit here was with the New Zealanders on their opening tour in 1927. He had the explosive knack of hitting hundreds at great, not always elegant, speed. Gloucestershire liked the look of him; Hammond was unconvinced.

Dacre's cavalier approach wasn't always in the team's interest. He was apt to give his wicket away at crucial moments. The chemistry between him and Hammond, who perhaps resented this Kiwi upstart flashing his bat at everything, could be quite ugly: even without a word being said. In a match at Cheltenham in 1934, when Dacre was wicket-keeper, Wally showed a rare eager willingness to bowl – but he appeared far more intent on curtailing the playing career of the stumper than the Sussex tailenders.

The incident was a rare show of petulance. Most people said Hammond's temperament was one of his great strengths. He bristled when he got bruised by the West Indians, Constantine and Martindale. He glared and probably harboured uncharitable thoughts for a long time when in the 1946 Test at Brisbane Bradman was considered to have been caught by Jack Ikin but didn't walk. But for most of the time there was an immutable phlegm about him. The emotions, like his private life, were hidden away.

It was Stan McCabe, that fine Australian batsman, who described him as 'the perfect cricketer, someone who did everything with the touch of a master.' The perfect cricketer:

there could be no greater compliment from such a source. So why, why, *why* was life so cruelly imperfect for him?

* * *

Maybe it's time to ask another question. Why the compulsion, on my part, to write about Hammond? After all, I saw him play only a few times, and then on Bank Holidays when his imperious off-drives were relegated in my imagination and schoolboyish idolatry as no more than pale imitations of those sweet cover boundaries from Somerset's opener, Harold Gimblett, then my especial hero.

Gloucestershire were never warmly embraced at Taunton. It was rather more than neighbourly rivalry, something to do with the collective personalities of the two teams. I can certainly remember more smiles from the Somerset players as they cantered round the field in vain pursuit of the ball. Bill Andrews once told me: 'We didn't much enjoy our matches with Gloucestershire. They were such miserable sods. I'd pop my head into their dressing room before play started to wish them good morning. It seemed to me that dear old Reg Sinfield was the only one who came back with any kind of greeting.'

The gut reactions of the famously flamboyant Andrews were often extreme, as scathing as they could be wonderfully generous in spirit. Individually, there were in those distant days some delightful members of the Gloucestershire side. But when you put them altogether and took them off to Taunton, their eyes glazed over and they could appear joyless. That at least was my impression, as a partisan Somerset native.

Jewish blood brothers, Bev and Dar Lyon, bared their teeth on one occasion, when Sinfield stone-walled interminably under orders and Gloucestershire won. Wally, like many of the finest stroke-makers, relished the Taunton wicket – and the food at The Castle. He had few friends within the Somerset club; indeed there was never much conviviality before or after matches.

It was Andrews himself who momentarily rearranged the chemistry. He was bowling at his own county ground, on a length, when Hammond braced the shoulders and hit him straight for six. It was the most exquisite and effortless of drives, demonstrating sublime mastery over a good county bowler who had done nothing wrong. The spontaneous reaction of Andrews was to shake his head in unreserved admiration and to applaud for ten seconds or more.

I have no idea whether Hammond noticed. The laconic Jack White, Somerset's captain, did. He walked slowly from mid-off and rebuked Andrews. Farmers from the Quantocks and beyond went to market and didn't concede sentimental ground when it came to buying a steer. Nor did bowlers go soft when opposing batsmen hit them for six. 'I didn't openly applaud Wally again although there were times when I wanted to, mostly off my bowling,' Andrews used to tell me. 'But Wally didn't return the compliment,' he'd joke. 'I'm pretty sure he vetoed my chance of playing for England just before the war.'

This isn't predominantly a cricket book, so my painfully limited experience of Hammond's batting is not important. By the time I first saw him, just after the war, the marvellous athleticism was disappearing. He had put on weight and, from my close-range observations at the lunch and tea breaks, the face was already looking middle-aged and blotchy. Was this 'the Bristol Prince' they used to talk so poetically about, I asked myself. Yet I still stood in fifth-form awe, just a few feet away, as he walked back onto the field. Tom Graveney and others talk unselfconsciously of how they worshipped him, of that extraordinary *presence,* and I know exactly what they mean.

I suppose I have wanted to write at length about Hammond since the mid-1950s, when I arrived to work in Bristol. That was when I first met Bert Williams, the Bristol Rovers FC trainer (or sponge-man, as these soccer craftsmen were still evocatively called). As a boy he'd steered the horse for his groundsman-father, Alf, to cut and roll the grass at the Eastville ground. By the 1919-20 season he was assistant groundsman himself. Bert was to live in a house just a few yards from a corner-flag. It was proudly painted in the club's colours of blue and white. Rovers never had a more loyal servant; he was with them for well over half a century. Hammond, who at school had shown exceptional gifts as a footballer as well as a cricketer, had signed forms for Rovers in 1921. Bert immediately took on a paternal role, which in fact continued when Hammond left football and concentrated solely on his cricket. Bert's wife did his laundry for 'a couple of bob a week'. There was always a pile of washing – the earliest signs of a clean and fastidious dresser were beginning to emerge.

Hammond had not benefited from a father who was emotionally close to him. There had been the strange nomadic army life in impersonal quarters. Then there had just been his mother. The gentle relationship between Wally and Bert could not have been more timely. Here was someone to confide in: whether about his sporting aspirations or the disturbing complexes of his emotional life. I gained the impression that Hammond talked more candidly to Williams than to anyone else in his whole life. The Rovers man was simple and yet wise. He was strong on human nature, with a sly East Bristol sense of humour.

'That's a smart old banger you've got, Wally. All the boys are envious of you. And they know why you've bought it.'

'Why's that then, Bert?'

'To take out them girls from the Prince's, the Hippodrome or the Empire in Old Market.'

Hammond would laugh. As ever, he gave nothing away. But his car, such a rarity among poorly paid young pros, would be spotted outside the local theatres late at night, as he waited for the chorus girls to do their final number and chase out of the stage door in perfumed high spirits. His romantic interest in one particular dancer was vaguely known to the Rovers boys.

The other players were never sure what to make of him. 'This lad's got something about him. But he won't stick to this – it's going to be cricket,' Bert told them. He himself puzzled over the enigmatic personality. It wasn't that Hammond was a good talker or particularly sophisticated, but his ambition, his eagerness to better himself socially, impressed Williams. And the handsome features appealed to the chorus girls.

It was from Bert I first heard of the nature of Hammond's illness during the 1925-26 tour of the West Indies. Before that I had read about the mosquito bites and hadn't paid too much attention to them. They didn't seem of any great relevance. Gradually I became aware of the innuendoes, the whispers behind the hand, the odious hints.

Long ago I thought about discussing the episode in print, and decided it was really no business of mine. Now, however, I have chosen to explore the illness and its medical and psychological after-effects at some length because I am convinced it helps us to understand our subject better. The biographer who researches and tries to interpret in depth a specific subject's actions is bound to be confronted at some time with the nagging question: are these words, is this conclusion, morally defensible?

I base my findings about Hammond's illness on admittedly flimsy medical evidence. The nursing-home records have been destroyed. Any references in the county's minutes have either been discreetly put aside or, more likely, expurgated. Some of his associates and friends outside the game refused to be forthcoming on this topic. There was loyalty in their silence. Against this I had conversations with relatives and friends of those who played alongside Hammond on that ill-fated tour of the West Indies. I spoke to cricket officials, to scores of pre-war players – from Gloucestershire and around the country – and they, almost without exception, confirmed my conclusions. This volume of concurrence surely adds up to something weightier than mere hearsay and rumour-mongering. Hammond nearly died – and it is time we asked why.

My long and intimate chats with Bert Williams, latterly just before his death in the old True Blue clubhouse at Eastville Stadium, where whisky-in-milk was his only apparent sustenance, have taken some years to reach print. 'Tell Wally's story truthfully and with affection', he had requested.

* * *

On a Monday in March 1969, I went on my own initiative as a freelance writer and cricket sentimentalist to an auction of Hammond items at the Cambray Auction Galleries in Cheltenham. It was a ghastly experience. I remember coming out, sitting in my little Ford Popular, and bursting into tears. Possibly that makes me a pathetic journalist but I hope it will not embarrass the reader. I think it was the only time I cried over my work. I then wrote a piece for the *Guardian*. The sub-editor didn't touch the copy. He put up a heading 'MEMENTOES OF HAMMOND SCORE £1,500 IN AN HOUR' and attributed the story to 'Our Correspondent'.

They were the first words I ever got into the *Guardian*. Journalistic baptisms are cherished and cuttings retained. Part of my report read:

> Guilt hung heavy in the Cheltenham auction room and the county ties remained discreetly out of sight. Not that the cricket addicts and sentimentalists who went along to pay for their memories had reason to feel guilty.
>
> The catalogue told us clearly that the auction was at the bidding of Mrs Sybil Hammond. Her late husband, 85 times a Test cricketer for England, was Wally Hammond, possibly the greatest allrounder of them all. And it was his mementoes that were being sold – the silver cigar box and tankards, the prints he once treasured.
>
> The inscriptions made one heady with nostalgia: 'To Wally Hammond from fellow members of the MCC team in Australia 1928-29 on the occasion of his marriage'. . . . 'In appreciation of our skipper, MCC-South African tour 1938-39'. And so on.
>
> Whichever lot you looked at, an immortal name was there: Warner and Jardine, Paynter and Pataudi, Hobbs and Sutcliffe, Hendren, Leyland and Larwood.
>
> It took just over an hour of strangely unemotional bidding. The memories cost £1500 and the pale-faced, unathletic cricket historians, weaned on *Wisden* and remote-control homage to the taciturn Hammond, shuffled away for their trains, nursing a small, cherished prize and murmuring that prices were high.
>
> There were few signs of Gloucestershire CCC committee members but perhaps some kindly West Country benefactors were buying mementoes for the county ground in Bristol where he stroked his maiden century in 1923.
>
> The auctioneer, who sacrilegiously confessed an ignorance of cricket, moved inexorably through the list,

> while a print of W G Grace (Lot 198), in his famous stance with toe raised, watched reprimandingly the redistribution of the treasures.
>
> Downstairs, an assistant said: 'They pay for the name, of course.' They also paid, in an inexplicable way, to purge their guilt – as cricket lovers – at the thought that the auction should have been held at all.

Mrs Hammond, then living in South Africa, didn't put in an appearance, and I was rather glad. I shouldn't have known what to ask her. The family were in a thoroughly bad way, financially.

It had seemed to me that Wally was worth more. I have a copy of the hurriedly duplicated catalogue in front of me as I write. A pewter tankard, inscribed to him from the skipper and manager, 1936-37, went for £22; a pocket spirit flask with his initials for £23. A cedar-lined cigarette box, inscribed to Wally from the Gloucestershire professionals on the occasion of his marriage, squeezed up to £54. As the marriage was Hammond's first, it is possible that Sybil, the second wife, saw the exercise as cathartic.

Most of the items had been gifts to Hammond. So many at the auction felt all the more uneasy when, for instance, a sauce boat was knocked down for just over £4, a fruit bowl for five guineas, an Edwardian engraved purse, with chain and ring, for £8 10s (shillings). True, a cigar box, inscribed to him and displaying the signatures of all the MCC team in Australia 1928-29, got to £200 – but it should have been more.

There was at least one poignant postscript to the sale. Andy Wilson, the former Gloucestershire wicket keeper who figured in an 8th wicket record stand for the county with Hammond, wandered one day into a jeweller's in Cheltenham. The director, who recognised Andy, said: 'I think I've got something here you'd like to see'. It was that lovely silver cigarette box, given to Hammond by the professionals to commemorate his wedding.

'I looked at it – and it filled me with sadness. It seemed so wrong to me that the personal possessions of such a great player should be on sale like this. I bought the cigarette box myself.'

The auction room at Cheltenham was not a pleasant place.

The ghouls were there, as well as the genuine addicts of the game. Rebuke and sympathy for Sybil Hammond were, as far as I remember, equally balanced. Many saw the auction as another cruel reflection on a devalued genius and an unfulfilled life.

Crippling financial losses have accounted for many sales and auctions that a civilised and warm-hearted society could have done without. George Sassoon, son of Siegfried, had to put the family stately home at Heytesbury in Wiltshire on the market after big reverses as a Lloyd's name. Boxer Henry Cooper, another Lloyd's victim, sat silently at the rear of the auction room as his gold and coveted Lonsdale belt went under the hammer. In Glasgow, the trophies and memorabilia of the former England footballer Ray Kennedy, suffering from Parkinson's Disease and still in his early forties, were reluctantly offered for sale. Yet I cannot be alone in believing that the niggardly £1500, picked up before commission, at the Cambray Galleries was the most melancholy scenario of all.

Almost as sad in its way was a letter printed in *The Cricketer* in the early summer of 1988. It came from Valerie Guareschi, one of Hammond's daughters from his second marriage, in South Africa. She wrote: 'Unfortunately, after the death of my father, my mother either gave away or burnt most of his things . . . . My son is very keen on cricket and of course the one thing that I really wish for is to see him become a good player. It seems such a shame not to have anything of value left of such a wonderful man. If anyone in England is in possession of anything regarding my father – trinkets, photographs etc. – I would very much like to contact them. I would like to purchase anything of my father's . . . .'

As I once attempted to write: 'Guilt hangs heavy . . . .'

Concern at the Quayside

The bells were ringing for matins on Sunday, 4 April 1926 as the *Ariguani* docked at Avonmouth.

It was the ship's maiden voyage. There was the invigorating smell of fresh paint. The light brown woodwork shimmered from elbow-greased polish, the brasses sparkled. And the captain, handsomely attired, preened himself as if inordinately proud to be carrying a team of English cricketers, even if they were not quite the best that the country could muster. He stood at the top of the gangplank to shake them all by the hand, as they stepped in a self-conscious line from the promenade deck in preparation for their descent to dry land.

Small knots of relatives, a reporter or two from the Bristol papers and stray supporters and onlookers, casual or curious, stood on the quayside. Understandably, they didn't recognise many of the players, huddled in their overcoats from the Severnside chill. That angular, distinguished-looking chap must surely be the Hon FSG Calthorpe, captain of Warwickshire and leader of the tour party. And, oh yes, that was certainly 'Tiger' Smith and the eternally affable Roy Kilner. And . . . .

But where was Wally? Mrs Marion Hammond, a striking figure formidably clothed to protect her from the early spring winds that swept in off the estuary, scanned all those bronzed faces which had for three months absorbed the baking, if fickle, Caribbean sunshine. The cricketers came down the well-scrubbed gangway, glad to be home again and, in most cases, impatient to pick up the waiting taxis for Temple Meads station in Bristol and then to head back to deserted wives and small children. Domestic loyalties and affections were already superseding the pleasant memories of an exotic, well-fetêd sporting itinerary.

Eventually Mrs Hammond spotted her son. Those supposedly stifling maternal instincts of hers caused her face to cloud instantly with concern. Wally was the last to reach the quayside, still gingerly gripping the supports as he stepped ashore. He was a shrunken figure, mostly obscured under his coat. Most of the players wore trilbies; he had a cap, wedged loosely against his ears. He looked listless and desperately ill. His mother could see that he had lost weight – as much as a stone and a half, as she discovered later. She embraced him, noting with alarm that his eyes were watery and unseeing.

'Oh, Walter, you look dreadful – whatever's the trouble?'

There was a long pause, as he appeared to be summoning up energy to speak. 'I got stung by mosquitoes out there. It's – it's left me with a terrible fever. I've been in bed for most of the journey home.' The voice was weak. Team-mates took his hand. 'This your mum?' asked the attentive Kilner. 'He's been in a reet bad way, Mrs Hammond. No proper treatment out there – and then not a doctor to be found on board.'

Freddie Calthorpe, captain of the touring party, came up to Mrs Hammond. 'Young Wally urgently needs someone to have a look at him. He's got a raging temperature. We've been giving him dozens of aspirins, which was all we could do. He wants something more than that.' It was an understatement; for much of the journey back to England, Hammond had stayed in his cabin, sweating and occasionally hallucinating. He had eaten little. When some of the other pros looked in to see him, he had waved them away. It was too much effort to talk.

His mother took him in a cab to his flat in Clifton, from where a doctor was called. As the young cricketer shivered and perspired simultaneously, slumped on his bed without either the energy or inclination to recall a single event of his first overseas tour, the GP solemnly felt the pulse and offered no more than a cursory examination. He rushed off to contact officials of Gloucestershire County Cricket Club and seek their urgent approval for a place to be found in a local nursing home. The doctor had noted alarming signs of acute delirium. Mrs Hammond snatched up clean nightwear and other essentials. Then Wally was tenderly helped down the stairs and into a waiting car.

The following day he had the first of a dozen operations of varying gravity. How can we say at this distance that one or two of them may have been superfluous, even counter-productive? The staff simply didn't know then what was wrong with him; they were working in the dark. They did their best to mask their concern every time Mrs Hammond looked pleadingly in silence towards them. One of Wally's legs had become grotesquely inflamed and it was learned later that an amputation was already being considered as a final option. His mother must have eavesdropped on the premature discussion. She had once been tardy in endorsing a livelihood in professional cricket for him; now it was her persistence, springing it would seem from intuitive thoughts of his burgeoning skills, mingled with a mother's love and panic, that ended any fears that he might have to lose a limb.

'I understand they'd almost given me up for dead at one point,' he was to tell his friends in the eventual days of recovery.

What he steadfastly didn't discuss with any of them, however well-meaning the enquiries, was the true nature of his illness: the reason for the nebulous, desultory statements from the county headquarters or the whispers which were already getting back to him. When was he first taken ill? We can't be sure. He maintained that his groin was strained while he was playing in Georgetown (British Guiana, now Guyana) in February, and that was probably quite true. Later he was said to have been bitten by mosquitoes 'in the same region', tempting one facetiously to wonder whether he was talking in the geographical or anatomical sense.

He played in the first of the three matches planned for Jamaica in March, scoring 12 and 17, moving awkwardly and in some pain, as observers in the team related. By now he was seeing a succession of doctors, who gave him conflicting advice or different treatment. None had any beneficial effect. A wise and wizened old man, working in the team hotel, told him to forget all about the recommended medics in Kingston and instead to go and see a self-taught and much revered native alchemist and counsellor. The wrinkled old man had him into his shanty surgery. He listened as the by now frightened

22-year-old listed the multiplying symptoms. He examined the much inflamed infection. And he told Wally: 'You must leave the country at once – or die.'

It all added to Hammond's growing panic. For the few remaining days of the tour, his condition worsened. He wanted little to eat. Consoling colleagues would wander into his hotel room and tell him that they, too, had been bitten by the persistent mosquitoes in the humidity of Trinidad and British Guiana. 'But not like you, Wally, you poor sod.'

One of his biographers, Ronald Mason, pondered the ambiguities and stated: 'It seems that both the origin and nature of the infection remained obscure.' Years later, Hammond himself went briefly into print on the subject. He wrote: 'I have only the vaguest memories of what followed.' He chose his words carefully and perhaps cosmetically. He adhered to the mosquito theory, though allowing that trace or two of mystery and uncertainty to remain. By now he was well aware of the rumours, but he had no intention of fuelling them.

'With the incurable optimism of youth, I would not believe, at least in the first stages, that so small a thing as a mosquito could do anything serious to me, bounding with health and fitness as I was. And when I took the thing seriously, it was almost too late . . . . My poisoning grew so steadily worse that it looked as if I should need an undertaker instead of a doctor.

'Just what sort of blood-poisoning it was I had, no one ever seemed to find out properly, and it was left to my constitution to see me through if it could. I had my first operation on the day after landing but I appeared to get worse and worse, and my life was despaired of . . . .'

People I have talked to about this passage, cricketing and medical men, unanimously concluded that there was a certain coding in Hammond's sketchy account, deliberately curtailed to a few vague paragraphs – even though the illness in the West Indies and the subsequent fight for life were the most traumatic experiences he ever went through.

The Worcestershire bowler Fred Root, who knew young Wally as well as anyone else on that tour, confined his printed thoughts to: 'Wally fell victim to a serious illness'. That looks suspiciously like tactful vagueness. 'Tiger' Smith, the

Warwickshire player, was another to write of Hammond's wretchedness in an equally vague, if eloquent, way. The party's senior pro was to say: 'I got malaria, but wasn't the only person to catch something!'

Edging somewhat closer, however euphemistically, Alan Gibson wrote: 'Early tours abroad for young and lusty cricketers are often hazardous . . . . [Hammond] nearly died because British doctors did not then know much about Caribbean infections . . . .'

It is likely that for some time only the doctors and consultants who attended him at the nursing home, an official or two from the county club who had been sworn to secrecy, and Hammond's circle of his closest mates – among them Bert Williams and Reg Sinfield – knew for sure the nature of his illness. His mother never did. Nor, of course, did the girlfriends who visited him. Nor did the thousands who were beginning to pay homage at the boundary-fences at Bristol, Gloucester and Cheltenham. To the general public, who had no idea at all how gravely ill he was, the odd paragraph in the papers – whether the *Western Daily Press* or the equally austere *Times* – it was just a matter of blood-poisoning which had maybe brought a few unexpected complications to prolong the cure.

A letter in one of the local papers, perhaps from an old soldier incapacitated by the ravages of malaria, read: 'The mosquito is a vicious creature – I can imagine what this young cricketer is going through.' But the truth was that Wally Hammond, though bitten by mosquitoes, was suffering from a far more insidious illness. He had contracted a form of syphilis or a related sexually-transmitted disease in the West Indies. Wretchedly, his body's reaction to the experimental treatment added to the tortures and uncertainties of his protracted recovery. My belief is that it permanently affected his mental make-up, his traits of character and even, up to a point, his career as one of the world's greatest cricketers.

Tour Triumph – and Trauma

Could anything have been more anti-climactic? During the summer of 1925 Hammond had fully justified the extravagant words of 'Plum' Warner. In addition to his emerging talents of batsmanship, instinctive and aesthetic, he had established himself as an allrounder – a genuine seam bowler and a superb fielder. His regard for sport was still refreshingly boyish: he enjoyed bowling, seeing it as no threat to the mental application needed for his run-making. When one of the Robinsons, Foster or Douglas respectively in terms of leadership, threw him the ball, he responded without any of the cussed indifference or reluctance that came later.

The 1925 season hadn't in truth started well for him. He scored no more than seven runs in his opening five innings. He had gone for a pair at the Oval, and that didn't often happen. Before too long, Maurice Tate also dismissed him cheaply twice in a month. All this time, Jack Hobbs was demonstrating the seemingly ageless mastery that had already spanned 18 years of Test cricket. Hobbs was in fact on his way to 16 hundreds that summer, beating W G Grace's record number of centuries en route. Young Wally idolised Hobbs, especially his cover drive.

Hammond had the temperament to play his way back into form. Ambition, particularly in the social sense, was not yet an obsession. He manifested self-confidence increasingly at the wicket, however wary he might be in a crowded room. Yet there were flaws in his early days as a county player. With the disdain of youth, he went for his shots with at times a disturbing lack of judgment. There had been too much rain and too few runs from him in 1924. His mentors at the Fry's ground in Bristol could be martinets. Those who knew him best said that he did worry, intensifying his work at the nets. By the end of the 1925 season he had scored more than 1800 runs, taken 68 wickets – a considerable improvement on his past record as a bowler – and held 65 catches, mostly in the slip area in tandem with Charlie Parker's foxy inducements to naïve batsmen. Occasionally he went into the covers. That was what the Bristol crowds liked – that was when they were most aware of his Grecian athleticism, the smooth rapidity of his running, his devastating returns to the keeper.

In the middle of August, at Old Trafford, he had a wonderful match – very much at the expense, psychologically, of Ted McDonald. The great Aussie opening bowler was feared and envied; dozens of aspiring schoolboy bowlers tried to copy the perfection of his action. In turn he demanded respect from what he saw as novice county batsmen. Hammond did not always relish sheer pace. He was apprehensive as he faced his first few overs from McDonald. But then, with an impudence rarely essayed against the Australian, Hammond began driving him off the front and back feet. It was bad for Mac's liver. He began to scowl and deliberately to pitch the ball short. Hammond, who mostly rejected the hook shot, was in glorious, contrary mood. He repeatedly leaned back to scatter the spectators behind square-leg. A handful of Manchester devotees are still around to claim they saw the six from Hammond which hit the pavilion roof that day.

This was the match when he and Alf Dipper (then almost 40) put on 330 for the third wicket. They were an unlikely pairing: Wally with his sweet natural movement and fine physical appearance, Alf with his grudging regard for coordination and quaintly limited repertoire. Hammond liked him. 'Never discount Old Dip', he used to say. 'If you want someone to stay in all day, he's your man'. If needed, Alf would stay in all week. He'd never spar or look wantonly for runs. Most of his scoring, as somnolently reliable as the old clock chimes in his native Deerhurst, were prods and pulls to leg. He was one of ten children, with the face and voice of a countryman. In his admirable county history, *Gloucestershire Road,* Grahame Parker tells the engaging, no doubt apocryphal, story of when Dipper played cricket with his young brothers in an orchard at

Deerhurst. There was an especially malignant bed of stinging nettles – and Alf would regularly pull to leg, sending the ball into the toxic reaches of the outfield as he built his improvised innings. Parker, formerly a housemaster at Blundell's School, had played for Gloucestershire – he scored a double century on one occasion – and was later president and first manager of the club.

Among the Gloucestershire chroniclers there has been a tendency to disregard Dipper because of his ungainly stance, his rejection of such niceties as the backlift and a seemingly stiff-jointed artisan approach. West Country cricket historians do well to heed the sage Hammond evaluation. It can hardly be an accident that Old Dip (did he always look gnarled and old?) scored 53 hundreds and almost 28,000 runs for his county. The Tewkesbury pubs were awash with congratulations when the customers basked in his albeit solitary Test appearance.

He made 144 in the county match against McDonald at Old Trafford. The partnership with Hammond (250 not out) took just under four hours. It was probably as animated an array of leg-side shots as Dipper ever made at county level. We can only imagine him, panting past the lithe Hammond in mid-wicket and muttering in rural supplication: 'Hure, 'old on, Wally . . . I bain't that young, yer know.'

The cricket writers, including those who fashioned their wordy prose with wing-collared punctiliousness, were by now taking an increasing interest in Hammond's career. Neville Cardus was leading the way. His viewing habits, as he snoozed or strolled at Old Trafford, could be uncertain. But he had been there when this young Gloucestershire batsman had put McDonald out of the attack. The hymnal of printed thanksgiving next day, poetically chiselled as ever, had implied that he dutifully watched every ball. There were no dissenting voices when Hammond was selected for the festival matches at Scarborough and Folkestone, as well as for The Rest against Yorkshire (taking the title for the fourth time in a row) at the Oval.

At Folkestone, playing for the Hon Lionel Tennyson's XI against Arthur Gilligan's XI he made 120 in a fairly relaxed atmosphere. Freddie Calthorpe, coming in off that comically distinctive, meandering run, bowled him, also at Folkestone, in the Gents-Players match. Soon he would be walking out behind Hons Freddie and Lionel in the West Indies sunshine.

The tour should have gone ahead 12 months earlier. Robert St Leger Fowler, a military man whose cricketing fame rested almost entirely on his deeds with bat and ball in the Eton-Harrow match at Lord's in 1910 (it was dubbed ever after as Fowler's Match), had volunteered to lead the party to the West Indies in 1924-25. But his health deteriorated, the logistics went awry and the MCC put things back for a year. Fowler had three games for Hampshire in 1925 but he was not to make the tour. By the mid-summer of 1925 he was dead, aged 34.

Such an attractive proposition as another Caribbean visit was pursued with enthusiasm, not least by those who made a habit of getting on the leisured, good-living winter jaunts. Indeed it could be argued that the composition of the eventual party was stronger on conviviality than balance. Social cliques were inevitable on these occasions and any glance at the list of amateurs suggested elements of an Old Harrovians' reunion. The pros exchanged knowing looks when they all met up. In dressing-room code, they were saying silently: 'We've got a bit of dead wood here – so we'll be doing all the bowling in that scorching heat out there. And on matting, too.'

Calthorpe broke the amateurs' pattern. He was from Repton, with a blue from all four years at Cambridge. Freddie was lean and lanky, 'a charming chap', as R E S Wyatt recalled to me with a generosity that masked erstwhile misgivings when Calthorpe, as skipper at Warwickshire, told him to stick to bowling. He was an easy mixer for much of the time and, despite demarcation lines that could be cruelly disruptive, even on tours, he got on pretty well with the professionals. They, in turn, respected him as a player. He did the double in 1920 and went on to captain England four times in official Tests. Up against the well-fleshed Tennyson back in the mid-1920s, the pros whispered merrily in their cups that Calthorpe looked positively under-nourished.

There were eight professionals on the tour. Most of them were yeoman performers, solid in achievement in this country. It still seemed odd that those who had drawn up the team had not seen the need for more than a single recognised fast bowler. George Collins, rubicund and muscular, was really the only one in the party. He played for Kent, like his father and grandfather before him; three years earlier, he'd taken all ten against Nottinghamshire at Dover.

Calthorpe and Tennyson, carrying the team between them, reckoned there was ample bowling talent around. Fred Root, with his beguiling in-swing and leg-theory, had just taken 219 wickets in a season for Worcestershire. For the off-spinner Ewart Astill, who could also turn the ball from leg, 1925 had been his best season. And wasn't there Kilner, pride of Wombwell and capable of the double four times in the 1920s, to introduce slow left-arm guile to complement his joyful native wit? Wally, too, of course, faster and more fearsome than he let on.

Kilner's Yorkshire colleague, Percy Holmes, should be full of runs after his 2453 in the season just finished, it was argued; and so should Lancashire's Frank Watson, who had ended up with three double hundreds and a triple one for his county. 'Tiger' Smith was there to keep wicket and bolster the batting. Here was experience, and 11 Tests behind him. It was rather less easy to explain why one or two of the amateurs had been invited. Doubtless, at that social level, a word in the ear often helped. When it came to some of these tours, especially the earlier ones, leisure, money and persuasive hints over the port in London clubs were frequently surefire recommendations. Cricket ability could be secondary, even at times when an overseas tour was sanctioned by MCC.

The journey out in December 1925 was inclined to be choppy, with inevitable days of widespread sea-sickness. Yet for 22-year-old Hammond such transitory distractions were obliterated by the sense of romantic adventure that lay immediately ahead of him. He was still in many ways a boy. When the pros sat side by side at the bar, he listened. There was more self-confidence from him on the field than off. But the old hands approved of the way he could already match them round-for-round. They noticed a trace or two of cockiness as the evening wore on, though they put this down to the last couple of shorts which were rather stronger than the boys' bitters he gulped down after a day in the field at Cheltenham or Gloucester. He was not boastful by nature – and the old campaigners approved of this.

They teased him gently about his girlfriends and the steady one he was supposed to have back in Bristol. 'Some of the lads say you like them show-girls when they come to your local variety theatres . . . .' They told him he was a good-looking lad and would do all right for himself out in the West Indies. Plenty of girls just starved of it. White kids, wealthy and spoilt. Dusky ones too. Got to be a bit careful, you know. But cricketers on tour have got it made. Wally was told that it was there on a plate for him. Bar-room banter.

He listened and said nothing. Never once in his life did he discuss personal matters with team-mates over drinks – or indeed anywhere else. He was, as we have indicated, a deeply private person. A girlfriend was never once mentioned by name; a conquest was never remotely gloated over. Whatever the demons that nagged away at those over-active sex glands, the knowledge and experience were not to be shared.

Lionel Tennyson was no stranger to London's late-night sybaritic terrain; his late arrivals, dishevelled and contented, at the Southampton ground for the start of play, made the point with a sense of mirth and mischief. He believed in corporate jollity. 'Lordship' busied himself during the outward journey on the *SS Inanda*, organising entertainment for the cricketers. Years later his contemporaries on that trip were still talking of the improvised orchestra he created from philistine material. Other passengers plugged their ears. Musical proficiency was virtually non-existent with the exception of Ewart Astill, who really could play the piano and was coerced into doing so with increasing frequency as the loquacious party rounded off their evenings with a sing-song.

And there was Roy Kilner, the most congenial of Yorkshiremen, to resuscitate those engaging, hoary tales of past North Country cricketers; the same tales he had trotted out a dozen times to lift a dour dressing room at Headingley or Bramall Lane. Why was it, one wonders in passing, that Yorkshiremen could appear so glum and saturnine even in the 1920s, when they were carrying off the championship pennant with perfunctory ritual?

It was going to be a happy tour, even more so if one or two of the amateurs, so far with not too much experience of the real world, would take a small democratic step down the rigid class ladder. Leonard Crawley had no inhibitions that way. He was just down from Cambridge and was no doubt pondering some sort of renewed cricketing future with Essex, following that spot of trouble over registration which caused him to leave Worcestershire. Lord Harris, notoriously eagle-eyed over matters of geographical allegiance and by nature officious, made his intractable views known to the Worcestershire committee. E W Swanton was later told by his friend, Crawley, that Worcestershire 'knew the game was up and decided to cock a snook at authority, pretending that the wire had not been delivered until the match was in progress. So Crawley had, literally, a last fine fling, making 112 out of 176 in a couple of hours or so. That, it was reckoned, would make the old meddler splutter into his tea as he read the stop-press.'

It's an appealing notion. Crawley was a wonderful cricketer and there is no knowing what, in different circumstances, he might have achieved. In a match at Leyton against Somerset, he was unusually circumspect at the start of his innings. It prompted Bill Andrews to turn to his inseparable mate, Arthur Wellard, and say: 'That bloke with the big moustache, whatever his name is, couldn't hit the skin off a rice pudding.' Wellard advised reserved judgment. 'And in the next over a couple of straight drives from Crawley screamed over my head to the boundary. Talk about approaching the green . . . .'

Bill, who became a great admirer of a man who could play the two sports, cricket and golf, with such brilliance, told me the story about the Leyton match when I edited his autobiography in the early 1970s. He also confided that he remained racked with guilt about a match some years later when he was playing briefly as a professional in Scotland. Bill was surprised to discover that Crawley was turning out for the opposition – and more so, that Crawley remembered him and shook his hand as soon as he reached the crease. 'Oh dear, I showed no gratitude at all. My first delivery reared up and cracked him very painfully around the ribs. He collapsed in a heap and it looked quite serious. I can't tell you what a relief it was when he recovered – he was playing for England in the Walker Cup the following week.'

Crawley represented his country four times in the Walker Cup. He was the English amateur champion in 1931. Eventually he chose to write about golf for a living rather than cricket; in terms of affection, it must have been a close thing. His fellow cricketers all liked him. There would have been no uneasy division between him and the professionals on the *SS Inanda*. He was a month younger than Hammond. They shared an interest in golf. Wally envied the articulate way Crawley could convey his enthusiasm for the game. They made plans for a round or two back in England. Hammond was proud of his plus-fours and his golf swing. At his best he could almost play off scratch. Gloucestershire team-mates told me they could recall the two cricketers going off with their clubs on Sundays, during Crawley's days with Essex. Some sort of friendship, however intermittent, had been built on the bumpy ride to the West Indies.

I asked Crawley's son, Eustace, what he had been told about the tour. 'My father didn't enjoy it much and didn't feel he was given too many chances.

He implied that Calthorpe and Tennyson stuck together too much. As for Hammond, I was, like my father, a tremendous admirer of him as a player.'

Hammond had assured his mother than he would treat the trip as an education. He had been told in advance that there would be ample time for sight-seeing, as well as parties and daily swimming; time to sample an entirely new culture, to savour the legends of the Caribbean islands. All his life he was, to say the least, sparing in his use of emotive language. So what made him sanction his ghostwriter's fatuous descriptive flights about his 'burning with desire to see something of the world and its people, and the glories of its seas and mountains . . . now cricket was going to take me almost to the Equator, and let me loose among the lovely islands where the buccaneers slit throats and gauded it with the black flag whickering at the main . . . . perhaps I should even discover a hidden hoard of thick gold doubloons . . . .' These somewhat flawed jewels disfigure

Hammond's first book; *Cricket My Destiny*.

But his excitement was real enough. And when he got there, all the evidence reveals how much he enjoyed, in his still gauche way, the parties and receptions, the dancing and, above all, the unrestrained flirting of the plantation owners' daughters, wives or other pretty members of the well-heeled colonial set. Back at the hotels, waiters who were toadying for tips were adept at sizing up the likeliest of the younger guests and, with furtive delight, would press addresses into receptive palms.

The carnal trade was rife in bigger towns. It was brazen and cheap. The cricket pros, most of them unworldly, would prowl the side streets, just like successive generations of gawky country lads exploring Soho for the first time. They moved in the safety of numbers, eyes popping out, enjoying the Caribbean cadences of the whispered invitations, daring and teasing each other, nothing much more. Wally used to stroll with them on these evenings of vicarious sex. The girls liked the look of him most of all. He was young and handsome. They assumed he was an affluent young Englishman and entreated him to part with his money.

In *Cricket My World*, Hammond amusingly writes of one incident:

> How well I remember my second match out there, when I made 238 not out. It was wonderful for me, barely of age and just beginning to triumph over one of the worst starts that any professional player's career ever had.
>
> I was certainly not prepared for the sequel. As I was walking back to our hotel with Fred Root, a negro pushed his way up to me, dragging at arm's length a coy black lady of about sixteen stone in weight – and she was no chicken, either.

Hammond went on to describe, in what I can only imagine was tactful language, the supposed fleshy donation on offer. Another double hundred like that, the good-natured pimp promised, and his mature, beaming companion could be Wally's – for nothing.

> She gave a bashful smile and I fled, pursued by the hysterical laughter of Fred Root. I didn't make another double century.

It was claimed years later by one of his steadier girlfriends back in Somerset that he lacked passion and a sense of romance, and that he hardly ever kissed her. On the other hand, every one of his contemporaries to whom I spoke about his interests away from the cricket field, referred – without exception and with no prodding from me – to his 'womanising'. It was not meant as criticism. But for as long as they could remember, it had always been there: the needs of the flesh. He was above all a physical creature. Almost straight from school, in his fledgling winter months with Bristol Rovers, he discovered he had the seductive body language – forget the fumbling conversation – to clinch a date with a pretty girl. He hardly ever paraded her in public. 'A secret feller was Wally with his women,' a Gloucestershire player told me more than once. 'Used to go off on his own. Never told us what was happening. But we'd see traces of lipstick on his collar.'

The older professionals with him out in the West Indies also found him 'a bit of a deep one'. On rest days or after one of the obligatory parties, he'd wander off for an hour or so on his own. 'Where've you been lad, then?' He'd grin and say: 'Just a stroll along the beach.' And they'd nod at each other: 'Ee, t'lad don't give much away . . . .'

As for the cricket, there was too much rain. Nine of the 13 fixtures were drawn. Hammond's fielding was a joy, much applauded by those who came to watch. He was by far the most athletic member of the party. When it came to batting, the matting wickets didn't appear to trouble him.

In the first of the three unofficial Tests, at Bridgetown (Barbados), only bad weather saved the West Indies from an innings defeat. The MCC got off to a marvellous start – or rather Hammond did. They scored 597-8 declared against bowling of markedly variable quality. Some of the home players looked too old for the sustained demands of the match. The young man from Gloucestershire had run straight into form, so much so that he was undefeated on 238 when the innings was declared. Tommy Jameson, as Irish as his name and probably better at rackets and squash than cricket, was out two short of his hundred, while Holmes, Astill and Smith all got past 50.

The temptation to dwell for a moment on Jameson is too

great to resist. Those traces of his Dublin brogue were prepossessing, the spirit was free. Touring was fun if you had the wherewithal; he'd gone with insouciant pleasure on S B Joel's jaunt to South Africa the previous year, and later was off with Hants team-mate Tennyson to India. There was a tour to South America, led by Pelham Warner, in between. Jameson was clearly something of a favourite of Ian Peebles, who loved telling the story of a fixture between Middlesex and Hampshire. Jameson had arrived from Ireland that morning, a trifle dishevelled, and had gone to Lord's only to watch. The carefree Irishman was hopelessly out of practice and his last net had been the previous season. But Hampshire were never averse to an extrovert amateur and Jameson found himself in the side. Peebles's first ball to him spun past his flailing bat and trimmed the bail which teetered but, helped by the wind, and to everyone's astonishment, returned to its groove. The next ball knocked over the batsman's middle stump as he sparred in comic despair. And in the second innings, the hapless, eye-weary Jameson was out first ball to Jack Durstan. As the affable Peebles used to say: 'Out three times in a match – to three balls. Must be a world record.' The benevolent pair, Peebles and Jameson, would have a drink on it whenever they met after that.

We must return to the West Indies tour. As a contest, the second 'Test' at Port of Spain, Trinidad, was by far the best of the series. MCC won by five wickets. Watson and Holmes were their top scorers; Hammond was out to a dodgy LBW for 48. But he had already made two half-centuries against Trinidad and, toward the end of February, a chanceless hundred against British Guiana at Georgetown.

Although he was missing because of his illness from the later fixtures, he still ended up in all matches with 732 runs and an average of just under 49. He bowled 205 overs and took 22 wickets at 26.4. His 15 catches were without ostentation, but still mostly brilliant. 'Plum' Warner was ecstatic, primarily about Hammond. The tour, given more respectability with a late win in Jamaica, had been voted a success. There was much favourable comment back in England about the overall improvement in the standard of West Indian cricket; full Test match status was to come in the following year. Writing in the

Morning Post, Warner said: 'Naturally a great deal will now be expected of Hammond, who must be near an England cap.'

Calthorpe reported: 'Young Hammond's fielding was quite exceptional. Nor did he give a single chance in his 238. it was a wonderful effort and took the people by storm.'

Many of the commentators made a point of how much the crowds, mostly untutored in the arcane ways of the game, enjoyed themselves. Some of the writing was couched in that unthinkingly patronising style that is perhaps even less attractive than racist cant:

> The niggers were highly amused with it [the tourists' bulldog mascot] for it occupied a prominent position at all matches . . . . These niggers will do anything to see a game of cricket. Keen almost to the point of fanaticism, they are learning to understand the game thoroughly.
>
> There is no class hatred in the Islands but sometimes there is trouble on the sugar plantations. Labour disputes and strikes are very easily settled however. When anything happens and there is a rising, or the niggers get out of hand, the employers organise a cricket match. There is nothing more attractive to the darkies . . . .

Ugh, such newspaper prose, normal and supposedly acceptable in those days, makes us now cringe. Of course there were still cruelly divisive lines. Many of the native population continued to live in primitive conditions, kow-towing still to the white-settler mentality, earning not much more than a pittance, suppressed and denied opportunity.

Yet cricket was gradually becoming a metaphor for joy and self-expression. Hammond, untouched by bigotry or the uglier strands of racial condescension that warped so much of colonial thinking, was to write: 'One of the things I shall never forget about the West Indies is the enthusiasm for cricket, which shows itself in all sorts of ways. The welcome for visiting players is tremendous and spontaneous everywhere. It is inspiring to find so many native families, groups and villages with their own matting wickets, industriously practising there all day long. I can think of no more joyous sight in the world than a village match out there.'

When he was quoted as saying: 'There is a childish innocence and kindliness about West Indians that I have not come across anywhere else on my cricketing travels', he seemed to be utterly sincere. Perhaps he was a little too ingenuous; perhaps his vision of the Islands was too easily falsified by the bulging reception tables, the well stocked cocktail cabinets and hotel pantries to which visiting cricketers were directed.

It is now time to return to Hammond's illness – the illness that confined him to his bed in Kingston and caused him to be an unfortunate absentee from those end-of-tour parties where everyone of importance wanted to see this Test player of the future.

Bedside Whispers

It is odd and significant that so little information was released from the nursing home or the county club about one of the country's most gifted and exciting young players. Retrospectively, one can appreciate how this possibly well-intentioned barrier of silence, compounded by varying degrees of unease and pomposity, only fuelled the rumours and innuendoes.

For some weeks, most of the Gloucestershire supporters did not even know that their new idol was in hospital. They had expected him to turn up for the early nets in 1926 and to be ready for the opening county fixture. But his continued absence gradually became a matter of concern. Every inquiry was diverted or answered evasively. 'Well, yes. Bitten by mosquitoes. Probably a touch of malaria. Blood poisoning. He'll be back before long.' But he wasn't. Not only was he missing from the early trial and championship matches; there was simply no explanation. Vague or meaningless statements, tucked away on the sports pages, were no sop.

On May 15, a bulletin was at last issued. It was carried by a number of papers and must have followed, we can only assume, a strident demand from sports editors, nationally and regionally, for information:

> It is generally known that Walter Hammond, the Gloucestershire cricketer and prospective Test match player, is still confined to his nursing home. Unfortunately, he has not made the progress which his many friends hoped he would, following his first operation and others that had to be performed. This afternoon we were informed that his present condition shows a little improvement.

The public had not in fact been told of his first operation. The bulletin made no mention of the nature of the illness. The address of the nursing home was omitted. A subsequent paragraph in the local papers said that it was not possible to deal with similar personal inquiries.

Such public taciturnity could not have been achieved without the compliance, it seems to me, of what I can only describe as the Bristol establishment, a tight-knit and arcane cluster which included the more rarefied levels of the city's legal, commercial and ecclesiastical life. This could be traced back to the days of maritime Bristol and the wealthy, influential merchants. One or two local newspaper figures paid homage to them, as did some elevated committee members at the Gloucestershire cricket headquarters. In the mid-1920s, amid political turmoil at home and the appalling evidence of desperate poverty outside the soup kitchens in Old Market, Bristol, there were surely more obvious issues for urgent discussion to accompany the evening brandies at the Merchant Venturers' building alongside the Downs in Clifton. But gossip was even rife among those privileged members who looked in vain for something about Hammond in *The Times* as well as in the Bristol morning and evening papers. 'Young Hammond is pretty poorly but it's better for everyone that not too much is made of it. Bad for morale at this stage of the season, don't you all agree?'

But the rigid code of silence, shrouding Hammond's condition in mystery, couldn't be sustained for ever. The local sports writers, who regularly penned their mostly august sentiments under such evocative pseudonyms as 'Quip', 'Scribe', 'The Usher' and even 'The Man with the Pencil', felt they had a journalistic duty to elaborate. They began to pester the officials at the county ground and were met by grandiloquent rebuffs. The *Bristol Evening News*, a relatively bright paper with a comprehensive cricket coverage, boasting 'a newsy page for sportsmen', appeared to accept failure with an infuriatingly anodyne item on 3 July. It baldly told its readers that Hammond had spent his 23rd birthday in a nursing home and 'every cricketer will wish him a speedy recovery from his illness'.

At this distance, we should surely be naïve in the extreme to accept that the mosquitoes alone were responsible. Public relations, under that particular guise, may well have been an unknown art and facility in the years between the wars. The imparting of news, however, should have been a matter of common sense and courtesy. Some caution over the exact phraseology would have been excusable.

I am reluctant to imply any sinister motives in erstwhile secretaries of the Gloucestershire club, but the fact remains that the 1927 county Year Book, covering the previous season is missing from the official records. The minutes for the relevant period can be found, though they too are bereft of detail as it affects Hammond. There is anxiety about a meagre profit (£249) on the 1925 balance sheet. The county decide they can't afford a coach and sheepishly agree to ask the local rugby club whether they can share their gymnasium. It is decided to start advertising home matches on the trams and buses.

On 16 June, the minutes record: 'The hon. treasurer submitted the draft of a reply to a letter from MCC, which contained a cheque for £78 towards the expenses of Hammond's illness. This was approved.' Nothing given away there. By 22 July, the minutes noted that the full accounts of the medical expenses were not yet available and the matter would have to be postponed until the next meeting. The treasurer was authorised to 'advance any moneys necessary to pay the accounts for Hammond'.

A special meeting was called at the end of July at the request of the captain. Any discussion of the postponed business of Hammond's expenses was omitted from the records. It seems that the meeting was primarily arranged to deal with some insubordination from Charlie Parker during a match. 'Lt. Col D C Robinson, the captain, gave details of what had occurred. Parker was then called in to state his case. It was agreed that if anything similar ever happened again, they would take drastic action'. Charlie, the club's beloved Marxist, was a fluent and engaging advocate and would have given a good account of himself on that occasion, as on the many others when his rebellious nature led to admonishment. His misdemeanour had been feverishly recorded by an outraged secretary in the minute book. Yet not a murmur about a player who had been on the point of death.

The 24 August entry was, by previous standards, positively expansive. 'The full medical and nursing home expenses of Hammond's illness were reported by the secretary, the Doctor's fees being £158-0s-6d and Nursing Home and Chemist's expenses £158-3s-2d. It was agreed that the chairman should see Sir Francis Lacey with regard to these expenses and ask for the sympathetic consideration of the MCC, both in relation to them and the salary paid to Hammond'.

Another special meeting was called, at the Liberal Hall in Bristol, on 28 September, to decide whether Hammond should accept an invitation to coach in South Africa through the winter months. 'After full discussion, it was decided to allow him to take the appointment'. A medical certificate was produced, stating that the trip would be beneficial to Hammond. What followed in subsequent meetings of the management committee was an apparent difference of opinion on the question of insurance, seemingly indicating a continued concern about his health and worries about his future as a county player. The committee backed the chairman, Horace Walker, in wishing to insure Hammond; a month later, for reasons not made clear, it was decided not to proceed with insurance. Maybe the members were reassured by the news that the MCC were forwarding another £100 to help with the medical expenses. 'Plum' Warner's influence had clearly been at work, following a visit to the cricketer's bedside.

Gloucestershire CCC's policy-makers were patently a bristly and autocratic lot. They turned down Sinfield's request for a modest increase in salary for the next year; they told that delightful general factotum, Bernie Bloodworth, he could expect £1 a week retaining fee and match pay of £5 a fixture as a player, scorer or 12th man (16 guaranteed), provided the salary didn't exceed £182; they brusquely rejected a request from Percy Fender for a donation to the Bobby Abel fund.

My final researches among the county archives, made available by the club's meticulous copper-plated record keeper Bert Avery, took me to the 1928 *Year Book*, covering 1927 and Hammond's return to the county scene. Here, surely, would be at least a smidgen of information about what had kept him so dramatically and almost fatally out of the game. There was a cursory reference to 'a season's absence owing to a most serious illness', but nothing else, apart from the fact that his salary would be £412 in 1927 – well up on Dipper's £312 and Mills's £300, and an eloquent line, surreptitiously slipped in, that he was being insured for £1,000, covering him for illness or accident in 1928.

On a more felicitous level, his productive return to runs in 1927 was praised with what looked like a surging sense of relief:

> He unquestionably stamped himself as an all-England cricketer and succeeded in equalling the record of W G Grace by scoring 1000 runs in May, this achievement being recognised by a public testimonial.

The *Year Book* joyfully listed Hammond's dazzling run of big scores in May: the 135 against Yorkshire at Gloucester, the 108 and 128 against Surrey at the Oval, the 187 against Lancashire at Old Trafford, and the 192 against Hampshire at Southampton. He beat W G's aggregate for the month by 26 runs.

If the true drama, as in the case of Hammond, is conveyed by what is left out in a dry journal of record like this, we should also pause and ponder on a fleeting mention of Fred Roberts in those same pages. He was a sturdy countryman from Mickleton, almost the extreme northern point of Gloucestershire and virtually into Shakespeare's terrain. He came to Bristol with his quaint Cotswold-beyond vowels and prodigious thirst, taking 14 wickets against Yorkshire in his first county match. In all, the affable Fred, left-arm fast, straight and untutored, took nearly 1000 wickets for Gloucestershire and then directed his energies and natural conviviality from behind the bar of a warm-hearted sportsmen's pub half a mile from the county ground. The cryptic note in the *Year Book* reads: 'F G Roberts, the old county player, has been made bankrupt. After discussion, proposed, seconded and carried, the sum of £10 will be used on Roberts' behalf.'

We have searched enough, mostly in vain, for an official identification of Wally's mysterious ailment. My conclusions have not been reached lightly, irresponsibly or sensationally. I have talked at length to venerealogists, general practitioners and medical historians as well as, just as pertinently, to those who knew him best.

The medical staff who attended Hammond when he was brought into the private nursing home in a quiet corner of Clifton were confronted by enormous difficulties. Their subject was no longer articulate in his feverish condition. However, even if he had any suspicions, this still unworldly lad, not so long out of school and inhibited by natural conventions, would have been reluctant to reveal them.

He had been placed in a small, airy ward, all to himself. There was an ambience of antiseptic cleanliness, symbolised by the starchy white of his sheets. Nurses crept in and out, taking his temperature or anxiously examining the discoloration of his upper leg. His mother was the only visitor allowed in the early days. She sat in silence beside his bed, periodically mopping his wet forehead. It was among the most tactile moments of their coolly affectionate relationship. She sensed that no one had any idea what was wrong with him.

Within 24 hours of his arrival, the doctors had lanced a septic swelling in the lymph glands around the groin area. Various additional operations involved further draining of the poison. There were of course no antibiotics in those days.

We can only surmise that suspicions eventually increased among the medical staff that he was suffering from a serious venereal disease. Their treatment would have been arsenic, mercury (an historically controversial antidote) or bismuth. It would have been administered orally or, more likely, by injection into the buttocks. Almost certainly, Hammond's illness was worsened by acute reaction to the forms of exploratory treatment that he was given. This is not intended in any way as a criticism of doctors, working to a minimum of information and possibily confused by the symptoms. It is quite possible that Hammond's resistance had already been lowered by mosquito bites and blood-poisoning earlier on the West Indies tour, and an infection of the blood even before he sailed.

Hammond was told later that only his exceptionally strong constitution pulled him through. He said of 'Plum' Warner's visit, 'when I was lying with my face to the wall' in the little ward, 'I had given up the struggle for life and I was, as 'Plum' said later, "in the shadow of death".' You couldn't be more graphic than that.

After a month or so, there were the first clear signs of recovery. Visitors were now encouraged. In came Reg Sinfield, stroking that boxer's chin and nose, religious and sweetly down-to-earth; in came Bert Williams, with training ground tales intended for ears that were no longer deaf. In came Billy Neale, after the milking, and one or two committee members from Ashley Down. In came Christina, his good-natured landlady from The Mall, in Clifton, and a long-standing girlfriend from the Hippodrome chorus was another visitor.

One surprise caller was that mighty hitter and peerless cover point, Gilbert Jessop. By then he was doing some journalism for the *Daily Mail* and had come to Bristol to report a Test trial match. It was actually something of a sentimental return for him, his first since before the war. He strolled round the large, rather soulless ground with Warner. 'Try to visit young Hammond – it'll cheer him up so much.' It was probably the first time they had met. Hammond treasured that kindly call, knowing that it was at 'Plum's' suggestion.

The small, dedicated staff at the nursing home, by now fully conscious of the potential status of their sporting resident, made no effort to conceal their relief as the surgeon's knife was finally put away. No longer was Hammond waving aside the food with a frail, token gesture.

In early June he was propped up in bed and passed a newspaper, to read that Gloucestershire had been bowled out for 58 by Sussex at the Wagon Works ground in Gloucester. Maurice Tate and Arthur Gilligan carved things up between them. But Sussex had made no more than 128 themselves. Percy Mills, by now bowling off-breaks and cutters, took six wickets, Parker the other four. Ah yes, thought Hammond, it was 'turning' at the old Wagon Works. He chuckled to himself to see that Bloodworth had been joint top scorer for Gloucestershire with 11; chuckled again when he was told Harry Tate was topping the bill at the Hippodrome. He hadn't chuckled for weeks.

His team-mates had given up any hope of seeing him again

that season. So they were surprised when he arrived, self-consciously, as a spectator for the match with Essex in Bristol on 12 July. He made his way gingerly into the dressing room at tea-time. His appearance embarrassed them. He walked slowly; his cheeks were sunken; there was affected bonhomie. He told them he'd be back full of runs for the next season. Then he rejoined his mother on a members' seat for a few overs. He had been booked in for a few weeks' recuperation at Burnham-on-Sea; after that he hoped the sunshine of South Africa would put him right again.

His appearance had upset the players. Not too many of them had realised how desperately ill he had been. Their welcome for him that July afternoon touched a level of warmth and humanity that would not often be surpassed. Cricket can throw up a rare, spontaneous goodness in the quirky human condition. The relationship between Wally and his colleagues over the years didn't always glow with the finer feelings. His homecoming to the county ground – he was *alive* again – was a rare beacon of affection to cherish.

He is by no means an exception among sportsmen. There was one popular and stylish Test player for England, briefly a county captain in the thirties, who was dogged by ill health and was generally thought to have had VD in addition to other ailments. Incestuous eye-winking dressing room asides implied that one or two of our post-war Test players were similarly diagnosed, though in their case they were quickly and discreetly cured by the then available marvels of penicillin. Several West Indian cricketers of repute, going back to the fifties, were also mentioned to me as sufferers. A medical confidence from within the profession revealed that a former British heavyweight champion, renowned for his physique and good looks, struggled painfully in the last years of his life from the apparent effects of syphilis.

The scandal of such infection was seldom allowed to surface in the case of Royalty. Henry VIII almost certainly had VD; Edward VII went to Vienna to receive treatment for his gonorrhoea; his eldest son, the wan and dissolute Eddy was indiscriminate in his bi-sexual proclivities – and suffered because of it. Yet it was officially pneumonia and not the pox that took his life at the age of 27.

Many members of the aristocracy, in this country alone, died directly from syphilis after no more than token or experimental treatment. Winston Churchill's father, Lord Randolph went that way. At least two popes, Alexander VI and Leo XI, were documented to have had some form of VD. So had Lenin and Woodrow Wilson, Boswell – ever willing to dally between the Diaries – Byron and Keats, as well as the composers Schubert, Delius and Smetana. Al Capone contracted syphilis as a young man and falsely thought the vicious organisms had been driven forever from his system. But they returned for their second and third stages to gnaw away at his brain.

Abrupt oscillations in personality and temperament so often came with the third stage. Flaubert, his facial features by then warped and mottled, was a classic case. He had caught the disease from one of the many prostitutes he subsidised as his uncontrollable outlet for lust, as well as scorn for the human race. There were, too, his fellow Frenchmen, Toulouse-Lautrec and Guy de Maupassant. The brilliant, stunted artist, died in mental confusion – from syphilis and, less so, absinthe. As for Maupassant, he died at the age of 42, his body and mind riddled with venereal demons.

Tertiary syphilis, in the form of GPI – General Paralysis of the Insane – got him in the end. That was what happened, too, in the case of Bram Stoker, indelibly associated with the fecund imaginings and Freudian misdeeds of Dracula. His great-nephew, Dan Farson, theorised how Stoker, frustrated in a marriage largely without physical contact, pursued vicarious eroticism in his novels. 'I received the distressing news that while his death certificate stated Exhaustion, it was revealed that he was suffering from GPI, presumably contracted when his wife Florence's frigidity forced him into the solace of prostitutes.'

It is possible that I have paused too long to trawl over the incongruous cross-section of sufferers in such discursive detail. But I hoped that in some way it would help to remove an outdated stigma, one I fought myself to reject firmly when people used to whisper to me: 'You know about Wally, of course, don't you? About him having a dose.'

For generations, maybe from the time, as one suspect theory

suggests, Christopher Columbus brought it from America just before the turn of the 16th century, people have pretended syphilis didn't exist. It was never a subject for polite conversation. There was positive daring in the manner Ibsen used it as an essential strand of his much admired play, *Ghosts*.

Up to 250,000 men and women a year in Britain alone receive treatment of some kind at VD clinics. Even twenty or so years ago, the medical profession accepted that gonorrhoea had become the commonest notifiable infectious disease in this country. Many of the genital ailments are relatively minor and syphilis itself claims only a few thousand victims. Nowadays the use of antibiotics usually offers rapidly effective treatment and permanent cure.

It wasn't so as Hammond lay, feverishly insecure, in a hospital bed in the mid-1920s. By then he would have reached the second stage of his illness. The chancres would have disappeared and the rashes returned. But, as every medical book on the subject seems to agree, the bodily signs could easily be confused with other forms of blood poisoning. We can't be sure when the doctors' suspicions were realistically aroused. But it is certain that they would have tried some, if not all, of the hesitantly prescribed forms of chemotherapy: arsenic, mercury, bismuth and iodides. One 'pox doctor', with whom I discussed the prevalent difficulties of those days, pointed out: 'The difference between the toxic and the therapeutic could be extremely narrow – it very much depended on the judgment of the medic'.

Mercury was probably given to Hammond in some form, by injection, orally or in ointment. It had been much used and advocated in the treatment of severe forms of VD, yet had a markedly controversial history. In an article for the *Journal of the Royal Society of Medicine* in 1990, Dr J G O'Shea, dealing with the subject of mercury and syphilis, quotes an authority as stating: 'The use of mercury in this treatment may have been the most colossal hoax ever perpetrated in a profession which has never been free of hoaxes.' The author himself accepted that mercury was ineffective in curing secondary syphilis; in the primary cases, it might occasionally have aborted the infection. But he pointed out that it had been the mainstay of such chemotherapy for nearly 500 years and that it remained in use until penicillin became available in 1940.

What interested me particularly were the long-term side effects of mercury-poisoning, known as erethism. They included personality change, moods of withdrawal, sudden outbursts of anger, impatience and exaggerated emotional response to circumstances. This leads me to the conclusion that Wally Hammond's condition was likely to have been affected more by the medical treatment he received than by the nature of the illness itself.

Discussions I had with Dr Colin Franklin, a retired GP who was born in Barbados and came to England to study medicine, proved of considerable interest and relevance. Hammond was his cricketing idol 'from the time I sat enthralled in the schoolboys stand at home in 1934 and watched him make 281 not out against a Barbados attack which included two Test match bowlers.' Dr Franklin went to school with Sir Frank Worrell; cricket was a deep-rooted part of his culture.

'Based on a description of his condition on the return to Avonmouth, I am 99 per cent certain that the true diagnosis in Hammond's case was *lymphogranuloma venereum*, a sexually transmitted disease, caused not by the syphilis organism but by another bacterium. It is common in the West Indies but in 1926 would have been very rare and little known in England. As far as I know, the specific diagnostic test only became available in 1925. The symptoms you detail are classical – namely high fever, anorexia, rapid weight loss, swollen, painful inflamed lymph nodes in the groin, almost certainly with the formation of sinuses and abscesses. Hence the surgical operations.' He added that the swelling of the leg was another common symptom. Dr Franklin has treated two patients with the disease, one in the West Indies and one in this country. *Lymphogranuloma venereum* is easily diagnosed today, he says, but would certainly not have been in the mid-twenties. His conversational postscript has a potent significance: 'There would have been a tremendous stigma attached to the sufferer and I wonder to what extent this contributed to Hammond's subsequent remoteness and self-imposed isolation?'

A discernible transformation took hold of him after he made

his first faltering steps of recovery from the bed in that nursing home of caring staff and perplexed doctors. In a matter of months he had ceased to be a boy. The youthful, impish eyes had suddenly given way to almost world-weary ones, strained, defensive, and for evermore, suspicious. From that ghastly proximity to death and those long hours of silent contemplation, as he lay in the private ward, feeling frighteningly alone and betrayed by fate, had come a strange maturity – earlier than nature intended. He was still only 23.

Hammond had never been much of a thinker. At school he had preferred whacking a cricket ball to the prosaic hours in the classroom; he'd enjoyed splashing through the mud of the farmyard with the Neales, during the holidays, rather than any visit to a library or museum, or putting his head in a book.

There had been a carefree indolence about him when he first arrived at the county ground in Bristol. Professional sport wasn't going to demand any particular intellectual effort on his part. That was when he started parting his hair in the middle, in the fashion of famous contemporary sportsmen, especially the glamorous First Division footballers who seemed to have so much spare time once their training was done: golf in plus fours, buckshee seats at the cinema – and, it seemed, not an anxiety in the world.

Wally had found there was plenty of good-natured teasing at both the county headquarters and at Eastville, home of Bristol Rovers. He smiled at the digs about his smart appearance – he was positively dapper by the standards of poorly paid professional sportsmen – and what supposedly went on in the back of his spluttering but serviceable old car. He was not adept at dressing room repartee and was hopeless at telling a joke in the style of the lecherous ones that did the rounds amid the pads and the shin-guards. But the team-mates all liked him in those early days: he had an appealing presence; he was modest; and everyone sensed that he was capable of becoming a truly exceptional sportsman before too long.

On his return to the pre-season nets in 1927, after the long enforced absence, the change in him was almost tangible. Other players looked at each other in unspoken eloquence. They couldn't quite determine what had happened. Some were effusive in welcoming him back, but Hammond's response was puzzlingly taciturn. Perhaps he was wondering how much they knew.

This transformation would not have been apparent to the general spectator. But I went to see an elderly Gloucestershire supporter in Keynsham. He had watched the county with loyalty and zeal in those very days. He had collected autographs and had studied Hammond, idolatrously, at close range. 'I noticed the striking difference in him when he returned to the club after his illness. Not till long afterwards did I personally hear the rumours. What struck me, quite apart from any changes in personality, was the marked manner his complexion had altered.'

As for the players, they remarked among themselves at the abruptness with which his boyish cordiality had at least partially disappeared. He was more withdrawn, less willing to share a harmless confidence. Laymen psychiatrists in the dressing room gave up trying to analyse the reason.

I am convinced that as he lay in his bed and later sat out in the sunshine near the windows of the nursing home, he took stock for virtually the first time, of his life. The analytical experience left him desperately insecure. That insecurity was never to leave him. He thought of his parents: of the military father he had known in the most casual, non-emotional way. He had lived with his parents in married quarters, a life as nomadic and unsettling as that of his father. Often there was time for no more than superficial friendships. His acquaintances at school were forgotten with the next posting. He grew up a soldier's son, and nothing could be more artificial or transitory than that. His father had died in action just before the end of the war. Wally and his mother shed their tears. But the father had frequently been away from home; it wasn't quite like the loss of an intimate member of the family. Mrs Hammond had always held the parental sway. She was a big, assertive woman; she arranged the schooling and made the decisions. There was the merest whiff of mystery about her own social life. Young Walter, in truth, knew precious little about her. The relationship, on her part, was well intentioned rather than intimate. She had never been in the habit of cuddling her son.

But during his hapless weeks in the nursing home she had been a constant visitor. She had badgered the nursing staff for reassuring news. She it had been who put an unequivocal end to tentative talk of amputating one of his legs. He was grateful enough for her attentiveness now. Yet why had she been so keen to send him off to Cirencester and boarding school? Why didn't she make greater attempts to dissuade him from his usual choice of spending the school holidays not with her but on a farm with a classmate? In any case, why did the young Hammond himself choose to put the Neales before her?

The self-imposed analysis, it seems to me, went on. Silly thoughts doubtless filled his head. Had he really been just an accident of birth? He was born six months or so after the marriage. The ways of the shotgun, in marital matters, can't always be kept from the children. Young Walter must have been left wondering how much he had really been wanted – and, indeed, whether Corporal Hammond and Marion had even intended to get married. We can only surmise how much feelings of insecurity eroded his early emotional life. We can only imagine how much he yearned for at least the semblance of an orderly and loving family life, emanating from the reassuring pillar of a stable and permanent home. He simply never experienced it.

In the mid-summer months of 1926, Hammond, still badly debilitated by his illness, unable to articulate the metamorphosis taking place, was being gradually gripped by a pervasive inferiority complex. He wished he could string his sentences together more eloquently, like 'Plum' Warner and the well-fleshed, well-educated senior members of the Gloucestershire County Cricket Club. He wished he was less awkward at the posher gatherings to which the pros were occasionally invited.

He would before long become acknowledged as one of the greatest cricketers in the history of the game. Yet privately he was to become preoccupied by a sense of failure. Indeed, to some extent, his life was later to bear this out – in the wretchedness of his business enterprises, in some of his social aspirations, in his personal relationships. It left him looking over his shoulder, at times needlessly suspicious of colleagues and friends. He confided that he thought one or two of them were always trying to gang up against him. That unshakeable impression of his must have been heightened during one scandal during an away match before the war. Hammond was accused of a disciplinary lapse. Major (later Colonel) Hugh Henson, the county secretary, was sent for. He hurried to the hotel, listened to the evidence of team-mates and hushed the whole thing up. It would be cruel, if not improper, to exhume the circumstances at this distance.

But we return to the complexes that tormented Hammond. He thought back to the irksome complications over his registration for Gloucestershire. Why did Lord Harris, the autocratic pillar of Kent cricket, with his punctilious regard for the rule-book, have to make life so difficult for him?

The more we study the outwardly rich and bountiful life of Hammond, the more we find evidence of the insecurity that bedevilled him. It was something I had the opportunity to discuss with Bob Wyatt, a quietly analytical observer of the human scene. He knew Wally well. 'And I liked him very much in many ways, finding him quite a kind person. But, of course, he wasn't very popular and, I always felt, was inclined to be shy . . . . Wally once stopped me going to South Africa, you know, in 1938. I knew I'd been selected. But he didn't like the thought of any previous England captain being in the side. It was a sort of fear of personal criticism, I suppose. Mind you, Gubby was the same'. This last was said with some affection; Gubby Allen was a great friend of Wyatt and his son's godfather.

As is so often the case with someone patently unsure of himself, Hammond offset his complexes subconsciously with intermittent shows of arrogance that could make him appear patronising, unfriendly and increasingly remote – especially in the later years of his playing career.

His moods could be sweeping and monumental. In his book, *The Cricket Captains of England*, Alan Gibson referred to a radio programme he introduced and linked, about Hammond, which went out shortly after his death. Many of the great player's contemporaries were interviewed. 'A word that kept coming up was *moody.* Even Tom Goddard, an old pal with whom he had shared rooms for years, used the word . . . . ' That, too, was my experience in researching this book. I don't believe a single cricketer with whom I talked could avoid this succinct assessment.

Ronald Mason is particularly perspicacious, in his biography of Hammond, on the subject of moods and preoccupations when discussing that last ill-fated tour to Australia just after the war. Here was abject inner turmoil. The moods hounded him like demons. Those colleagues who suffered because of them should perhaps have made more allowances. The moods were frequently misinterpreted, seen as personal slights. It's possible some of them were, of course. R C Robertson-Glasgow, that elegant and scholarly observer of sporting humanity, once wrote that during Hammond's Test failures in 1934, he had seemed almost bored. Mr Mason asks whether this is evidence that 'in face of stress or failure, he retired into a protective shell of reserve'.

Hampden Alpass, a Bristol solicitor, knew Wally well and actually went on holiday with him a couple of years after the illness. 'He was terribly moody, even in those days. I wouldn't necessarily choose him for a friend but he had many good points. And such grace with every movement. It was just those inexplicable moods . . . .' That is the point. The moods and the uncommunicative propensity had not been noticeable before he went off to the West Indies and returned to the hospital bed. It seems entirely reasonable to conclude that they emanated from his illness, either from the disease itself or the effects of the treatment.

His diffidence had always been there; but once he used to grin and to enjoy banter, as well as Charlie Parker's radical idealism spiced with Prestbury profanities, or Reg Sinfield's uncomplaining accounts of sadism, in the guise of discipline, once perpetrated against him and his fellow cadets on the *Mercury* training ship by C B Fry and his formidable wife. 'Lucky to have missed that, Wally,' Reg would say, eyes twinkling as he stroked that long Jack Hulbert chin.

As the 1930s approached, Hammond forgot how to smile. It is wrong to say he made enemies. The players detected the marked change in personality but their vast admiration of him as a cricketer never wavered. They marvelled at the way he played the spinners on the most inhospitable of wickets; they went on cheering, like schoolboys, his peerless cover drives; they jumped to their feet, on a score of balconies around the country, to acknowledge his latest hundred. They just couldn't work out why he went out of his way to withdraw from them. It simply got worse. 'What's he got against me?' asked George Emmett, someone with a similar army background, who found himself dropped down the order without too much explanation. 'When am I going to hear a murmur of praise?' asked George Lambert, who couldn't have been far off a Test call and was almost as fast as anyone around.

The attitude was sustained after the war. The Graveney brothers symbolise the dichotomy: idolatry and the touch of resentment. Tom went weak at the knees, seduced by the Master's mere presence. Ken was more critical. 'It seemed to me Wally was always brooding. Once I found myself alone in the dressing room with him. He was in one corner and I was in the other. Twice I tried very hard to strike up some kind of conversation. I got no reply at all – and finally gave up.'

It was not so long before that that Ken had taken a week off work to turn up in the nets in the hope of impressing Gloucestershire. He would prove to be a useful and deceptive swing bowler who once took all ten against Derbyshire at Chesterfield. It was the occasion when he spontaneously produced a priceless quote: 'And I don't believe that bloody spire is crooked, either!'

In the nets this unknown bowler found himself bowling at Hammond. It was an awesome experience. But to everyone's surprise, he conjured up a beauty to knock over Wally's off stump. Silence, with maybe a polite collective clearing of the throat from the knot of onlookers. 'He said nothing, just as if nothing had happened. Charlie Parker, then the coach, put the stump back in.'

Hammond was to become known as The Silent Man: it was a silence unexplained. Len Hutton loved to tell of a 700-mile car journey in Australia during the 1946-47 series – it was something of a privilege actually to be travelling as a fellow player with him. The manager, Major Rupert Howard, was the usual companion. 'Do you know,' Hutton used to say, 'for the whole of that long, boring car journey, with Cyril Washbrook and myself, the only words Walter said to me were "Keep an eye out for a garage – we need some petrol". '

There are many other examples. Denis Compton was to write of the way that Hammond's aloofness came through when batting with him. Communication was practically non-existent. Compton recalled the time when, as a 20-year-old, he made only his second Test appearance, at Trent Bridge, and was caught at deep square-leg for 102, compiled in no more than 135 minutes. He'd put on more than 200 with Eddie Paynter for the fifth wicket, England were 487-5 and Middlesex's emerging hero was bubbling with excitement. The shot that cost him his wicket had so nearly been a six. But Wally took him aside: 'Don't you ever do that again. When you play against the Australians and make 100, you take a fresh guard and start again . . . . ' Compton accepted that the advice may have been sound. He, was a good deal less sure about the way, and the moment, Hammond chose to express it.

Up to a few days before he died, Reg Sinfield, Gloucestershire's first pro to complete the double, was talking cricket. I sat in his bedroom, at the home of his son and daughter-in-law, while he so engagingly wheeled away – like erstwhile overs at the College ground – in anecdotal joy. He showed me again the grip for his off cutters and asked me to read the scriptures to him. Reg was a church sidesman in the village of Tickenham, near Bristol. He was incapable of a thought that lacked charity. He probably liked Wally more than some of the others. 'But, oh dear, he'd go solo for a couple of days. None of us could fathom what was up. He was a man of few words . . . very few words. And you just didn't know how to take him. I think he suffered from some form of depression.'

Cornishman Jack Crapp, another Gloucestershire cricketer without a malicious notion, was apt to be inhibited in the presence of Hammond. 'I have to be honest – only once in his whole career can I remember him saying anything helpful to me. He came down the pitch and murmured: "The Hollies leg-break isn't turning!" That was something.'

The tragedy was that gentle Jack Crapp and the others desperately wanted to embrace Hammond. They hoped in vain that he'd remain one of the boys. Unfortunately Hammond became increasingly selective in his choice of company. This leads us to the undeniable fact that he was a snob. His mother was also inclined that way; she enjoyed the social side of army life that went with her husband's promotion. She loved making something of an entry at the county ground in Bristol, in the dicky seat of Wally's car – or having tea with the committee members. And, like her son, she acquired an accent and speech mannerisms appropriate to her social aspirations. There will be opportunity later to delve more interpretatively into Hammond's striving for social grandeur – and those tortuous, honest moments when he privately feared that he wouldn't make it. We earlier reflected on the lonely hours he spent, during that period of slow recuperation, ruminating on a still young life but one disrupted by confusion and doubt. He had been endowed with a strong and gifted body; he was not to know the extent to which that body and, more so, the mind and temperament would react to the trauma of his illness. Nor had he any idea of the perplexing ambiguities of personality that were to follow.

Dr K C P Smith sat only a few feet from Hammond as he waited to bat in his last, ill-conceived appearance for Gloucestershire in 1951. He was the medical adviser for the county club during part of the 1950s and 1960s, soothing nerves and offering gentle counsel which at times had little to do with runs and wickets. He is now a consultant psychiatrist and is in effect co-originator with his son, Dr Michael Apter, of the academically acclaimed 'psychological reversal theory'. Much of the ground-work was done by Ken Smith, in Bristol. His son, formerly Visiting Professor of Psychology at Yale, is the world's leading authority on the theory. This is no place to discuss the theory, except to say that in essence it is concerned with the motivation of pairs of opposites – 'the serious and the playful, mastery and sympathy, acceptance and rejection, other and self'. The pair lecture extensively and the tormented if gifted life of Wally Hammond has a habit of finding its way into the papers Dr Smith and his son deliver to both specialist and lay audiences.

'The whole of Wally's life centred on the basic need for mastery in cricket; the need for him was individual rather than team,' says Dr Smith. 'He sought social mastery and excitement. There is, for instance, the suggestion that he married in the first case largely for money. I believe there is a physical basis to our temperaments. The consultant physician who attended him when he came back from the West Indies, Dr Richard Clarke, was to examine him again after his recovery and restored strength. He told me Hammond was the most perfect physical specimen he'd ever seen. In my mind, I associate a body like that with satisfaction, something to be used to surpass other competitors.'

Ken Smith grew up in Bristol with the Gloucestershire and England left-hander, Jack Crapp. They played cricket together in the park as schoolboys and were later in the same club side, Willows CC. When Dr Smith took on his role with the county club, he renewed his chats with Crapp. 'Jack also told me that of all his partnerships with Wally, only once was he given a helpful word. Hammond had made a thorough study of opposing bowlers. This knowledge was unrivalled but he rigidly kept it to himself. It gives some idea of the great batsman's self-containment. To him, such self-concern was a preferential state of mind . . . . As far as his own cricket was concerned he was almost entirely professional (serious), though occasionally playful, according to the mood or circumstances. He was playful only when security was assured'.

Dr Smith gave two examples from his own experience of rare playfulness by Hammond. In a county match played at Clifton College, when the pressure was off and a win was a formality, he saw this magnificent fielder move almost casually from slip to the leg-side of the wicket keeper to take a catch and immediately pop the ball into his pocket. This piece of lightning legerdemain became a Hammond trademark: he later used it occasionally even in big matches.

'In another match, when Gloucestershire were cruising to victory and Wally was at the wicket, he was presented with a full toss. He lifted his bat as if it were a tennis racket being used in reverse. And he flicked the ball over the wicket keeper's head for the winning boundary.'

But this kind of playful informality was merely an example of Hammond's remarkable physical dexterity. He was incapable of this kind of liberating spontaneity in his human relationships.

Ken Smith recalled: 'The county secretary, Colonel Henson, once pointed out to me what he felt was the basic difference between Hammond and Graveney. If he mentioned to Hammond that a big crowd was expected for the Bank Holiday match and he'd like him to be at the wicket all afternoon, he could be relied on to do so. With Graveney, it was more a matter of chance. That indicated the degree of power and control (mastery) in Hammond's case, incorporating skill, knowledge and strategy. Yet being short on sympathy, his leadership was sometimes lacking.

'To me he was a master, not a leader – he lacked the quality of sympathy needed in a leader'.

When he carried that fundamental control of his into his private life, in the opinion of Dr Smith, he was troubled and confused by a number of setbacks – complications over his registration for Gloucestershire, the appalling mishap on the West Indies tour, the shaky marriage to his first wife, Dorothy, the measure of criticism that accompanied his change of status from professional to amateur . . . .' And at the very moment many were considering him the greatest batsman in the world, up popped a certain Don Bradman to upstage him'. There was also the war to take away some of his best years.

The self-doubts and paradoxes in Hammond's life are rich material for any student of psychology. Reversal theory, say the Smiths and their team, does much to explain many of the inconsistencies and changes that often dogged his path. Ken Smith, coincidentally a Squadron Leader in the RAF stationed in South Africa for some of the time Hammond was there, goes to pains to make it clear that any professional conclusions he may reach don't in any way imply any personal condemnation of a marvellous cricketer. 'I saw many of his hundreds in Bristol and elsewhere and thrilled to them. Looking back, it was like going into a room full of Rembrandts'. You couldn't ask for anything more figuratively apposite from a person who loves art and is married to an artist.

PART II

BOY AND MAN

Mystery of the School Holidays

William Walter Hammond was in uniform for his marriage to Marion Crisp in Buckland parish church, on the outskirts of Dover, on 3 December 1902. He was in the Royal Garrison Artillery, stationed at Dover Castle, and inordinately proud of his two stripes. It was a small congregation, colleagues from the army and their wives, and family friends. The whisper among the relatives was that they had had to get married. There were doubtless discreet glances towards Marion as she stood with her soldier groom in the centre aisle. Their son, Walter Reginald, was born in June 1903.

Bombardier Hammond was 23 and had been in the army for five years. He was neat in appearance, receptive to the normal rigours of military discipline, and was ambitious in his chosen career. His own father had been in the building trade. William saw better prospects in the Artillery. Conditions of pay and status had improved; he looked forward to an overseas posting. In the meantime, he was an instructor in arms. He had a facility for teaching the rudimentary skills of army life. As an instructor, he also liked the authority that went with it. He had met Marion at a village dance. She was well-built and not lacking in admirers among the local soldiers. Her father was a clerical worker for the railways. Home-life was modest but self-sufficient. The Crisps had good standing in the locality. Marion's pregnancy would have been an embarrassment.

The young couple had married quarters. It was a relatively relaxed posting. Marion pushed the pram and mixed with other soldiers' wives. When William was promoted sergeant, she enjoyed the open social nights in the mess. She had plenty to say; no one could have suggested she lacked self assurance.

'How about that posting abroad?' she used to ask. It came when Walter was approaching five, ready for school. Hong Kong seemed more than a world away in those days of slow sea travel and an absence of information or knowledge about foreign parts. All the same, the Hammonds agreed it sounded like an exciting place to be stationed. They stayed there for three years, followed by three – up to the outbreak of the First World War – in Malta.

Malta had some importance in Britain's imperial affairs. Young Wally loved it there: the sun on his back, the improvised cricket, the swimming. He was essentially a physical boy, incessantly hitting or kicking a ball. In the water he already swam with the vigour of a teenager. His parents noticed the stomach and calf muscles that were forming ahead of their years. Education for a soldier's son abroad came from the army itself. The syllabus was not extensive; and the boy had no complaints on that count. 'He's never going to be a scholar', said Marion, who had harboured hopes that her son would fashion a successful life for himself, away from the oppressive aura of khaki. Wally liked the open air. He went camping and learned to tie knots with the Scouts. He made up the numbers on the days when soldiers organised a cricket match. When the papers arrived from England, his parents watched the way he turned at once to the sports pages – to read of Ranji's deeds for Sussex, Hobbs' for Surrey.

There is one insight regarding Wally's early days in Malta. His parents were in a position on occasions to make use of a nanny or child-minder. In my research I talked to Mrs G Munday, of Weston-super-Mare, whose mother had had that particular responsibility. Mrs Munday's grandfather had been a sergeant-major in the Royal Artillery, himself stationed in Malta. In later years, her mother would tell her about a time when she took young Walter to school. 'He'd play me up. We had to go through some kind of tunnel on the way to school. He would get so far and then run right back to the entrance again.' But as far as one can tell, he was a fairly obedient child. The scorching sun suited him temperamentally. His body bronzed quickly and there were days when he would have passed as a Latin. In his innocence he probably thought he was destined to live the rest of his life on that seemingly carefree island.

Then the war came. In August 1914 the Hammonds sailed for England. It was quite a hazardous journey; the Bay of Biscay was at its most challenging. Weakened by sea-sickness and worried by the war, they reached home. But the family was to be disrupted, in effect for ever. William went off to France; Marion had friends in Southsea, the southernmost suburb of Portsmouth, and found a flat there. She had no idea of the carnage that would follow in Europe but, like so many soldiers' wives, she wondered whether she would see her husband alive again.

Mrs Hammond was a natural organiser. 'Make sure you find a decent school for our lad,' had been among her husband's last words. So she arranged for him to go to Portsmouth Grammar School. Within a year or so he was playing for the 2nd XI at cricket. He spent his evenings on Southsea Common rather than getting down to his homework. The boys at school noticed how much bigger and better developed he was than most of them. They were surprised how rapidly he'd made the 2nd XI. Some found him 'cocky'; it seems reasonable to conclude that shyness and social unease, already burdening him, may have been misinterpreted.

He didn't stay long at Portsmouth Grammar School and we can't be sure why. His mother apparently had the theory that he would benefit from becoming a boarder, living far away from her. But that may have been a rationalisation of her own preferences. At all events, there has never been a wholly satisfactory explanation of why she sent him to the smaller grammar school at Cirencester in Gloucestershire. He had a distant uncle who ran a garage in Victoria Road, Cirencester, but I'm not convinced that that was a real consideration. It has also been suggested that it was because the school had a reputation for turning out agricultural students, and that Mrs Hammond was beginning to think that her son might end up a farmer.

Portsmouth Grammar School was surprised when she told the headmaster what she planned. She wrote to the school at Cirencester – most delightful of environments for any growing boy – and discovered that the fees for boarding were reasonable.

She told Wally what she proposed and he shrugged; he hadn't enjoyed the increasing academic pressures in Hampshire in any case.

He was one of 50 boarders. As part of the ethos of turning out hardy young men, conditions at such grammar and minor public schools could be quite spartan. Boys had to get used to cold water for washing; they kept warm in the class rooms by wrapping up well. But discipline was still more relaxed than at Portsmouth.

It was a school for both sexes, and Wally was an immediate hit with the girls. One who was there at the same time remembered how the girls' tennis sessions were invariably cut short so that Hammond and the rest of the schoolboy cricketers could have longer practice.

Mrs E M Gough, a teacher for 40 years, was a pupil with Hammond at the school. She told me how in those days the boys' and girls' departments were strictly segregated. 'It was very much 'us' and 'them', with a high wooden fence between us. The girls' fifth form was on the upper floor and we were able to look out on the boys' playground and no doubt signal to them. Some of the girls used to meet Wally Hammond and his friends in the evenings – I couldn't, as I lived in a village three miles away!'

From other contemporaries of those schooldays came memories of his visits to the Goblin Tea Rooms in the Market Place. 'Whether the attraction was the fare provided in the tea rooms or a pretty member of the staff, I never really knew. But I had my suspicions,' one local lad was to write to me more than sixty years later.

A second boy at the school in those days was to tell me that on one occasion Wally had gone into the town without permission. He was spotted, with a girl, by the school caretaker-groundsman and reported. This led to a severe reprimand. My source remembered the incident graphically; it became something of a talking-point in the school and the embellished story was that the young hero, shamed by a sneaky caretaker, had wasted no time in seeking him out to deliver a few choice, precocious words.

Hammond's arrival at the grammar school was soon to be

clouded by sadness. He learned, not long before the end of the war, that his father had been killed in action. By now, William had progressed by way of sergeant-major to the commissioned ranks. He ended up a major: a conscientious soldier, who gave orders assertively and showed personal bravery, like so many. The headmaster called Walter into his study and gave him the news. 'Here's your train fare. Now go home for a few days to comfort your mother.'

It is unlikely that anyone, through his eventful life, ever saw Wally cry. He was not an outwardly emotional creature; his feelings were seldom seen. Perhaps he momentarily wept when told, in kindly words, that his father was dead. Their relationship had never been an emotionally demonstrative one. Once or twice they played cricket together with a tennis ball on the grass in the surrounds of Dover Castle. But there were to be no homely conversations. In the years of the war, Wally had barely seen his father. Family greetings at Christmas time were the only real signs of affinity.

Hammond the boy badly needed a father. He needed a mother, too. For long periods he was without either. Marion made a fuss of him on occasions, though the rationale of sending him off to Cirencester eluded the boy. It was another unhappy and influential strand in his life. He was neither cursed nor blessed with too much sensitivity. Back he went to school after the day or so of family grieving. He learned how to dance and his natural body rhythm made him the most sought-after partner in the school dances. Success was a good deal less evident in the class-room. His marks were usually low, though the mild-mannered rebukes of the masters didn't appear to bother him too much. There were always the playing fields and the school holidays to look forward to.

The way he spent most of his holidays was another mystery. He used to go down to the farm belonging to the family of Billy Neale, a fellow boarder and steadfast pal. Other times he stayed with the Mills family in Cirencester. They had links with the school and Cirencester cricket; they must have worried about his apparent reluctance to go home to his mother, and befriended him. There were also occasions when he spent a few days of his holidays with Tony Bubb, at Compton House, Newent. It was an impressive building, with its Adam fireplaces and fine portico. Bubb, four years older than Hammond, was a keen cricketer and was later to be sounded-out about becoming the secretary of Gloucestershire CCC. His daughter was told how much the visiting schoolboy enjoyed riding in the dog-cart and on the ponies. She wasn't aware of any family links, though her grandmother's maiden name was Hammond.

It was a curious, almost non-existent home life for Hammond. Again we can only wonder why his mother – later to become so considerate in his welfare and a proud observer of his feats on the cricket field – didn't insist on seeing more of him. Travel from Cotswold country to the Hampshire coast may not have been easy in wartime, but that can be no excuse. Nor can the fact that he came to love trudging through the thick farmyard mud in Billy Neale's gumboots. It goes deeper than that. But there was always his sport to obscure, at least for the time being, any worries about rootlessness, and to lift his spirits. It wasn't just cricket. On sports day he would win the mile, the sprints, the long-jump and the cross-country. Those sturdy leg muscles and the expanding chest served him well. Envious classmates suggested in stage whispers that he might consider giving a chance to someone else. He was soon in the soccer team, too. But it was still cricket at which he excelled. 'Pat' Fraser, the bachelor headmaster, had spotted the exceptional promise at once. He would trot across to the nets after school to offer advice. His encouragement stands with that of John Tunnicliffe and George Dennett, coaching mentors we shall come to later. Mr Fraser believed in a broad education, one that reserved a place for hitting fours through the covers.

By his second year at Cirencester, Hammond had walked into the cricket XI. He was now opening the innings with Billy Neale, striking the ball firmly as the Head had suggested. The fixture list, for a small grammar school just after the war, wasn't an onerous one. Cirencester played the local villages and other schools of comparable size. Approving ancient scribes from the local weekly papers, august organs liberal with their space, came to watch on their days off in 1920, as Wally's statistics became a matter of general excitement. They went away to extol the remarkably mature style of this well-built teenager.

Hammond's first hundred came in the parents' match. He followed it up with six wickets. The faded record books tell us that in one fixture, when Cirencester batted appallingly and were all out for 40, Wally batted through the innings for 36 not out! The much-quoted 365 in a house match is less impressive. Everyone already knew that he was the best batsman the school had ever had. The runs for the boarders' house were plundered in just under two hours. He hit 24 sixes in ludicrous dominance. House matches at schools all over around the country were laden with monumental individual totals. Hadn't A E J Collins driven *The Times* to apoplexy with his 628? Yet so often the bowling, the fielding and almost certainly the scoring, were painfully suspect.

Hammond left school at the end of the summer term in 1920. His mother, by now showing an increasing interest in and concern for his future, started writing to farming friends on the Isle of Wight and the mainland. Her son adopted a phlegmatic attitude, irritating to Marion no doubt, toward the necessity of earning a living. As he said goodbye to his classmates, he played a game or two for Cirencester CC – and scored a century for them.

'What you going to do, Wally?' asked the rosy-cheecked Neale, himself resigned to a life of early-morning milking and manual work on the family farm. He would have liked young Hammond permanently with him in the Berkeley Vale. But the farm didn't have scope for another hand – and Wally certainly wasn't cut out to be just a labourer, however much he took to the rural life during the school holidays.

'Tubby' Witchell, also at the school and three years younger than Hammond, was a member of that informal cricketing coterie. He knew the headmaster had recommended Wally to Gloucestershire. 'It's my ambition, too,' he used to say as the boys shared the cream cakes and eyed the waitresses at the Goblin's tea-rooms. And he made it. 'Tubby', who came from Dursley, had a solitary match for the county a year or so after leaving the grammar school. He did rather better for Wiltshire in the Minor Counties championship.

It wasn't unusual for schoolmasters to press the claims of their best players on members of the county committees.

Gloucestershire went through the motions of following-up with token enthusiasm. They were really in no position to recruit more young professionals. There wasn't enough money to pay them. The early post-war years were fallow times. But 'Pat' Fraser's persistence was rewarded. In August 1920 Hammond was included in a Club and Ground game. He played as well as anyone, batting into the 60s and then taking two wickets. 'How old is this lad?' committee members were quickly asking. 'Only seventeen – and he's just left school.'

It was ascertained that his father had been killed in the war and his mother was living in Southsea. 'Don't waste any time. Go and see her and get the boy signed up.' For Leonard Olive and Walter Pearce, pillars of the county club, it was to be a nice day out on the south coast – and a productive one of historic significance. The two of them, Mrs Hammond and a mostly silent Wally, sat rather stiffly round the drawing room table. There was much grandiose talk of a new career and what might be achieved. Well no, the boy could expect no more than a very modest salary to start with. But the club would help him find some digs and would keep a kindly, paternal eye on him.

Mrs Hammond was far from convinced. Her father had been a nicely dressed clerical worker; her husband had been a major in the army; her aspirations were reasonably high for her boy. She knew a few gentlemen farmers who paid others to do the hard work. The Neales were gentlemen farmers in their way. But cricket . . . . that was no living, surely? There was much talking and much tea-drinking. The impasse was frustrating for the Bristol delegation. In the end, Wally himself was asked what he would like to do. 'Play cricket,' he answered without hesitation. Those two eloquent words concluded a protracted discussion that had appeared to be getting nowhere. The lad's signature of acceptance, witnessed by his mother, was delivered in triumph to the county headquarters.

'You may not hear anymore about it,' Mrs Hammond told Wally in conscious tones of pessimism. Yet before the summer was out, the 17-year-old was making his first-class debut during the Cheltenham Festival, against Lancashire and Leicestershire. He fielded energetically and batted with melancholy brevity. He did slightly better when he went on to Worcester for his third, entirely unexpected match.

His initial impact, then, was minimal; his name meant nothing to anyone apart from the Cirencester pupils and a proud headmaster. 'We'll get you in the nets before next season,' said a generous-spirited Percy Mills, that reliable medium-pacer who showed equal skill in helping young players, whether at the county ground or, later, at Radley College. Mrs Hammond was altogether more pragmatic. She still rather resented the way Gloucestershire had coerced her into agreeing to his becoming a fledgling county cricketer. So she continued to ponder other employment for him. When it came to harvest-time, he was sent off to the Isle of Wight to assist on the farm of a family friend. He stayed over there for much of the winter, nominally giving a hand during the week and playing football for both Cowes and Ryde Sports on Saturdays.

Then came the letter, asking him to report with the others to Nevil Road in preparation for the 1921 season. He collected up his basic schoolboy kit and his mother, with some misgivings, bought him a new pair of boots. It was the start of a new way of life. He was entering an adult's world. It was time to have a place of his own, a poky, functional room just off Stapleton Road, from which he could hear the trains going by. With the independence of youth, he had coins in his back pocket. He took fish and chips back to his flat; he went with his new mates for an occasional pint of 'Georges'. He noticed the way Charlie Parker and the others ordered their beer. Before long he was doing the same. 'Pint of bitter – and a glass with a handle'. It was a habit he never lost, although he later tended to drink more spirits. When he briefly returned to England in the 1950s and was taken to a pub in Tetbury, a friend observed the nostalgic request to the barmaid: 'A glass with a handle, if you don't mind.'

The county headquarters was quite a culture shock for him at first. He retained vague, indirect memories of army discipline as it affected his late father. There were sharply defined divisions and disciplines in the life of a soldier; so there were, he discovered, in the life of a professional cricketer. At Bristol, the amateurs outnumbered the pros. They remained segregated at meal-times. Their accents and vocabularies were different.

Wally pricked up his ears and liked the sound of the amateurs' vowels. But he couldn't understand why they had so little to do with the pros, who were by far the better players. They ignored a newcomer like himself almost completely. Foster Robinson, a famous local name and at that time a decade short of his knighthood, was the captain. He was not the most gregarious of fellows but he liked the style of Hammond. Mr Fraser's recommendation had gone personally to him, after all. It must be taken as some kind of affection for Hammond that Robinson named his dog 'Wally'. They used to joke that it stalked and deflowered the female canine population.

In the net and practice sessions of the early 1920s, Wally was enthralled by the language and cynicism of the older pros. Parker littered his envied wisdom with the 'cussing' of the Prestbury hayfields, where his father had struggled to make some kind of living and bring up a big family. Alf Dipper was so wonderfully rural and uncoordinated that it was hard to see how he got into position so quickly for those cross-batted shots when he was in the mood for diversions of aggression. Harry Smith would explain how a Bristol lad from Fishponds could end up profitably spending his winters chasing down the wing for Bolton Wanderers, no less.

This was all education for Hammond, so much more than he had chosen to extract from the grammar school textbooks. He didn't say too much and wasn't sharp enough – ever – for dressing room repartee. All the time he absorbed the technique being offered in the nets. Like all talented boys, he was arrogant enough to ignore some of the counsel. In truth, as a lad still two years short of twenty, his instincts knew more about cricket than those of many of his older team-mates.

Two tutors he respected immensely were John Tunnicliffe and George Dennett. It's a good moment to acknowledge their influence. For part of 1922, when there were problems over Hammond's registration for Gloucestershire and the county had to decide how best to stall, he was sent along to Clifton College, ostensibly to help a little with the coaching. The idea was that the coach at the college, John Tunnicliffe, would also find time to put Hammond right on one or two points of his batting. The rangy old cricketer had been a fine batsman in his day. He had played nearly 500 times for Yorkshire, once scoring a double hundred in 1898 at Chesterfield, where he figured in that world record opening stand of 554 with J T Brown. He was a shrewd coach, loving the game as only a Yorkshireman can. His unofficial pupil from the county staff was never good at asking for advice or reassurance. But Tunnicliffe was, as Hammond admitted more than once, the most perceptive coach he ever had.

Dennett was less dour, a slow left-arm bowler coming towards the end of a solid and under-valued career for Gloucestershire. He was a modest, always amiable man. It was hard to prise from him the fact that he was the county's first bowler to take 200 wickets in a season, or that his nagging off-stump precision had brought him all ten against Essex in 1906. His record surely entitled him to Test recognition: but you never heard him broach the subject. His voice belonged to Hardy's Wessex.

George's interest in Wally was instantly avuncular. He spent hours bowling to him in the nets, and that was when the shy Hammond became a peerless player of slow bowling. Twenty-four years older than the young professional, there was probably more rapport between Dennett and Hammond than, whatever the circumstances, between Wally and his father. Observers sensed a sort of vicarious parenthood here. In the days when Hammond lay critically ill in the Bristol nursing home, gentle George Dennett would be a regular visitor – just like Bert Williams, another surrogate father.

But we return to the 1921 summer. The punctilious Lord Harris, that intractable stickler for the letter of the law, had ascertained that Hammond shouldn't be playing for Gloucestershire at all. Someone had small-mindedly reminded the Canterbury despot that this precocious lad had been born at Dover. There was a sharp exchange of letters with Gloucestershire's officials; the upshot was that Hammond had to serve a two-year qualification. Lord Harris was never forgiven by Gloucestershire, or by Hammond, who later wrote: 'I was livid – and I was also perfectly helpless'. It was one of the injustices, cruel and illogical as he saw them, that punctuated his life.

So championship matches were out of the question in 1921;

there was no immediate chance to build on his burgeoning reputation and, in the process, to obliterate those minor failures at the tail end of the previous summer. He played instead for Gloucester and other club cricket, but it wasn't quite the same. The psychological momentum was being disturbed. His two first-class matches were against the Australians; neither time did he distinguish himself in the least.

The Tourists came to Bristol in June. They were in great heart, a superb all-round side. The night before, when Hammond was doing some ground staff work, Foster Robinson had told him he'd be playing. There was another surprise when the Gloucestershire batting order was announced. Wally was opening with Old Dip. And he was out, almost in the next breath, for one. That was dispiriting. But he was again selected when the Australians played at Cheltenham in the August. Once more lack of first-class match practice went against him. Now he'd been dropped to No 5 in the order. He was out for O and 1. Jack Gregory, with the fastest delivery he'd ever faced ('He absolutely frightened the life out of me') knocked his stumps out of the ground in the first innings; then he was one of Arthur Mailey's ten victims in the second. There need be no disgrace in failing against that kind of illustrious opposing company.

Mr W L A (Bill) Coleman, of Braunton, North Devon, has been a member of Gloucestershire County Cricket Club for many years and is a collector of cricketana. Some time ago, going through a scrapbook he had bought, he found an article written for a Bristol evening paper in the 1930s by 'Blue Feather'. This was the pseudonym for H E Roslyn, who had been writing about Gloucestershire cricket from the days of W G Grace. Mr Coleman already had in his possession a collection, passed on by his father, of earlier articles by Roslyn, which had appeared in the *Bristol Times and Mirror.* Roslyn, a well-known West Country sports writer of his day, was associated with the Gloucestershire club from 1887 and accompanied them to almost every first-class ground in the country for many years. He later became a member of the management committee. For more than thirty years he was the honorary secretary of that esoteric and distinguished artistic body, the Bristol Savages. Wally was later enrolled as a member, receiving not a blue but a green feather.

Mr Coleman is assembling a miscellany of Roslyn's absorbing, intimate articles into book form as a collectors' item and he has given me permission to quote from one of them, touching on Hammond's early days and the problems over registration:

> I well remember my first meeting with Hammond on Clifton College Close. It was on the morning of a match with Old Cliftonians in August 1920, arranged to fill out the week. As a preliminary to an introduction, Foster Robinson handed me a letter from the headmaster of Cirencester Grammar School, recording some of his pupil's feats.
>
> They were so remarkable that it was evident he was well worth looking after. Yet his appearance was not impressive. Rather tall for his age, he was all arms and legs, and so nervous at meeting so many strangers that he could hardly say a word. Still, there was something about him which at once aroused my interest; and that was deepened when he came to bat.
>
> What I first noticed was the easiness of his stance. This, coupled with confidence, enabled him to meet the ball with the full force of the bat, and make strokes with a sureness unlooked for in a novice. Before being caught off the bowling of Percy Robinson, 60 runs stood to his credit.
>
> It was assumed he would in due course become a regular member of the team. No formal engagement was entered into, and that omission nearly cost us his services. One morning I received an urgent summons to an emergency committee meeting. Somebody had learned that Kent had invited Hammond to join their staff. They were keen to get him because he was born in Dover, and they might well offer better terms than we could afford. But we were determined to forestall them. Two of our officials went to see Mrs Hammond. They took with them a contract and did not leave until it was duly signed. That did not end our trouble. Kent objected to Wally's qualification. The MCC upheld their objection, so he had to stand down for two years.

During the Somerset match at Taunton in May 1922, Sam Woods – never particular about the qualification of some of the recruits he enlisted – expressed indignation at the ruling of the authorities at Lord's. He said Somerset would support Gloucestershire if they ignored it, and urged Foster Robinson to include Wally in the engagement with Derbyshire at Gloucester, which opened later in the week. He was sorely tempted to do so; and on reaching Gloucester at a late hour, there was a conference in my bedroom at the New Inn. It was solely the uncertainty as to what would happen to Hammond if the MCC were defied that induced us to observe their mandate. If any other course had been adopted, it is quite certain he would never have captained England.

During his probationary period, he figured in a few games outside the championship with far from flattering results. Some of us, however, never lost faith in him and when his trials were over, he justified our confidence by scoring 110 and 92 against Surrey in the opening match of 1923 at Bristol. From that day he never looked back.

Committee member Roslyn's account is as authentic as any we are likely to get on the bad blood between Gloucester and Kent. There does seem to have been a clear intention on Kent's part to poach Hammond, even if the birthplace was the county's only – and tenuous – claim on him. They had the rule-book on their side. And Lord Harris was thundering away before long in dogmatic pedantry. The popular version of an unedifying rumpus is that Kent objected to his registration only after he had become ensconced at the county ground in Bristol. But the rumours that Kent had been targeting him themselves before that, albeit in a fairly casual way, may have had genuine substance.

Chasing Down the Wing

Hammond was coming up to nineteen. He had never been one to pause and question things: the carnage of the trenches, why his father had to die, whether there would be a better, more harmonious world after the Armistice. The curmudgeonly attitude of a county, whose headquarters were almost 200 miles from Bristol, jolted him. He was just about to make some kind of living for himself, by hitting and bowling a cricket ball, and some distant authority was attempting to block his aspirations.

'Bloody Harris', the politically truculent Charlie Parker would say to him, 'what does he know about young lads like you – just out of school and with only a few bob to spend? Went to Eton, he did. Then he were Governor of Bombay'. There was distaste in every syllable. 'And he runs Kent cricket – no one else gets in a word. Has spent his bloody life getting after poor sods who he reckons *transgress,* because they got a funny bowling action or because they was born and spent a few days in another county. Wanted you for Kent, the crafty old bugger.'

That would summarise Parker's view of the affair. 'Transgression' was a favourite word of his. His voice belonged to Prestbury but the vocabulary was extensive. He'd already been in trouble with the Gloucestershire committee himself. They would tap the mahogany table with mounting impatience and say: 'We hear you've been transgressing again, Parker – you must control that temper or you'll be leaving us.' He didn't leave, of course, till he'd played more than 600 matches for the county, audaciously threatened 'Plum' Warner with fisticuffs in a crowded hotel lift and defended his corner in life with fearless indiscretion, to the chortling delight of his fellow pros.

Hammond listened to Parker. It was said that in the years to come he always seemed to try that bit harder against Kent. He listened to Parker – and he listened to Harry Smith, the wicket-keeper. Harry, a Bristolian, was almost as talented at football. He was a professional at both sports. 'Two football clubs here in Bristol, Wally. Why don't you see if you're good enough. I'll put in a word for you. We can all do with a few extra bob in the winter'. Bristol City appealed more to Hammond, but he joined the Rovers instead. They had heard about his prowess charging down the wing at the grammar school; they also took a surreptitious look at him playing a game or two in the first division of the Downs League in Bristol. He was signed for the start of the 1921-22 season.

Bristol Rovers were enthusiastic about their teenage capture. They sent Bert Williams to meet him off the train. 'I didn't even know what he looked like – but I recognised the school scarf he was wearing. I'd found some digs for him and took him straight there'. Hammond's career as a professional footballer lasted for three seasons. It wasn't memorable; he made 20 first-team appearances and scored twice. The new manager at the club, Andrew Wilson, a Scottish international who had played for Sheffield Wednesday for 20 years, was a shrewd judge and suspected that Hammond had a wayward loyalty to soccer. It was a reasonable assessment. The rigorous training disciplines weren't much to his liking. His football was essentially instinctive; he didn't consider he was going to benefit much from the recurrent exercises and rudimentary moves that the old-fashioned Mr Wilson dreamed up.

Bert Williams had quickly become one of Wally's confidants. He could see that the newcomer had more natural talent than most of the gruff, good-natured pros around him. 'Give it a go, Wally. If Patsy Hendren can do it, so can you.' In fact, these two fine cricketers opposed each other just once on the football field, Bristol Rovers against Brentford. Rovers won; but their record, on the intermittent occasions that Wally played, was undistinguished.

The almost filial bonding which Williams extended to Hammond offered something that the young cricketer missed in his own home life. When the winger arrived for training in the morning, the white-coated Williams was invariably the first and most welcome figure he saw. In addition to his Rovers duties, Bert was unofficial masseur to an army of rugby, tennis and squash players, to athletes and to cricketers from the county ground. He kept them all, including Wally, amused with tales of the intermittent floods at Eastville and of the time he once swam in five foot of water, in his best clothes, to rescue a canary from the dressing room.

At times Wally's partner on the right wing was Joe Walter, another Bristol boy who went on to play for Huddersfield Town in their great championship-winning sides of the mid-20s. Nearly seventy years later, he would come to watch Rovers again and be persuaded to talk about Hammond.

'We got on well together. Not that any of us knew him too well. He was one of those who didn't hang around after training or a match. He'd get dressed and clear off. Maybe there was a bit of shyness about him. He certainly didn't like people talking to him about cricket. As a footballer he was very clever with the ball. He nearly always made use of it. He understood me and I understood him. But cricket, I felt, was going to be his future. He'd avoid a heavy tackle or anything like that. Some at the club thought he should have taken a few more risks. But he told them straight he didn't want to be injured playing football.

'There was something very strange about him, you know. He never wore ordinary shin-guards like the rest of us. He used to have a pair of cricket leg-guards. He had cut the bottoms and the tops off. We all used to laugh about it, seeing him pull his stockings up over. His legs would be all out here, really big. But of course, there was some sense in it. You can get a very nasty kick on the shin.'

Joe Walter was a cricket fan and would go to the county ground in the summer months specifically to watch his right-wing partner. He got the impression that, at Eastville, young Hammond was just a little stand-offish. Wally was to admit himself that he didn't have too much in common with the majority of the Rovers professionals. Most of them were older than him, ready to do almost mechanically what they were told at training – it was a continuation for some of army ritual, in a way – and then wander off home to the wife and kids. There was no sign of social ambition. The occupants of the dressing room at the county ground had more compelling personalities.

Yet Bert Williams would remember that, in their inarticulate styles, the footballers appeared 'in awe of him'. They sensed that he possessed a special sporting aura. They looked at each other when they heard he'd chosen to find new digs in up-market Clifton; they gazed enviously at the second-hand car in which he arrived for training. They agreed without a murmur of dissension that he was the fastest player on the books. In more relaxed moments of training, they would have unofficial races with spikes on. Hammond won in a jaunty stroll. One or two of the team supposedly fancied their golf drive. Wally had recently taken up the game, encouraged by affluent businessmen in the city to whom he'd been introduced. A challenge was arranged. I heard the story from various sources, including trainer Williams, a man with an infallible memory and not given to embellishment.

'It was a question of who could hit the golf ball the farthest. I was a witness. Wally placed his ball on the centre circle and aimed for a gas workers' platform. It was way outside the ground. I can remember it vividly – the ball actually landed on the platform where the fellers were having their sandwiches. It was an incredible drive. I don't think anyone else attempted to compete after that.'

In his last season with Rovers Hammond's social life was taking off. He was even beginning to borrow money. And a £12 demand from the Inland Revenue devastated him. He couldn't have been that stand-offish or proud, because he discussed his plight with some of the players. Jimmy Walton had the solution. He was a wing-half who had just arrived from Leeds United. Although a useful player, he only stayed at Eastville for one year. Jimmy was remembered as an incorrigible gambler: horses, cards, pitch-and-toss. It was a variation on the latter, regularly played by a crowd of the pros after training, that gave Walton his idea. 'Give me a quid, Wally, and I'll pay your tax bill for you,' he said in his persuasive County Durham voice.

He did more than that. According to Bert Williams, ace gambler Jimmy Walton turned Wally's pound into £35 in a matter of days. It probably needed a lucky investment or two on the horses, in addition to the tossing of coins in the Rovers car park.

As Hammond's salary with Gloucestershire modestly increased, so his regard for soccer lessened. He saw no real point in turning up each morning for training at the Rovers ground when Andrew Wilson had no intention of playing him regularly in the first team. His two snatched goals, against Reading and Exeter, were hardly landmarks in his career. Rovers were a poor side, mostly in the lower half of the Third Division South. The Eastville crowds, though loyal and raucous, brought no tingle of excitement to him in the way cricket spectators' more dignified applause for a cover boundary did. In any case, he was ready to opt for independence and relaxation in the winter months.

It was to be cricket only from now on. The first glimmers of celebrity were emerging. The Neales still made a great fuss of him. What a sporting dynasty that was, emanating from Brookend Farm and carrying on for Wally at Breadstone Farm, down the winding country road from the A38. He stayed with Billy as often as he could. He listened, over the years, enthralled to tales of the Neale clan: of Hastings, finest of horsemen, boxing referee, lover of the arts; of brother Maurice, who played alongside C B Fry for the Blackheath XV, and then for the Barbarians; of 'Tiny' Neale, 6ft 4 inches and 17½ stone, a police constable who regularly totted up 100 points in a rugby season for Clifton, was a champion police boxer, and held a pilot's licence. As the Neales ruefully admitted: 'We'd have been better farmers if we hadn't devoted so much time to sport!'

Though not quite a romantic about country life – it wasn't in his nature to be overtly a romantic about anything – Wally loved the atmosphere of the Berkeley Vale pubs of those days – the Fox & Goose, the Plume & Feathers and the old cider houses like the Apple Tree, just up the road from Breadstone Farm. Billy Neale remained Wally's most steadfast friend through his life. He first played for the county himself as an amateur in 1923 and, maybe reflecting the fickle economics of agriculture, turned professional in 1929. He was an uncomplicated , good-hearted man, who did the milking before setting off for the county ground. But ill health troubled him increasingly, and he died of kidney failure aged 51.

The friendship with Hammond had been cemented at Cirencester Grammar School. In turn, they showed their affection for the school. Whenever it was possible and there was no clash of fixtures, they turned out for the Old Boys' annual match. By the late 20s, Wally was back there playing in a trilby. He had seen pictures of Somerset's John Daniell and some of the others who showed a liking for flamboyant headwear. It seemed to him a kind of symbol for the established and slightly superior player, usually an amateur.

Alec Maslin went to Cirencester Grammar School a few years after Hammond. He watched the much-discussed Old Boys' match when the Gloucestershire cricketer was out first ball. He came out of the army and went to live in America and Canada. In the mid-1960s, he referred to that particular game during a writing course he was taking:

> Wally Hammond, one of England's most famous cricketers, arrived on the sports field of Cirencester Grammar School. We kids turned discreetly to watch the burly Hammond and our dignified headmaster – his old coach – chat happily as they strolled towards the pavilion. Hammond, the Babe Ruth of cricket, was at the peak of his batting career. He had now returned to play for the Old Grammarians in their annual match against the school.
>
> Bill Neale, another disciple of brighter cricket, was also playing for the Old Grammarians. Consequently, the School XI had been reinforced with two or three members of staff. Among these was Ernie Flexen, a laconic war veteran with a lean, brown muscularity, the idol of every boy in the school.
>
> A tense, expectant crowd waited for the game to start. We kids discussed yarns of Hammond's schoolboy prowess – how he had hit balls over the railway embankment, or across the brook. We darted envious glances at the school XI, resplendent in their white flannels and coveted scarlet caps and blazers, as they mingled with the celebrities.
>
> Flexen was to bowl the first over, for he was pacing the distance at the railway end. Two batsmen tripped briskly

down the pavilion steps to be met by a tide of clapping, for they were Hammond and Neale. They smiled in acknowledgment and strode to the pitch, Hammond to the batting end, where he adopted an easy stance.

Flexen made his leisurely run and delivered a ball of good length. His intention was to give Hammond the vulnerable alternatives of stepping either backward or forward. Over-confident, Hammond advanced and drove the ball straight back like a cannon shot. Flexen thrust out his bare right hand instantaneously with the hope of stopping a certain boundary hit. Leather met hand with a sickening smack but – miracle of miracles – Flexen brought off an amazing catch. He had caught and bowled the great Hammond with the very first ball of the match.

Hammond, already halfway up the pitch, was incredulous. But he was the first to congratulate Flexen, and the crowd howled its delight with both of them. He trotted back to the pavilion, smiling sheepishly, no less surprised than Flexen, who stood grinning in disbelief while he nursed his aching hand.

Hammond's quick dismissal demoralised his team-mates, and only Neale's cool survival to the end of the innings prevented an utter rout. In the second innings, Hammond and Neale treated us to the colourful cricket we had expected earlier.

It was a memorable game. Hammond and Neale provided the glamor [sic] and the headmaster took pride in his old pupils. But the lasting glory belongs to Ernie Flexen, because we had witnessed his great feat, linking his name with Hammond for evermore. Flexen: a schoolboy's idol whose feet were not 'part of iron and part of clay'.

That would have been one of Hammond's first appearances in an Old Boys' match. His appearance created quite a stir. The boundary was lined with present and past pupils and, it seemed, rather a lot of the town's curious and excited population. The catch of Mr Flexen, who had himself helped with Hammond's coaching at the school, took on epic proportions. Accounts of it have now gone into the local tourist trade literature along with the documented deeds of the Romans. Mr Maslin's evocative memoir, written far from the cricket field he revisited, and titled 'No Feet of Clay', brings authenticity and schoolboy romance to an afternoon which has threatened to veer towards fiction.

Earlier in this chapter we remarked that Hammond's social horizons were widening as he settled in at the Nevil Road ground. Indeterminate form and the unscheduled complication over registration had curbed his progress. But the soothsayers of the Bristol committee rooms were in no doubt. They valued the calm words of appraisal from George Dennett. Gilbert Tunnicliffe was now the club secretary; he shared the enthusiasm of his father, John, who not so long ago had painstakingly gone over the whole technical repertoire of batsmanship with Hammond when the two of them had sipped their mugs of tea together at Clifton College, while waiting for the boys to come for net practice.

Invitations were starting to arrive for him – to cricket club dinners, hospital dances. For a time he became part of a tennis-playing set at Bath. There was nothing untoward at that stage but everyone agreed he was quite a catch. For Wally this was nice, wholesome, giggling middle-class life, a new experience. And he decided it was very much to his liking.

The Depression wasn't far away. Back in Bristol, the churches and the socialists were holding their regular meetings in Old Market. There were the soup kitchens and the soul-searching. And the self-delusion of the flapper-culture.

Still the tea-dances throbbed with shrill, giddy, giggly vivacity. In Bath, Norah Guest had her 21st birthday party at the Weston Hotel in Newbridge Road. She was a popular girl and the party was full of laughter. Wally Hammond was invited. He accepted and was rarely off the dance floor. I talked to Mrs Guest, charming as ever at 92, still having 'a gin and martini and a cigarette a day'. She said they all grew up in the very relaxed social life of Bath. Wally was often over there. 'I was very flattered when he accepted the invitation'.

Innocent it may all have been. But all this female proximity was beginning to give him ideas. One of the crowd was Marjorie Davis. He was obviously fond of her and gave her an inscribed picture of himself. Marjorie's daughter, Mrs Betty Collins, told me that her mother actually turned down a proposal of marriage from him. Marjorie's brother, Edgar, knew Wally – or 'Tommy' as everyone in Bath called him – well and confided to Betty: 'You know that she could have had Tommy if she'd wanted him'. He made numerous visits to Bath and often saw her. Instead she married the last organist at the Assembly Rooms before the splendid building was blitzed.

Mrs Collins had one personal recollection. 'Whenever he came to the family house he would drop a large white handkerchief over a nude figurine that stood on the mantelpiece. It was his idea of a joke and it was repeated each time he came.' So he *did* possess a sense of humour – a quality sparingly demonstrated in his life, and dismissed as non-existent by some of his team-mates at county and Test level.

Perhaps it was a period in his development when he felt he could still laugh. He had pretty, well-spoken girls in Bath eagerly waiting their turn to dance the Charleston with him. He was getting invited to the tennis parties. The old banger he drove with spluttering pride gave him some kind of cachet as well as mobility. He was beginning to play golf, with a borrowed set of clubs. It wasn't at all a bad life. He had every reason to smile and, with mock modesty, to cover the naked figure on the mantelpiece. The neuroses weren't yet bearing down on him.

The 1924 season beckoned and that infuriating ban the MCC had imposed on him was over. Now it was time to start making runs for Gloucestershire. And, with equal ardour, to chase the girls.

PART III

THE CRICKETER

County Days Between the Wars

If only the Bristol wicket had been endowed with human qualities and had access to a good libel lawyer, litigation would have made it rich. It was maligned by many – from 'Farmer' White and Dar Lyon to Jack Meyer and Brian Close. 'RJO' likened it to the sands at Weston-super-Mare. But unloving words were expressed not only for Nevil Road. 'Gubby' Allen went to another Bristol ground, Packer's, with Middlesex and said the wicket was quite appalling, one of the worst he'd ever seen. This was in the final county match of 1924. Gloucestershire had been bowled out for 31 and Middlesex for 74. The atmosphere was throbbing with pejorative comments. Committee members fidgeted; the secretary kept his door shut, although the Middlesex amateurs recurrently banged on it. As for the groundsman, the scapegoat as ever, he felt like shooting himself.

Hammond's season had been undistinguished by the standards of what had been expected. He had taken a hundred off Somerset at Taunton and failed by four runs to score a hundred off Oxford at Bristol. Cheltenham had been a disaster for him, with a rare, embarrassing pair against Worcestershire. Between innings against Middlesex he was caught mooching around the boundary on his own. 'Remind those bastards from Lord's what you can do,' said Parker, the class struggle as relevant to him as his latest bowling figures.

He did that with a display of style and technique that demonstrated how well he was capable of playing on the most fiendishly capricious of wickets. It was 'Gubby's' first memory of Hammond – and he retained it with much admiration. The boy batsman dominated Gloucestershire's second innings, mocking Middlesex's public misgivings about the state of the square. 'He may have been dropped a couple of times but it really was quite a magnificent innings.' It allowed Hammond to reach his 1000 runs for the county, and rekindled a wavering enthusiasm for the game. Psychologically he may still have been suffering from the after-effects of that registration snub.

At times his form had been as fickle as the weather in that 1924 summer. He realised he had not heeded enough of the technical counsel given him by Dennett and Tunnicliffe. He was inclined to be too cavalier, too inclined to waft with a handsome, if wanton, flourish of the bee. 'You're not playing for the grammar school now, Wally. Settle in before you start going for your shots like that. You won't get any second chances or sympathy from the old sweats around the country.' In fact, a number of the bowlers reckoned they had already worked him out; they believed he was too incautious by nature to establish himself at a higher level.

His mother kept the cuttings and when he thought she wasn't watching he would glance down the statistics. He had started his career proper the previous year with such timely brio, scoring 110 and 92 against Surrey at Bristol. He appeared to be announcing his arrival in the most dramatic fashion, inviting the regional scribes to reach for their dictionaries in liturgies of lilting prose. Since then, he decided, he had stumbled into some kind of decline.

Was there, at that stage, some fatal flaw in his concentration? How else did he account for being out in the 90s against Surrey, Derbyshire, Warwickshire, Yorkshire and Oxford? Bob Wyatt had got him caught for 99 at Edgbaston. There had been too many casual, cocky shots when a hundred had looked a formality. Those early aberrations may partly have accounted for the haughty way he later rebuked Compton and others for, as he saw it, giving their wicket away.

In 1925, he continued to worry about his form, although he was still too young to be undermined by the negative forces of self-criticism. He spent more time in the nets. Everyone marvelled at the instinctive grace, the effortless movement into position, the orthodoxy of the shot. 'You're safe, son. They'd play you for your fielding alone.' He was then more often to be seen in the covers. Nothing ever got past him. And the ball was returned sweetly to Harry Smith's gloves; the wicket keeper needed to move no more than a foot. But Hammond knew he was also in the side to score runs.

Deep into the season his first century came at Maidstone. But Old Trafford in August was worth waiting for. Worth waiting a hundred years for, according to Cardus, taking his very first look. Hammond's 250 not out is often cited among his finest innings. There are several apparent reasons for that. Cardus's prose is one. It would have been handwritten as usual, and the *Manchester Guardian* sub-editors back in Cross Street, would rightly have indulged him; maybe checking a classical allusion but not daring to alter sentiment or syntax. Another, more valid, reason for placing the innings on such a shimmering pedestal was the manner in which Hammond destroyed the dignity and credence of Ted McDonald, who with Jack Gregory had formed the most devastating opening attack thus far seen in test cricket.

The Australian had come to Old Trafford by way of the Lancashire League. He had a peerless action and a tetchy temperament. No upstart batsman was going to take him apart. He fired straight and true; he narrowed his eyes and dug the ball in malevolently short; now in compounded despair, he varied pace, length and line. He heard Mancunian voices teasing him with the irony of it all, in that native manner they have of applauding an heroic opponent. Mac, with his joints aching and face grimmer by the over, bristled at this overt impartiality. He didn't believe in that; nor did he believe in allowing callow 22-year-olds outrageous flights of arrogance.

No one of that tender age should be allowed to lean back and hook him with such matter-of-fact facility for six. It wasn't just the occasional liberty; the more McDonald pitched short, the more Hammond heaved him away. It was an extraordinary sight, adventurous and playful at a great bowler's expense. We must find it desperately hard to understand why he was to eliminate the hook shot from his repertoire. He was to justify this by emphasising that the hook was an attacking strike fraught with danger. So it is, as every unimaginative cricket coach will tell us. But danger and risk are part of sport and life itself. Yet who are we to dare criticise ageless geniuses like Hammond or Hutton for rejecting the maverick hook shot?

In that joyous, extraordinary match at Old Trafford, Hammond and Dipper put on 330 in less than four hours. It was a partnership to rhapsodise about – if you came from the West Country. Dipper was faster than usual, not so much though, in scoring 144. It only expands the compliment to Hammond's zest and unfailing style. This was the match when, in effect, he had become known to a nation. It was wonderfully iridescent and audacious – but there would be other innings with which to compare it, some even better.

One was on his return to Old Trafford in 1927. He was fit again, physically rejuvenated after the horrors of his illness. The face had lost its boyishness, the features had hardened just a little. But he had put back the missing weight: and he had become a cricketer again, one now on the way to becoming imperishably great.

The 1927 season opened for him in stunning fashion. In a matter of weeks he was the talking-point on every sports page. He surged away towards 1000 runs in May, starting with a hundred at Gloucester and then one in each innings against Surrey at the Oval, where he mocked the vastness of the playing arena and hit the ball out of the ground. In no time he was back at Manchester, where he had dared to wreak such havoc two years before.

Those eulogistic essays by Cardus and the others were simply superseded. He drove five boundaries in a row this time off McDonald and every elderly Lancastrian continues to claim he saw them. In the first innings Hammond had gone for 99, taken at the wicket off McDonald after some surprisingly circumspect overs. In the second innings he stayed for three hours – and made 187. This supplanted the previous labels of adulation and became 'the greatest innings seen at Old Trafford'. It merely confirmed the earlier impression. To the brilliance and impudence of his onslaught against Lancashire's finest in 1925 had been added another layer altogether: one of maturity and adulthood. McDonald and his savaged confederates grudgingly acknowledged it. Hammond had saved the match for

Gloucestershire virtually on his own.

And on he went, electrifying the crowds, as he devastated the bowling of Hampshire at Southampton, of Somerset at Taunton and of Northampton at the Wagon Works. Each time he got to the 190s, leaving a growing trail of bedraggled bowlers whose only fault was, for the most part, to pitch on a length. By now the speed at which he moved into position was such that he no longer needed to wait for wayward deliveries.

He'd scored 1042 runs in May, even though Gloucestershire made a late start in the season; he ended with 2637 runs for his county (average 71). The first of the Test trials had come for him. *The Wisden Almanack* had rightly given him the accolade of recognition among the chosen five for the year.

There were many individual feats in 1928, not least Test elevation and double hundreds at the Oval, at Chelmsford; and at Bristol against Glamorgan, who were to suffer more than most at his hands – hands which could be brutal, it must be said, as well as artistic. Tommy Mitchell, the Derbyshire leg-spinner, was just one of the many bowlers driven to distraction. Tommy, good enough to play five times for England, was sometimes known as the merry-hearted cricketer. There wasn't much merriment in his big heart on the day, close to tears, he asked his skipper if he could leave the field. A mauling from Hammond had been too much for him.

In the minds of ancient West Countrymen, the season would be remembered for the Cheltenham Festival. Never did a week of cricket belong more enthrallingly to a single player. The sun shone and the ball kept skimming down that perceptible slope, through the iron railings and across the road towards the hospital. That was if it got that far: dozens of onlookers peered through those railings whenever Hammond was batting. And in 1928 at Cheltenham he overshadowed everything else. He was as omnipotent as any county cricketer, including Dr Grace, can ever have been. The only thing he didn't do, it seemed, was lead the prayers in the Gothic Chapel.

Surrey were the first Festival opponents. Hammond scored 139 and 143, two breathtaking demonstrations of off-driving, according to the local newspaper reports. The Surrey bowlers simply gave up trying to defend the boundary at the bottom of the slope, so effortlessly, almost comically, did he place his exquisite shots between the fielders. Not content with his performance at the crease, Hammond took ten catches in the match.

Cheltenham always seemed to project a certain academic primness about its matches on the College ground. Schoolboys would come back off their holidays to watch, there were invariably old military men of high rank, and the clergy. A ripple of applause was invested with infinite dignity. But, by jove, Hammond invited a shedding of some of those inhibitions in that glorious summer.

Worcestershire were the next visitors. It was a convenient and popular fixture; they brought their own supporters over the hills and down to the Regency town. Some of them anticipated another feast of runs by Hammond. They had it slightly wrong; he made only 80. Instead, he *bowled.* As Parker had found (he'd probably have stomped off home to Prestbury a couple of miles away if he had discovered otherwise) the wicket encouraged spin and controlled pace. Wally may have been a reluctant bowler but he was a versatile one. He allowed Bev Lyon to twist his arm to join the attack. He settled for off-spin, intermingled with cutters. Everyone who watched said he was unplayable that day. In just over ten overs, he took 9 wickets for 23 runs. The somewhat aggrieved Parker got the other, assisted by a short gully catch from Hammond. Worcestershire went in a second time. By now the wicket had eased – but Hammond pegged away for 33 overs to take 6-105.

I go to county historian Grahame Parker, and so many more with long, loving memories, for the sum total of Wally's harvest at the College ground. In the two matches, he made 362 runs, took 16 wickets and held 11 catches. Has there ever been anything comparable?

He finished 1928 with 2583 runs for the county. Gloucestershire themselves were in a bonnier state. Bev Lyon was taking over as captain, a bespectacled democrat. He was a high-powered business man for Rediffusion, apt to take an occasional liberty in the pursuit of a compromise over conflicting professional and cricketing diaries. He fielded bravely at short leg, propounded ideas on the game that were as ahead of their time as were Bernard Shaw's social commentaries. Most importantly of all, he got on well with Hammond and the rest of the team.

Lyon had a flair for blending exceptional individual talent into an effective unit. Apart from Hammond, he had the vastly gifted and nationally under-valued Parker. And Goddard, who had at Lyon's sagacious behest given up any notions of being a fast bowler, to re-emerge – his appeals more sonorous than ever – as an off-spinner. He would go on to take, in all, almost 3000 first class wickets and play eight times for his country.

We have already remarked on Hammond's attempts to model himself on Lyon. He tried to dress like him, speak like him. In some of the pre-war team pictures at Bristol, Bev wore the well-cut clothes in which he had arrived at the ground. There is some pictorial evidence that Hammond did the same. The rest of the players were in their flannels. On just one occasion, probably over an adventurous variation in conventional tactics, Lyon was criticised in the professionals' changing room by Hammond. It took the players by surprise; it was unlike Wally to find fault publicly with his skipper. He looked in vain for verbal support and realised at once that it had been a thoroughly unwise opinion to express. Several of his team-mates remembered it as a singular gaffe. Their spokesman (who else?) was Parker. One old stalwart recalled: 'Charlie took Wally apart that day. He also loved Bev and hated any back-biting'.

The 1929 season coincided with his wedding. There was also the reassuring glow that came with the pleasing aspects of his first Australian tour, just completed. The presents were still unpacked when he travelled to Edgbaston for a free-scoring double century, quickly followed by a hundred against Essex at Leyton. The South Africans came here and he took two hundreds off them in the Tests. Gloucestershire, too, fancied their chances. They missed him, not least his fielding, when he was needed by England. Yet only in late summer did the county's prospects of the title slip away.

Gloucestershire had become an attractive side. Lyon, blessed with imagination, was a chancer. There was no mileage in his mind for a drawn match. The wins multiplied and oppositions were inclined to recoil from his cunning entreaties 'to make a game of it'. Rather too many of them had been seduced by his charms, allowing Gloucestershire to romp home.

In 1930 they finished second to Lancashire. Hammond composed a pretty two hundred against Oxford University at The Parks and failed by a single run to reach it at the Oval. In between, he played a few reckless shots and was not always at his tingling best. He was, however, beyond any question, in that historic tie with the Australians when they came to Bristol. Old misty-eyed Bristolians, some of whom had queued for hours to see the match, could recite the complete scoreboard years later. They were lucky to get into the Fry's ground; hundreds were turned away. Romantics and many of the West Country players preserved and framed copies of the game's epic statistics.

Hammond's 89 in the second innings, against some excellent and fiercely competitive Aussie bowling, was a treasury of technical skills that ensured the tautest of finishes to this low-scoring match. He had gone cheaply in the first innings; this time he grafted, he farmed the bowling, he gave a flawless demonstration of concentration while the young Bradman watched from the covers. Harry Smith, at number 6, gave him reliable support. Mostly it was just Hammond, in another class and doing nothing that offered the merest risk.

Those who spend winter nights compiling lists of his finest innings – the most subjective of exercises – must include his 89 runs in that late-August fixture against the Australians. He was finally bowled by an absolute beauty from the slow left-armer Hornibrook. His innings utterly lacked dynamics: and yet it still takes its place, because of the thoughtful, selfless manner he fashioned it, with those that will live for ever in Gloucestershire folklore.

The Australians were left to score 118 to win. Lyon could have opened his attack with Barnett and Sinfield, not the most fearsome pairing it must be said, against the Tourists. He banked on the slow spin of Parker and Goddard instead. They took all the wickets between them. Parker, cap on and sleeves buttoned at the wrist, was never more parsimonious, and took 7 for 54; Goddard, poker-faced, gripping the ball in that big fist of his, was in good voice. And that Barton Street voice thundered triumphantly for the final time as – after agonising maidens in a ground of momentous silence – Hornibrook played defensively, missed and was judged to be bang in front. Umpire Buswell, the former Northamptonshire wicket-keeper, was in no doubt.

It was estimated that there was a crowd of 17,000. Most of them spilled in indescribable joy onto the field, all doing their best to hoist the ungainly Goddard and Parker, outwardly the least emotional of men, onto their shoulders. Hammond, another adept at keeping personal feelings obscured, was to admit that this tied match provided him with his most moving sporting experience. An admission indeed.

Hundreds of words of jubilant, figurative prose have been written about that fixture. Bristol would never again have such a crowd; two sides, one of them with timelessly famous names like Ponsford, Bradman, Kippax, McCabe, Richardson and Grimmett, would never again be able to sculpt a match of such exquisite shape.

Team spirit, an often elusive state of harmony, was at its peak at the county ground in those days. The Gloucestershire players had the greatest difficulty making their way to Temple Meads station that night: they had a fixture next day at Swansea's St Helen's. As soon as they waved goodbye to the hundreds of spectators, who had followed them in a state of mesmerised adulation from Nevil Road to the station platform, they sank into their reserved-compartment seats. Almost in the same movement, Lyon was reaching for his hand-luggage, and out came the hurriedly acquired bottles of scotch. The captain, arch democrat that he was and sitting completely at ease with the pros, believed in celebration. Each swigged from a bottle, passing to the next man in thirsty rotation. 'Here's to Charlie, Tom and Wally', the skipper toasted. No one could have disagreed with that.

Lyon was in confidential mood as he moved onto the second bottle. 'We didn't quite beat those Aussies – but I'd like to see us win the championship before I have to pack in this job.' They had assumed, and hoped, he would continue as the captain for years. The county never had a more popular skipper. He put a few catches down at short-leg but was a fearless close fielder as he crouched almost in the block-hole. In the middle of the batting order, his approach was punchy and eager without, in his case, too much sophistication in technique. He was an average county cricketer but a shrewd skipper – and a master when it came to fellowship.

'I've got my business to think about. Can't give the time to too many more years of cricket. May have to phase myself out gradually. Wally here can step in while I'm away.' The two had doubtless discussed this eventuality. Charlie, more senior as a pro, would hardly have been captaincy material with his wayward disciplinary record. Tom didn't have the authority or enough positive tactical sense for the temporary job. Wally was the obvious deputy: his technical knowledge was vast, he was essentially a team man, and everyone knew that he would relish the kudos that leadership provided.

In evenings with Bev, at a hotel bar or when they dined together, Hammond revealed that he hoped one day to be making enough money outside the game to be able to play as an amateur. And then he could be Gloucestershire's captain as well. 'But don't mention it to anyone, Bev. I wouldn't like that to get around at the moment.'

In fact, Lyon continued for another season or two. His tactics remained challenging, and Hammond knew inwardly he could never be half as daring. In 1931, with the compliance of the Yorkshire captain, Frank Greenwood, Lyon engineered a freak declaration and what amounted to a one-innings match. The authorities were appalled, but Gloucestershire's rebellious visionary was never bothered by the predictable responses of the game's stuffed shirts.

'We made a game of it, Wally. And we got maximum points. If they don't approve of what I'm doing, they'll have to change the regulations.' That, in fact, was what happened. Hammond would not, by nature, have rocked the boat. He had a sneaky regard for his idol's impudence, but had neither the vision nor imagination ever to emulate it. And he had no wish to antagonise cricketing friends in high places.

But back to his county cricket. Hammond ended the 1931 season with centuries against Glamorgan and Northamptonshire. There had been five hundreds in all for Gloucestershire, and six more came in 1932. He saved his finest for Liverpool at the end of that summer. It seemed as though he plundered the Lancashire attack with ritualistic purpose. Those earlier feats at Old Trafford were, in 1932, followed by 164 against them at Cheltenham College, and 264 at Liverpool. This was the summer when All India came to Bristol to play the county at Clifton College. Grahame Parker remembered the match for the cheeky manner Hammond took a catch on the square leg boundary. He clearly wasn't always in the slips.

'It was odd to see him out there. Talking to a lady on the boundary, too', added Parker, smiling at the memory and no doubt imagining the extramural scenario. 'Suddenly Amar Singh picked up a short one from Reg Sinfield and belted it, flat and square, towards Wally. Hammond was standing only a yard or so inside the boundary and he actually took the catch one-handed across his chest. He'd judged it perfectly and didn't have to move. I suppose anybody else would have caught the ball two-handed . . . and still probably fallen flat on their face.'

The wide-eyed Grahame Parker, just 20, down from Cambridge and in his first season with Gloucestershire, applauded with boyish incredulity. 'It was the last first-class match at Clifton College, you know,' he told me. 'As for Wally fielding out there, well I suppose he'd only have done that for a lady!'

What possessed him to take the catch, with such ludicrous ease, one hand casually placed across his torso? Could it have been a rare flight of arrogance? Was he showing off in front of an adoring spectator? According to his novice team-mate, there never appeared to be the slightest danger of the ball being dropped. It contrasts sharply with the absence of ostentation or boorish histrionics in his play. That public jauntiness at the Close was in no way typical; nor was his isolated, perhaps misinterpreted, treatment of an Oxford player, fielding in the covers to the great man.

'Don't worry, old chap. I won't hit you.' He said it after a succession of off drives that eluded the eager, sprawling fielder. First the ball scorched one side of him, then the other. The undergraduate, renowned at that level for the sharpness of his reflexes and the nimbleness of his movement as he patrolled the covers, was made to look comically superfluous. Hammond may well have made that remark to him as a spontaneous joke.

Some, hyper-sensitive in their youth and fearful of making themselves look silly in front of their dons, claimed that the comment was needlessly haughty. They were almost certainly wrong.

The correspondence columns of the newspapers rumbled away during the 1933 domestic season with liverish reaction to the Bodyline tour. The tones of the argument were jingoistic as well as moralistic. In the Gloucestershire dressing room, the pros crowded round Hammond for an intimate account of what had really happened out there. He shrugged, told them he didn't really approve and left it at that.

His principal pursuit that 1933 summer was to make runs. Some said he was hardly ever away from the crease – but they must have forgotten his ducks against Somerset and Yorkshire which he threw in to assure us he was mortal after all. For most of the time he batted like a dream. Leicestershire, Glamorgan, Derbyshire and the West Indians (when they came to Bristol) would grudgingly accept the ethereal simile. He took double hundreds off all four of them. At New Road, Worcester, he scored a century in each innings. He was also less contrary about his bowling; Surrey and Nottinghamshire, in particular, wished he hadn't been.

That added up, including 3323 runs in all matches, to a commanding prelude to his 1934 benefit. Schoolboys queued up to sell the modest brochures or to take the buckets round the ground for his special match against Hampshire over the Bank Holiday. The overall benefit receipts came to slightly more than £2,600, a timely boost to a bank account which was inclined to be ravaged by regular bills from his fashionable tailors in Clifton and other social commitments. He enjoyed spending money.

My late sports editor in Bristol, George Baker, who retained a schoolboy's hero-worshipping regard for Hammond despite recurrent professional snubs ('I always understood he was responsible for the clause put into Test players' contracts that they wouldn't talk to the press') went along to report one of the various club matches arranged in 1934 as part of the benefit.

'It was played in the evening at the small, historic Downend ground, on the edge of Bristol, and literally stopped the traffic. The Gloucestershire team had arrived straight from the county ground and by the time Wally came in to bat, the crowd had spilled all over the surrounding roads. Buses and cars were marooned. It was impossible to move.

'He didn't let anyone down. He stroked and smote his way to a ton in no time at all. The memory of such magic lingered for years.'

The season itself was adorned with memorable double centuries at the expense of Kent, Notts and luckless Worcestershire. Glamorgan, who must have regretted their short, traumatic journey to the Wagon Works the previous year, worked out a plan of Celtic cunning to avoid a repetition in 1934. They told Jack Mercer to attack the Master's leg-stump. The strategy worked, restricting Hammond to a paltry 302 – without once needing to withdraw the blue-silk handkerchief from his right trouser pocket to wipe away the sweat.

Earlier that summer he had also murdered 'Tich' Freeman when scoring that 290 at Tunbridge Wells. Les Ames played in that match – and remembered. 'It was a perfect wicket and poor little Tich had absolutely no chance. He was hammered all over the place. It was typical and often brilliant batting by Wally against slow bowling. And remember that Tich was, in my opinion, one of the greatest leg spinners of all times'. (The diminutive Freeman took over 3750 wickets with his leg-breaks and googlies during his first-class career.)

Ames, by now a Test colleague and increasingly a friend, had played against Hammond for the first time seven years earlier at Dover. He stumped him, too. 'Wally got his usual hundred against us and what comes back to me is one unorthodox stroke of his against Hardinge, our slow left-arm bowler. Hardinge had been given some awful hammer previously and now he was bowling very wide at Hammond. Suddenly the batsman swivelled round and hit the ball left-handed over the heads of the slips. It infuriated our bowler, who ticked Hammond off.'

So the batsman, essentially a text-book practitioner who seldom chose to improvise, was essaying the reverse-sweep in the mid 1920s.

His 100th century came in 1935, after no more than a dozen years (and he hadn't strapped on a pad in England in 1926). 'W G' took more than twice as long. The milestone was passed with a minimum of fuss. Hammond had been out of sorts missing nets with permission and spending hours stretched out across the lockers in the changing rooms. Recurrent sore throats dogged him and he seemed to have permanent tonsillitis. His form suffered. When Somerset arrived at the county ground in Bristol, he took Sinfield aside. 'I'm feeling rotten, Reg, and my confidence is going out there. Should I give it a miss for a few weeks?'

Sailor-boxer Sinfield, the team's most hardy member, sniffed at such defeatism. 'Hit your way out of trouble, Wally. Get out there and smash the ball about for the first 20 or 30. Then settle down to your normal game.'

They found themselves at the wicket together. Sinfield approved as his partner started hitting the Somerset bowlers back over their head. Soon Hammond was 50 . . . and then 116. The ripple of applause was more dignified than vociferous. Why were West Country spectators often unnecessarily reserved when they had every right to show their joy? They had done it rather better at Ashton Gate, across the city, in the days when little 'Fatty' Wedlock, Bristol City's first England international, had risen like a giant to out-jump visiting centre forwards seemingly twice his height. Grace had enjoyed the acclaim as he stuck his left toe characteristically into the air and pulled the four that gave him his century of centuries in 1895. The flunkeys charged onto the field with the champers; he took charge of the committees that immediately set to work organising his dinner and the latest subscription list; he made sure there were plenty of locums around to look after his surgery while he extended his absence from medical duty.

For Hammond the feat was just a passing event. Statistics didn't preoccupy him; he left his mother to paste-in the reports. After that historic hundred, he was invited along with his teammates to share a celebratory drink with the chairman and secretary. And that was about it.

He captained the pros in the Gentlemen v. Players match that year, and whacked a late 252 at Leicester. His doctor was saying to him: 'You're going to need those toxic tonsils out'. Hammond went into St Mary's private nursing home in Bristol, where another patient was Len Creed, a former chairman of

Somerset CCC, who was having his appendix removed.

'It was my 17th birthday and the greatest thrill for me was the news from my family that the great Wally Hammond was in another ward. I picked up a pencil and paper and summoned up enough courage to knock on the door of his small, private ward. The nurses had a word with him and I'm not sure he was too keen on the idea. But then he had me in and signed his name for me. I was pretty tongue-tied and it wasn't exactly an easy conversation. I retreated with thanks – and treasured the signature for years.'

His slow recuperation from a painful throat operation meant that Wally missed some of the early games of the 1936 season. It wasn't a summer to enjoy; too much rain, too few runs in the West. Gloucestershire, in fact, at last woke up with the sun. They bounced from their traps and ended the season like unbeatable greyhounds. And so they were, with six wins out of seven, to end in fourth position in the table. It had been a quite splendid run, incorporating Cheltenham, ever a resolute friend when needed most.

The last match of the season was at Gloucester. There could have been nowhere else than the beloved, soulless Wagon Works for Tom Goddard's benefit. His carpet shop was only a mile or so up the road. Players used to joke that if wife Flo wasn't too certain about a price, she could always shout to Tom for a second opinion. For the benefit match, against Nottinghamshire, his Gloucester friends – some from the local pubs where he regularly played skittles and let go a shout of LBW vintage every time he aimed for the 'landlord' – rallied loyally but the Wagon Works trifled wickedly with his affections. The weather decreed that it would be a spinners' wicket. It wasn't the fault of groundsman Arthur Paish, a former slow bowler for the county himself and one who in 1899 had spun out 137 opponents. He drank with and was a member of the same bowlers union as Big Tom. And by the end of the first day of the match, he was spluttering his apologies.

'Sorry, Tom. How was I to know it were going like this? Trouble is, you can never tell at Gloucester.'

'I relied on you, Arthur. And here it is, bloody breaking up. Never going to last for three days. And that's hundreds down the pan.'

Hammond overheard the plaintive conversation. He had seen Notts bowled out by late afternoon – and the early Gloucestershire wickets had gone, too. Goddard's face, always saturnine, was longer than ever.

'Don't panic, Tom. I'll make sure the match lasts. For a start, I'll bat all day on Monday.'

There were cracks in the wicket; the ball kept turning. The bowling demanded utter concentration. As for the faithful who had come to boost Tom's fund, they couldn't decide what they wanted most – some entertaining batting to justify their decision to take a couple of days off work, or Goddard at his match-curtailing best. Hammond was as good as his pledge to the angular, laconic old mate with whom he used to room. He batted for six and a half hours and scored 317 runs. It was yet another wonderful performance, in which he vigilantly defied the spinners, not to mention Bill Voce, and yet managed to play his strokes with artistic freedom. Goddard came out of the pavilion to meet him as the batsman came in. 'Worth more than a pint, that, Wally'.

A lifelong Gloucestershire supporter, Mr R W Spencer, did not miss a ball of that triple century. In the course of the research for an HTV documentary on Hammond, Mr Spencer came up with a delightful story which reflected a warm, welcome side to Hammond's personality. 'Although I loved cricket as a small boy, I wasn't always able to attend county matches. When I returned, Wally came and sat beside me. He asked me why I hadn't been lately and I told him my meagre pocket money didn't run to it. Soon after that, I received a schoolboy membership card by post. I was never quite sure who sent it to me but I always felt it must have been him.'

Hammond topped the national average again, inevitably, with 3252 runs in 1937. Much was happening, in addition to the 217 against Leicestershire. He was in the process of restructuring his life. There was a business directorship and the announcement that he was proposing to play in future as an amateur. Not everyone was surprised; yet you could hear the buzz of astonishment, cynicism, misgivings around the country.

'I told you – he's too good for us.'

'Now you know why he was toadying to 'Plum' so much.'

'He's going to get the England captaincy – and he's just not cut out for it.'

You could eavesdrop on such remarks in every corner of the dressing room, every pub where the game's devotees gathered.

And by 1938 he was leading his country against Australia, he was leading The Gentlemen against The Players, he was elected to MCC. The Gloucestershire management committee extended life membership to Wally and to the woman to whom he was still nominally married. The county had every reason to bask in the formal elevation of their most famous player.

By then double centuries were almost commonplace. He followed his 237 against Derbyshire with 271 against Lancashire (yes, them again), both at Bristol. He went to and returned from South Africa. At the county headquarters, a rubber stamp was really all that was needed to appoint him as captain. He succeeded Basil Allen, a hunting Man of Mendip. Not everyone enthusiastically approved. On one occasion during a Gents-Players match at Lord's, Warner turned to Allen:

'Basil, that Wally Hammond of yours really is a wonderful chap, isn't he?'

'If you want my honest opinion, 'Plum', I think he's an absolute shit.'

The incident came to me from three impeccable sources. I include it here, not so much to indict Hammond as to illustrate the diametrically opposed opinions about his character. Was it a peevish, retrospective salvo from Allen, country squire, joint master of the Hunt, a person who didn't like the idea of professional cricketers getting above their ordained station? Or was it a fragment of straight talking about the human condition from one amateur to another during the tea interval?

In that last summer or two before the war, Hammond composed the sweetest of centuries in each innings at Burton-on-Trent and, for the second time, lambasted the Glamorgan bowling for 302. Wilf Wooller was just one to suffer on that occasion at Newport. His innocuous swing made no impact at all, but he lived to tell the tale many times in print. 'It was truly glorious stuff to watch'.

As the war loomed, 'Podge' Brodhurst, son-in-law of H S

Altham, MCC president and influential cricket author, gained his Blue for Cambridge and played the first of his half dozen games for Gloucestershire. 'It was at Maidstone and I was pretty windy. We batted first and lost several cheap wickets, including Wally's. I was nervous and was next in. Wally was sitting next to me, a complete newcomer. How I'd have loved a word of gentle encouragement. He said nothing at all. I went out and made 50 or so. So did Desmond Eagar, I remember. I felt we'd done quite a good job. Wally was the skipper but again he ignored me when I returned to the pavilion. I was a little surprised.'

Players reacted in many different ways to him. Alpass, the lawyer and part-time cricketer, was one of the relatively few favoured with helpful advice. 'I was out there in the middle with him, facing Voce and Larwood. I'd been hanging around, most unhappily, for 20 minutes. Wally noticed my plight and between overs he chatted helpfully to me. At the time he was batting so easily and, at the other end, the ball kept whistling past me. I wasn't getting a touch. He told me that if they were pitching outside the off stump, I should leave well alone. I had to be honest and admit that they were far too fast for me and I had no idea at all where they were going to pitch. Wally went on to his hundred and, although I didn't stay for long, I appreciated the trouble he took to try to give me added confidence.'

He'd farm the bowling with disdainful skill. That could be the most unselfish of gestures if the attack was on top and his colleagues were, as was often the case, in acute trouble. On the other hand, Charlie Dacre resented being allowed a limited strike and sometimes showed a reluctance to run a single at the end of an over. Andy Wilson was altogether more generous. In 1938 he featured in a record eighth-wicket stand of 239 for the county with Hammond. 'He told me to run when he called me – and I don't think I got a ball for six overs!' The little left-hander had no complaints on that count: he stood and watched in admiration, many times, from the other end.

Sinfield got on better than some with Hammond; he even worked up some kind of whimsical rapport with him, and not many could say that. When Hammond became Gloucestershire's captain, he would take Sinfield out with him to study the strip before the match started and the toss had been made. He appeared to need a second opinion from someone he could trust: 'What do you think, Reg? Do we put them in?'

Reg told me that one day, as the pair strolled back to the pavilion, he asked Hammond why he asked him what he thought. 'Because it's for you, Reggie, you've got to bowl the buggers out'. In a side bereft of bowlers, he frequently had to open the bowling and batting.

It was from Sinfield, too, that I heard the classic story concerning another fine cricketer useful, like Reg, with his fists in the ring, J W H T Douglas, who led his country on two tours of Australia. 'We were playing Essex and Joe Hipkin was the bowler when Wally came in. He was slow left-arm and he was unwise enough to give Wally an early half-volley. It was given a tremendous crack and Laurie Eastman, fielding in the covers, threw up his hands to save his face. And the ball stuck. Everyone looked at Wally but he didn't move. Johnnie Douglas went up to the umpire quite deliberately and said 'How was that?'. The umpire, in some confusion, told him it was a bump ball. Johnny had a few pointed words with Wally.

'At the close of play we were changing when Johnny Douglas opened the door and asked where that so-and-so Hammond was. Wally was tucked away behind the door and didn't say a thing. Next day, as we were walking out to field, Wally called to Bev Lyon and said he'd like a bowl. It must have been one of the very few times! He was given the ball and came in from the top end. And when Douglas's turn came to bat, Wally was adding a few paces to his run. I've stood up to Larwood and others but never seen anything quite like this. He bowled like a demon. He hit Johnny black and blue. Had to admire the way he didn't flinch – but then he was a fine amateur boxer. I didn't ever see Wally at that fearful pace again.' Sinfield allowed those vivid blue eyes to twinkle. 'Mind you, I felt a bit sorry for Douglas. Hammond was caught in the covers all right and should have been given out'.

We aren't privy to any evidence of earlier antipathy between Hammond and Douglas. Exception was clearly taken to the tone of the Essex skipper's voice as he stormed into the Gloucestershire dressing room. The implication was that

Hammond had cheated, that he'd refused to walk when he really knew he was out – and that a weak umpire had sided with him.

That suggestion of dubious integrity may well have infuriated Wally. It was a brash condemnation of him in front of his team-mates. But I still believe that the pair must have sparred verbally before. It was a view shared by Sinfield.

Another Essex player, Ken Farnes, best and brightest of the amateur speed merchants in the years running up to the war, was subjected to some unmitigated brutality at Hammond's hands. Again the body language gave the warning that battle-lines were being drawn up. Farnes had brains enough, as he showed at Cambridge; he'd have been advised not to take on Hammond in the way he did during one home Essex match.

Gloucestershire's star was not well and had asked to be excused the fixture. His likely absence was not only bad news for his team; if it was an away fixture, the treasurer at least of the opposing county would also despair. Hammond pulled in the crowds like no one else in our domestic game. His achievements in the Tests had turned him into an icon. Cricket spectators all round the country demonstrated a refreshing interest whenever he was playing. They didn't mind if their county lost, provided he paraded those off drives and scored a hundred.

When Essex discovered that he was unfit, they sent an urgent telegram to the Bristol headquarters. Could someone persuade Hammond to change his mind? They followed up with phone calls, suitably pleading and fawning. 'You know what his presence means to us on the gate. If he's only half fit, he's better than almost anyone else in the country'.

Gloucestershire persuaded him to play. He walked out to bat with a pallid face and a heavy heart. And he found himself facing a sequence of bouncers from Farnes. The Essex bowler was not only decidedly fast: he could dig them in. Whether or not he was aware that the batsman was running a temperature, his approach was bellicose and unsentimental in the extreme. Hammond began dodging the rising ball. His evasive action was increasingly accompanied by long, smouldering looks down the wicket. He was telling Farnes that he would have to be punished for such a challenge.

Around the Essex ground the cognoscenti sensed there was

trouble coming. Who dared to say that Hammond was fearful of fast bowling and the rising ball? Hadn't he taken Ted McDonald apart in a style that Old Trafford had rarely seen?

When it came to Farnes' next over, Hammond very deliberately took a new guard. We shall never know whether the bowler grasped the significance of it. The England batsman suddenly stopped ducking. Instead he began slogging – and doing it with panache. He was picking up the pitch of the hurtling ball, stepping out of his crease and hitting back over the bowler's head for fours and sixes. It went on for some time in this destructive and fiercely eloquent mode. George Lambert was there and claimed that Hammond's language that day was as ripe as his timing was faultless.

Lambert was one who didn't really know what to make of his captain. He hated to see him, silently stationed at slip, glaring at the normally chirpy George when his line was awry and too many runs were being given away. Often the willing bowler had been kept on too long and would have welcomed a little respite himself in a more sedentary corner of the field. Yet his admiration for the great cricketer was boundless. When he arrived first in the West Country from London, he would watch the pre-season net sessions in hypnotised fascination. He used to watch Hammond select a bat from the many sent to him by the manufacturers. Then Wally would invite the whole of the county's bowling strength to try to get through his defence. 'It was one of the numerous occasions when, in a sort of party piece, he'd use the edge of his bat only. And we still didn't get through him.'

Players like Lambert came to interpret the code of Hammond the Batsman. If, at the crease, he twirled the bat before taking guard, he was in good spirits and the runs were going to come. When he gave the merest wave of the bat towards a deckchair on the distant boundary, it meant a female admirer was there.

Through the 20s and 30s he ' Gloucestershire cricket. The trams and buses were jammed with impatient fans, cheered by the news that he was at the wicket, and determined to snatch a cherished glimpse of him after they left work. Many travelled miles to see him. A 14-year-old lad, Ken Brown, was typical; he cycled from Bradford-on-Avon in Wiltshire. 'There are so many memories – of Wally taking on Larwood and Voce, or cheekily playing J C Clay between his legs for four . . . of George Lambert polishing the ball at one end, and Tom Goddard rubbing it on the ground at the other.'

Many correspondents told me of the ingenious methods devised, the intricate grapevines of communication used to discover the state of play at the county ground and indicate whether a frantic dash up the busy Gloucester Road was justified after work. The one recurrent question was: 'Is Wally still in?' His presence mesmerised a city. Idolatry on this scale wasn't limited to Bristol. An elderly cricket fan, Bill Curtis, used to spend his school holidays during the 1920s on his cousin's farm in the Cotswolds. The cousin had a horse-drawn milk float and, at the time of the Cheltenham Festival, he would complete his round earlier than usual. 'Then we'd take the float up as close as we could to the College boundary wall, give the old horse a nosebag of chaff and oats, and get a perfect view. My cousin would nearly break a blood vessel with excitement if Wally was batting. If, later on, I got a bit bored, he d turn in disgust towards me and say "We ain't goin' yet – top up that there nosebag!"'

Nothing was more touching than the memories passed on to me by an elderly lady who in the 1930s was with crowds of other children at Muller's Orphanage – that grey, forbidding row of Victorian buildings that look out over the county ground in Bristol. 'Cricket was such a big thing in our young lives. We got a wonderful glimpse of so many great players, including Jack Hobbs, as we peeped out from the high windows. Do you know, it never seemed to rain in those days.

'Discipline was very strict and some of us got caned for causing a bit of disruption in class as we passed on the latest score. Wally was our hero – he brought a touch of glamour to so many of us boys and girls. Our dads would come to Muller's on visiting days but we used to think they only came for a free look at the cricket from the playground wall. For years I lost track of my hero, Hammond. Then I read of his memorial service being held in Bristol Cathedral. I'd have liked to go but I didn't because I felt someone would have asked me why I was there. I did send up a little prayer instead.'

There must have been dozens of children who pressed their faces to the lofty windows of the orphanage. Amid the bleakness of their lives, Hammond was the metaphor for excitement and a fuller existence. That same pensioner wondered aloud whether Wally would have been knighted if he had played in a later age. Nothing came his way in terms of honours. It was an omission, surely, that would have been rectified if he had stayed longer in this country.

The Test Match Career: Bodyline and All

Wally Hammond played 85 times for his country, 20 of them as captain. He had a spectacular series in Australia under Percy Chapman, won matches almost on his own and fashioned several innings that will garnish for ever the deeds enshrined in the record books.

Some commentators have asserted that he was a bad tourist. This is not a fair conclusion, and it may have been unduly influenced by the way he behaved on his final tour of Australia in 1946-47. In truth, he entered into the spirit of conviviality whenever it was time for the England players to relax. He joined in the practical jokes, though he was never an instigator of this kind of waggish therapy, and drank his full share at the bar without any unseemly repercussions.

Until he received the nod from his mentor, Pelham Warner, to change his status – and to assume the England captaincy as culmination of the process – he could be one of the boys at least to the extent that his natural diffidence and fluctuating patterns of temperament would allow. He enjoyed being in the company of our finest players. At a score of cocktail parties and receptions, attractive hostesses gently flirted with him. There is not too much evidence that in the first ten years of his Test career he responded. Maybe overseas lessons had already been too painfully learned.

He had been pencilled in for serious consideration as an England candidate in 1926. That visit to Australia was out of the question, of course; he was probably past caring, at the time, whether his chance would ever come again. But it did the following year, when the 1927-28 party was announced for South Africa. There was no Hobbs or Hendren, no Tate or

Larwood. The attack was a negligible-looking one, even more so after George Geary hobbled off in the second Test. When Hammond's Test debut arrived at Johannesburg immediately before Christmas, he obliged with a five-wicket haul on matting, and a half-century. That was better than Bob Wyatt, who made his first Test appearance in the same match, and had only a duck to show for it.

Hammond had not yet wholly regained his strength after his illness; he'd also been sapped by a rigorous domestic season, however reassuringly successful, before the tour. It was in no sense a memorable series, either for England or the debutant from Gloucestershire. He cracked along, in his most insouciant manner, for an undefeated 166 against Border and for 132 against Transvaal, but these were exceptions.

Nor, on his return to England, did he excel in the three matches against the visiting West Indies. Warner was playfully chided by his chums at Lord's. He scratched his bald head, embarrassed that others should think he was 'potty about Hammond' (Wyatt's words to me) and said: 'You've seen what he can do for his county. Just be patient and he'll do it for England as well.'

Bob Wyatt came to know Hammond well. He studied him at close quarters on tour, noticed the shyness, the complexes and a grey kind of personality. There was much he liked about him. 'He might not eventually have wanted me, a previous captain, playing under him in a Test side. But I had found him very good indeed under me – no trouble at all. He once asked me to stay with him at Failand. We were playing at Cheltenham and he drove me in his Riley to his home near Bristol, very fast and very dangerously. It wasn't usual, of course, for an amateur like myself to be invited to stay with a pro. I remember he was very anxious for me to come. We'd been together on tour by then. Possibly we had something in common. Just like him, I wasn't terribly good at handling the press. Molly, my wife, used to say I always had a stern expression on my face and this gave the wrong impression. It was really that I was pretty shy, too.

I warmed to him in various ways. He showed great concern for me when that ball from Martindale just took off and broke my jaw. But he shouldn't really have ever been appointed captain. I didn't agree with that. He was a bit out of his depth socially, didn't seem comfortable. My objection was nothing to do with him having been a professional – I was largely responsible, after all, for Len Hutton being made captain of England.'

One could detect signs of mutual respect. Hammond approved of Wyatt's stubbornness and refusal to budge over matters of team selection. He envied the spunky challenge in RES's voice when, during the 1934-35 West Indies tour, he turned to the MCC treasurer Lord Hawke and asked: 'How about some decent expenses for the amateurs?'

'Goodness me, you don't need them, do you?'

Some of the amateurs genuinely did. 'In the end we settled for a niggardly £25. And most of that went on tips!'

We have mentioned Hammond's successful attempts, in the earlier years of his Test career, to integrate in the fullest sense on tour. Wyatt was approaching his mid-90s when I was lucky enough to be invited to spend an afternoon with him at his Cornish home. Gritty as ever, he had survived strokes, hip and back trouble. He sat happily through the afternoon session till the tea interval. There was a line of *Wisdens,* crouching prominently in the gully area. We stopped for toast and raspberry jam at 4.30 prompt and then resumed the by-ways of nostalgia. 'Oh yes, Wally did have a dry sense of humour – as I discovered to my cost on the night before our joint debuts in South Africa.'

Who said Wyatt had a stern face? The details of the prank came back graphically, amusingly, to him. 'I was very keen to do well and deliberately went to bed early, about half past ten. Several of the team decided to go for a walk. Suddenly, at one o'clock, I woke with a start to find a girl in my bed. I spluttered and asked her what the hell she was doing there. Her odd reply was that she was a 'sweetie from the sea'. At the same time, members of the tour party materialised from the wardrobe and other dark corners of my bedroom. Half the team seemed to be there. They were all in on it. The girl, Rosie I remember, had met them when she'd gone for a midnight bathe. Someone had kitted her out in Eddie Dawson's pyjamas and told her to slip into bed with me. When I batted, I was lbw before I'd scored.

And I never heard the last of it. I discovered that Wally was one of the perpetrators.'

He was in no doubt at all about Hammond's finest innings, the 240 against the Australians in 1938 at Lord's. 'I'd go further and say it was one of the greatest innings ever played. He didn't make a single mistake. Everything was made to look so easy. That driving of his through the covers had to be seen. How I wish some of the present-day players could have seen how it was done.'

Wyatt never once in his life went in for cant. Amid such affectionate shafts of nostalgia, he would switch subjects and shake his head with disapproval. 'I didn't much like the way he treated Stephens, one of the younger Gloucestershire professionals – he could be rather patronising to him, make fun of him when he brought him in to silly-point. Things like that.'

Dickie Stephens was never destined to be more than a pocket-sized journeyman pro. Much of his cricketing life was spent as 12th man, though he still made more than 200 appearances for his county. He was an uncomplicated left-hand bat from the city of Gloucester, and was an agile fielder. It's not likely he would have minded if his skipper placed him within bootlace distance of a troublesome batsman.

But just as the observant Wyatt would digress, so do I. We are considering Hammond, the Test cricketer. After South Africa, he went to Australia for the first time in 1928-29. Percy Chapman was a popular captain. He could take a joke about his fleshy waistline, and made sure all the players had a drink when it was time to relax. There was much good humour, always easier to rustle up when you were winning everything. The parties were fun, not submerged in protocol. Percy drained his glass and made jolly, ambassadorial speeches at the official functions. The whole party relished the informality of the schedule.

On the field, Hammond had rapidly struck form with a hundred against South Australia and a double one against New South Wales. In that latter match at Sydney, he first became familiar with the name of Bradman; a short, frail young man, given no more than a cursory mention in the papers before, who had nearly scored a century in each innings. As it was, 87 and

132 not out were to prove ominous portents of things to come.

In the second Test, at Sydney, where the Hill's raucous occupants actually allowed habitual barb and sarcasm to make way for something approaching admiration for the enemy, Hammond scored his first century for his country in a Test match. The spectators were openly amazed at his facility for driving so freely off the front and, more frequently, back foot. His 251 was said, almost unanimously by the writers, to be 'full of charm'. The Hill residents didn't go that far. To them, it was just 'bloody good for a Pom'.

He could do nothing wrong. At Melbourne, in the next Test, he was just as monopolistic with another double hundred. The headlines in the Australian papers reflected the concern over someone who was a newcomer to most of them and who couldn't stop scoring runs in the most entertaining and assured style. In the fourth Test, he simply continued; there was a century in each innings, and he ensured a narrow win for England. Douglas Jardine was in one lengthy and crucial stand with him. Hammond noted how competitive his partner was. Some batsmen, altogether more congenial by nature, chat and joke their way through long partnerships; it eases tension and breaks boredom. Jardine and the young man from Gloucestershire dispensed nothing more than a mutual nod of approval. They had a job to do and that, especially for Jardine, meant a rejection of anything that might border on frivolity.

Hammond's Test aggregate of 905 runs (average 113) was a new record. How was he to know that Bradman had such covetous designs on it?

A final word about that series and Hammond's burgeoning brilliance during it. In 1980 the peerless English farceur and cricket buff, Ben Travers, was persuaded to reminisce in print about the game he loved. He had accompanied our team on that relaxed 1928-29 tour, dining with the players and hardly missing a ball. Hammond, like the majority of the team, was very fond of him; indeed it would be difficult to summon up an uncharitable thought to level against the gentle, civilised playwright. Wally knew where Travers would be sitting and liked to wander along for a chat during the lunch interval.

In his book, *94 Declared*, Travers relates that Hammond

showed him the bat he had just used to score 251 runs. 'Nowadays, in the TV close-ups, one sees bats festooned with the blots of impact. Hammond's bat was unmarked, except that plumb in the middle of the sweet of the blade there was a perfectly circular indentation.' Travers goes on to describe how the great cricketer, pads still on we assume, would come off the square, take a seat next to him and borrow his field glasses. 'He would say nothing, merely hold out his hand for the glasses. There he would sit, the field glasses making a detailed tour of the Ladies Enclosure, until a few minutes before play was due to start again. Then he would say Thanks and disappear. Laconic.'

Various writers have picked on the insight. I, too, was to chuckle at the incident when, a few years earlier, I was privileged to have it related to me directly by my Aldwych idol. Travers had lived formerly at Withy Cottage, Berrow, in Somerset and, over my ingenuous journalistic decades I had rung him for spontaneous observations on the state of Somerset cricket. They were given willingly and warm-heartedly. He must have been in his late 80s when the BBC in Bristol discovered he was staying in a local hotel, and they sent me, armed with a slightly cumbersome Uher tape-recorder, to interview him.

He arrived, beaming, in the hotel lounge – at a surprisingly sprightly lick, certainly as fast as any military medium bowler. He was dressed as a country gentleman and his fine head of grey hair was groomed as if straight from a Denis Compton ad. He was courteous as ever, took infinite pains over personalised autographs for both my children, and talked with schoolboy enthusiasm about the game of cricket, and Hammond in particular.

'Of course, he liked the ladies. Well, he must have. Why else would he have wanted to borrow my field glasses in Sydney to look at all those lovely beauty queens out there?' He paused as if consumed with what might be seen as a minor betrayal of confidence, and added: 'Mind you, I never saw evidence of any ladies on his arm, though he was still a single man at the time.'

By 1930 Bradman was here, in person, stealing thunder and headlines. Hammond, by comparison, was doing his best to come to terms with Clarrie Grimmett. Not many had taken

Clarrie too seriously at first; but by now, balding and inelegant to watch, he was taking his place among the great wrist-spinners. Hammond could read his googly, less so the penetrative top-spinner. As a contest at Test match level between two dynamic world-class batsmen, the 1930 series was, for Hammond, a demoralising experience. Bradman had not simply broken the records – he had seized the psychological initiative. And he would never let go.

It was out to South Africa again in 1930-31, and some dreary cricket. The hosts won the opening Test and the others were drawn. The New Zealanders were here in 1931 under the captaincy of Tom Lowry, Percy Chapman's brother-in-law, who had made a lively impact during his incumbency at Taunton and bade farewell in Bristol to Somerset at just about the time Hammond was arriving. Wally gave the Kiwi bowlers an unenviable time at the Oval, so much so that for one traumatic spell they lost all pretence at length and line.

England returned to New Zealand for a couple of Tests immediately after the Bodyline tour, to which we shall briefly return later in the chapter. There has been a disproportionate number of drawn matches in Christchurch and Auckland over the years. Hammond did his best to get a result, however. He scored 227 in the first Test and 336 not out, his highest, in the second.

The fascinating psychology of the game refuses to go away. That innings of 336 – against, it must be said, a palpably weak attack – beat Bradman's 334 at Headingley on the Australians' last visit. Who would dare say there was not predestined intent from the young Englishman, beginning to imagine, if not to hear, the snide little asides about his Antipodean rival? Gubby Allen remembered Hammond breaking his bat during that monumental innings. 'He knew I used a light one of the kind he favoured. He nipped mine out of my bag and he smashed it. Not sure he ever replaced it, but I've no complaints at all about that. His bat is in a case in the Long Room at Lord's, you know.'

The New Zealanders, saved by the weather, were perhaps unlucky to be on the receiving end of England, off the emotional leash imposed by the bitterness and anger engendered as a result of Jardine's lethal leg theory. It was like a pleasant postscript, devoid of contention or much importance, to pay New Zealand a call on the way home. The home bowlers viewed their bowling figures, totted up Hammond's 563 runs from two innings, and probably didn't share the sentiment.

Back in England, the obsession with bodyline showed a reluctance to recede completely. The West Indians briefly tried their own variation and Hammond was cut on the chin at Old Trafford. He was not enamoured but didn't bellyache. Soon there were reconciliations, in any case; hands were shaken and simmering resentments forgotten.

The West Indians carried too many passengers in their side and were badly balanced for that series. Learie Constantine was committed to his League side and missed the first Test. Martindale pegged away, at times dangerously. George Headley carried the batting. This he did quite beautifully. Someone once said to Wally: 'You're going to have to call yourself the White Headley'. He hated that as much as Viv Richards did, years later, when he was dubbed the Black Bradman. They are such fatuous comparisons after all. (In any case, the dubious title had already been bestowed on Headley during the 1933 tour.)

In 1934 the Australians were in great heart as they regained the Ashes at the Oval. Hammond was rarely in good heart. His Test form was modest, he was gargling all the time with salt water for his incessant sore throats – not eased by the numbers of cigarettes he smoked – and was being given the first warnings of a troublesome back. 'What did the doctor reckon it was, Wally? Lumbago? That's for old men!'

Once or twice in the mid-1930s, mischief makers suggested that Hammond might benefit from a break at international level. Dismissals to bad shots, lapses of concentration, the look of a sickly man all contributed to the speculation. But 'Plum' Warner remained an unwavering advocate – and all the marvellous statistics accumulated over the previous ten years couldn't be discounted. At his worst, he could still send a four between cover and extra, a piece of art , gift-wrapped for the gods.

He next went on the 1934-35 West Indies tour. We can only

guess at the Caribbean memories that hurtled back to haunt him. He had loved so much about his first journey there; the Barbadian sun would bring the colour back to his cheeks. Wyatt was the skipper, coming up with surprises like asking Jim Smith and Ken Farnes to open the batting – in addition to the bowling. Hammond belted 281 against Barbados in the second match of the tour, out of a total of 601. Jim Smith, the big, uncomplicated Wiltshire lad from Corsham, had gone into the tour party on the strength of one full season for Middlesex, during which he took 172 wickets and finished sixth in the averages. He was a village boy and his head was in a whirl; only the other day he'd been selling scorecards with Compton at Lord's and now he was batting with Hammond. Smith went in at No 11 in that match. In three-quarters of an hour, he and Wally thundered 122 runs. No one could slog more excitingly than Big Jim. He was soon outscoring Hammond, who sat on his bat handle and winked at his thick-muscled partner.

Again Test success was modest for Hammond. And so it was in the following home series against South Africa. Some concern was now being expressed in high places; this in turn was stilled by two gritty innings, of 63 and 87 not out, at Headingley. And when the Indians arrived under the Maharajah of Vizianagram in 1936, he plundered 167 at Old Trafford and 217 at the Oval.

By now his tonsils were out and his sore throats had stopped. He was conscientiously doing special exercises to prevent, as he hoped, any recurrence of lumbago or sciatica. He looked forward to the next tour of Australia, under Gubby Allen. It was never to be in the least confrontational, in the mode of the last, bitter one. The teams mingled cordially. Bradman was by now captain; he, of course, was courteous rather than effusive or jocular.

Australia came back to win the last three matches, two of them at Melbourne. Hammond had rediscovered the effervescence in his batting. He began with an early sequence of hundreds, with centuries in both innings at Adelaide. His appearance confirmed the transformation, which must surely have been attributed to improved health. Charlie Barnett, his erstwhile pal from the Berkeley Vale, shaped one glorious innings at Queensland; Hammond was extravagant in his public praise, and he meant it. The sparks of schism weren't yet flying. He was just as generous in the case of 'Chuck' Fleetwood-Smith, a left-arm googly bowler of rare talent, who surely deserved a more felicitous finale than the skid-row one that fate dealt him. His delayed Test chance against England had come in that 1936-37 series, and he was desperately difficult to play in the third match, on a Melbourne wicket bedevilled by heavy rain. Hammond made 32 out of 76 and he invariably nominated it as the best innings of his life. 'I was out to a most wonderful catch by Len Darling. The crowd cheered for five minutes . . . . We lost the Test and Fleetwood-Smith took his place in Australia's regular side.'

Hammond went out of his way to compliment the unusual left-arm bowler and to confide the extent to which he had, under orders, done his utmost to destroy Fleetwood-Smith's Test career even before it had begun. There is a thread of unsentimentality, usually justified, in sport. Many careers have been stifled by ruthless opponents with the foresight to look beyond the game in hand. Fleetwood-Smith had been on the point of making his debut for Australia back in 1932. He was a bowler with a highly personalised style, capable on the right wickets of being a match-winner. The selectors were ready to blood him. And England had heard about it. Or rather, Douglas Jardine, heart as cold as a fishmonger's slab, had eavesdropped.

He told Hammond. 'I want you to murder him. We don't want him ever to play for Australia. Now's the time to destroy him. It's up to you, Wally'. The unscrupulous yet astute order couldn't have been acted on more conscientiously. Against Victoria, Hammond attacked the raw unsuspecting bowler with a fury not too often repeated. Fleetwood-Smith had to be withdrawn from the attack. The England batsman scored 203 that day at Melbourne. As for the disheartened bowler, it took several years before he resurfaced, considered strong and experienced enough to take on England.

By the time the Australians returned to England in the summer of 1938 Hammond was in charge, a trifle self-consciously but not lacking praise – at that stage – for the way he handled his bowlers and set the best example himself. Many established Test skippers have said it is easier leading your country than your county. Hammond had the advantage of fine players around him. In only his second match as captain he scored 240 at Lord's. And yes, this was the one every historian cherished and every pre-war pundit pretended he had seen. Cricket's elite had assembled to watch. Pelham Warner needed to say nothing: he had been wondrously vindicated. His protégé was not only indisputably our best batsman but was England's captain as well. It was the fulfilment of 'Plum's' dreams.

When Hammond walked to the wicket, Ernie McCormick had taken three wickets in 25 balls. He was pounding in off 30 or so paces with the appearance of the most aggressive fast bowler in the world. And so he might have been, if he could more rhythmically have sorted out his delivery stride to avoid all those no-balls, and if he hadn't been plagued – like Wally – with back trouble. There was nothing too much wrong with his delivery at Lord's. Hammond was his only serious problem. The new captain batted for six hours; the tragedy was that those six hours could not be recorded for posterity. Some say they will never be emulated.

On to the Oval: for Hutton's 364 and a mighty innings win. Joe Hardstaff, who made 169 in England's total of 903-7, had like Hutton taken specific orders on how to bat. There was to be inexorable application in a match of mathematics which would make no concessions at all to Bradman. Had something of Jardine rubbed off on the new skipper?

Now it was Hammond's turn to take England to South Africa. Four of the five Tests were drawn. The rubber was decided at Durban, the third Test, when England won by an innings. Farnes bowled beautifully; Eddie Paynter hit a double century in pugnacious triumph. The matting wickets in South Africa had gone by now, and there was plenty of heavy scoring. It was most pronounced, in the much-quoted last Test. The game's history is laden with freakish and bizarre happenings. Yet, when apart from this, did a Test last match for 10 days? It was known, of course, as the timeless Test but was worth more than a cliché. There was much good batting, heroic deeds, inopportune thunderstorms, cables of inquiry to Lord's, confusion and fatigue.

The 1925-26 West Indies Tour: (*above left*) The simple scoreboard at Bridgetown for the first Test says it all. Hammond had immediately run into tremendous form, dominating the innings. They all liked Ewart Astill, seen here (*above right*) with Hammond on a sightseeing trip and (*below*) going out to bat in Barbados. Note the splendid headgear.

The MCC and Trinidad sides. *Front row*: W St Hill, J Small, F Grant, E St Hill, C Fraser. *Second row*: E J Smith, V Pascall, C A Wiles, Hon. F S Gough Calthorpe (Capt.), S Dewhurst (Capt.), Hon. C H Tennyson, H L Dales. *Third row*: Andrew Cipriani, P Holmes, Roy Kilner, G C Collins, W E Astill, A V Waddell. *Back row*: L Constantine, C T Bennett, F Watson, Major T H Carlton Levick, W R Hammond, G John, L G Crawley, Capt. T O Jameson.

Nothing could have been more carefree for Wally than the early weeks of the West Indies tour. Here he is (smoking) on a fishing trip. He was already popular with the ladies.

Little wrong with the backlift – but the Bristol Rovers ground still seems an unlikely venue.

In the year of his first wedding, 1929, Hammond was a scratch golfer.

The England Test side of 1930 against the Australians at Nottingham. *Back row, l to r*: G Duckworth, K S Duleepsinhji, R W V Robins, F E Woolley, M W Tate, R J Tyldesley, J C White, E H Hendren. *Front row*: H Larwood, W R Hammond, A P F Chapman, J B Hobbs, H Sutcliffe. Duleepsinhji and White (*behind*) were left out but came in for the next Test, at Lord's.

Back in 1932 when Gloucestershire had some of their early nets at the Memorial Ground, home of Bristol rugby. *Left to right*: Hammond, Neale, Stephens, Dacre (partly hidden), Barnett, Goddard and, batting, Dipper.

Cold expressions . . . cold weather. *Left to right*: Sinfield, Goddard, Hammond, Parker and Bev Lyon.

The press conference at the Cheshire Cheese in Fleet Street, London, where it was announced that Hammond would in future play as an amateur (as a necessary move towards the England captaincy).

The famous 'doodlebug' shot at Lord's during a one-day match between the RAF and the Royal Australian Airforce. Jack Robertson is batting, Andy Wilson is keeping wicket and Wally is at first slip. They all dived for cover as the V1 cut out.

The streets of Bingley were jammed with well-wishers on Wally and Dorothy's wedding day in April 1929.

Dorothy arrives at the Parish Church on the arm of her father, Joe Lister.

With Dorothy in the mid-1930s.

Hammond sits between his mother – such an enigmatic influence in his life – and Mrs Tom Voyce, wife of a local rugby hero, during the 1927 Cheltenham Festival.

Wally's mother, always fashion-conscious, talking to the Gloucestershire skipper, Col. D C Robinson.

Wally with Sybil on their wedding day in 1947.

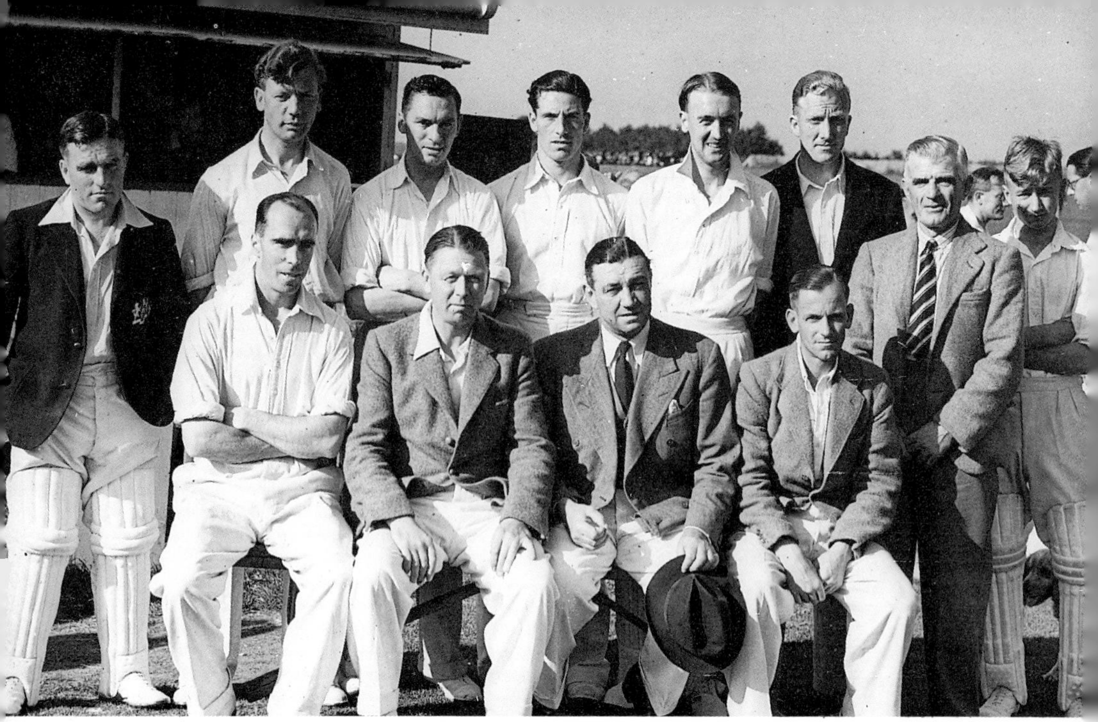

Gloucestershire CCC, just over the war, in typically serious demeanour. *Back row, l to r*: Andy Wilson, Monty Cranfield, Vic Hopkins, George Lambert, Alf Wilcox, Colin Scott, Bernie Bloodworth, Arthur Milton. *Front*: Jack Crapp, Billy Neale, Wally Hammond, George Emmett.

Grim resolve as Hammond goes out to bat with Bob Wyatt.

Hammond greets former skipper Basil Allen at Gloucestershire's first practice after the war.

A rare picture of Wally, the reluctant bowler, in a Bank Holiday match against Somerset.

Hammond with two of his fast bowlers, George Lambert and Colin Scott, who were sometimes given a hard time by him.

In action during the second Test against India at Old Trafford in 1946, at the time when it was announced that he would lead England in the following winter's Ashes series against Australia.

His last sad, ill-advised appearance for Gloucestershire in August 1951. He walks alongside Sir Derrick Bailey as they lead the county side onto the field against Somerset.

In 1952 Hammond made an appearance in one of the Duke of Beaufort's matches at Badminton. A notable front row: Lord Cobham, R E S Wyatt, Hammond, Gubby Allen and Tom Goddard. The team also included Roly Jenkins, Bill Andrews, Charlie Barnett and B A (Ben) Barnett.

WALTER HAMMOND MEMORIAL FUND

COMMENTS FROM HIS CONTEMPORARIES

"Please remember Wally Hammond — the greatest all-round Cricketer for the last fifty years"

—*B. H. Lyon*

"I still rate Wally Hammond as the greatest Batsman I ever saw. His technique was so complete, so superb"

— *Denis Compton*
(*Sunday Express*)

Cable from Sir Donald Bradman:

DURING HIS ERA WALLY HAMMOND WAS UNDOUBTEDLY ENGLAND'S GREATEST CRICKETER. I AM VERY DISTRESSED TO HEAR OF THE NEED FOR THE HAMMOND MEMORIAL APPEAL FUND AND FEEL SURE CRICKET LOVERS WILL GENEROUSLY RESPOND.

DON BRADMAN.

The Walter Hammond Memorial Fund has been created and formed as a Trust for administrative purposes, and the benefits of the Trust will be extended to Cricketers throughout the Commonwealth (or their dependents) whose need for support is approved by the Trustees, and the first beneficiaries will be Walter Hammond's widow and three children. PLEASE SUPPORT THE FUND GENEROUSLY.

A plea for help – with kindly words from Don Bradman, Bev Lyon and Denis Compton.

In all 1981 runs were scored and bad weather beat England in the end. There was some question about whether they should cancel their return sea passage and find other means of transport. But the tour management had a succession of meetings and decided they couldn't keep the ship waiting. At this distance, it seems absurd and amateurish in the extreme.

They were only 40 runs short at the end. Hammond made 140; Bill Edrich, loyally retained by his captain, at last made some Test runs, 219 in defiant, admirable style, full of pragmatic pulls and intrepid hooks that had served him so well when he raced in the previous domestic season to 1000 runs in May. As a schoolboy I'd charted Edrich's melancholy sequence of scores for his country and couldn't understand why he hadn't been dropped. There was a certain amount of personal conflict as I spread my cigarette cards on the bedclothes before I went to sleep. Bill, hair parted in the middle like so many of them, was always near the top of my pile. His white shirt hung loosely across his shoulders: it could have been the one he wore for Tottenham Hotspur reserves. And Spurs were my favourite soccer team. Why did life have to be so agonisingly difficult for a naïve village lad who suspected that Edrich should probably have been tearing down the wing at White Hart Lane rather than playing for England at cricket?

Never once, in a newspaper article or a book by Bill, did I come across a sentence that was less than generous to Hammond. His admiration was in the Les Ames class. He had every reason to be grateful for the way his England captain disregarded the clamour of criticism and kept the Middlesex player in his side. Who knows the effect it would have had on him if he'd been rejected by his country in those immediate pre-war years?

The 10-day Test was effectively abandoned; it would be wrong, it seems to me, to give it a more decisive official ending. In no other sport could there have been such a surreal contest. Back home, the music hall and radio comedians revised their scripts with topical allusions. Even Max Miller said it was all double-Dutch to him; that made a change from his customary double-entendre. Alan Melville, the South Africans' captain, shook Hammond's hand warmly. There hadn't been a moment's serious acrimony, if we ignore one little dust-up between two of the players who traded oaths after coming off the field. Melville could see his opposite number developing into a fine skipper. A lot of people were saying the same, based on the sketchy, undemanding early evidence.

Good-natured mischief on my part will not allow me to ignore an incident on the tour, mentioned to me by Jim Swanton. 'Hugh Bartlett was a magnificent player in 1938 and a very attractive chap. But at Bloemfontein, he made the cardinal error of showing a good deal of interest in the girl Wally had his eyes on. An unwise thing to do – to cross the captain like that!'

Now all that remained, before the war put paid to dozens of vibrant sporting careers, was the visit of the West Indians in 1939. England won at Lord's; the matches at Old Trafford and the Oval were drawn. Constantine dazzled and was caught predictably off a skier. Hammond obliged with 138 at the Oval, to give a fragrance to a disquieting, ersatz summer of cricket when spectators tried to delude themselves that things were normal.

Even in the dressing rooms, where players waiting their turn to bat liked to have a therapeutic musical background of Roy Fox and Lew Stone on the wireless, they were now tuning-in, instead, to the news bulletins. Not too many shared the hopes of the political appeasers. By the end of the season, the European distractions got irreversibly in the way. Cricket was only a game.

Yet who would have dared to call it that in 1932-33? We can't by-pass that eventful and ugly tour of Australia without some kind of comment.

The England party was a formidable one, singularly well balanced. Hammond was co-opted as a selector; he was never a forceful advocate in the committee room. His knowledge of the game and quiet common-sense in tactical matters could be useful. His vote was not idly cast when it came to the composition of the team for a specific match, in specific local conditions, and against specific bowlers.

The circumstances of the Bodyline Tour have been examined and dissected ad nauseam. They have been fictionalised and dramatised, often both at once. Every conceivable argument has been dusted off at every conceivable anniversary. There is really very little more to be said on the subject. England won the series 4-1. By the middle of January the two-way cables were threatening to set the airways alight. Splenetic exchanges and diplomatic tension, fanned by bitter anger on one side and pomposity on the other, brought embarrassment and rancour. Jardine's leg-theory had escalated from the cerebral to the physical. Larwood, then the fastest and most accurate bowler in the world, had been reviled because under orders he had pitched the ball short, in line with the body. It is unlikely that anyone in Australia's understandably complex-ridden history has ever been hated with a greater intensity than Douglas Jardine (Winchester and Oxford) was then.

The whole point of the tactic was to neutralise the threat of Bradman. In this it was uniquely successful: the Don's series average of just over 56 was by far the lowest in his career. Stanley McCabe's 187 at Sydney – one of the greatest innings in Ashes history – was the only truly convincing Australian riposte to the physical battery offered by the bowling of Larwood, Voce and Bowes.

Jardine had planned the bodyline approach on the voyage out to Australia and had discussed it with members of the party. Our concern here is with Hammond's participation. Years later he was to reveal just how much he disapproved of bodyline. Yet that was a retrospective judgment; like a number of the members in that tour party, he remained silent and seemingly acquiescent at the time. What else was a pro to do, of course? He wasn't usually consulted on matters of policy. Can we imagine the forbidding Jardine calling the professionals together and asking: 'What do you think, chaps? Are we being beastly to the Aussies?' Everything suggests that what he *did* say to the team was: 'We've got to keep Bradman quiet. And this is the way.'

Gubby Allen's antagonism to the theory was never disguised. In one interview with him, I was surprised at the extent of his condemnation. 'From the start I was dead against it. Dead against it. Dead against it.'. He recalled the way Hammond and Ames knocked on his hotel door and told him they were uneasy about what was going on. They didn't think it was in the interest of the game. 'No, it damn well isn't,' he replied.

It was no more than a nominal protest. Neither of the two pros had rebellious blood in his veins. They also felt they owed a certain loyalty to their captain. 'I suppose you could say that Wally and I went along with it,' Ames was to recall. Wyatt himself went more and more off the idea, while never denigrating Jardine, 'a great captain, who used his bowlers magnificently and was a splendid example to us in the field'. He told me of a meeting he attended back at Lord's following the tour. 'I don't like to see intimidation, with the ball buzzing round people's heads – no one plays the game to be killed. At that meeting, I advocated a line halfway down the wicket. I argued that bowlers should be compelled to pitch over it. Failure would result in a no-ball. Sir Stanley Jackson, who was to become chairman of selectors when I was captain, wouldn't agree with my suggestion. He didn't give a reason. But my views haven't changed all these years after. I believe in a certain amount of legislation to cut out intimidation.'

Wyatt talked to Hammond more than once about dangerous short-pitched deliveries. The Gloucestershire man would hark back to the day he was cracked on the chin. If opponents wanted to play that way, he wanted no part in it. Jardine and Wyatt were both batsmen of immense courage. Hammond was perhaps slightly less so. In the next chapter we shall discuss this aspect at rather greater length. It is sometimes argued that, as a popular figure, he should have spoken out in support of Gubby; that he and one or two others showed moral cowardice. But that is an absurd view; Wally never spoke out in his life; polemics passed him by. Abused and scorned, the England party's reaction was to close ranks. The players mentally barricaded themselves in – and left others to do the talking and write the strident headlines.

Technique of a Prince

There is something crass, fraught with imponderables, in making comparisons between sporting giants from different eras. How do we measure the skills of Hammond alongside those of Grace, or of Botham alongside those of Jessop? Yet sweeping claims and counter-claims are made in our natural desire, but vain quest, to establish the 'best of all time' in any field. It is too easy for supposed witnesses to line up and make their judgments – and for history to accept their word. I am thinking, for instance, of the popular view that the game never produced a finer off-side batsman than Hammond. We can be virtually sure of this, but never absolutely certain. Many of his contemporaries, at Test or county level, were convinced of it. So were many of those who opposed him in international arenas. All of us can think of half a dozen other candidates, wonderful exponents of the scorching drive through the covers; but none was better, technically or aesthetically, than Hammond.

The great coaches and tutors have been misty-eyed in praise of his perfect balance and poise. There was no flourish or swank with him at the crease. He minimised movement: still and vigilant as a sentry at Dover Castle, yet ready to move like lightning to the pitch of the ball. His appearance, freshly laundered, creased, the personification of classical athleticism, had its own magnetism. The shots were unfailingly worthy of the man.

When, some years ago, I edited the autobiography of Somerset all-rounder Bill Andrews, *The Hand That Bowled Bradman*, the exuberant pro wrote of a match when Jack White brought him in to silly point. It was hardly an enviable prospect when Hammond was the batsman and was denting the hoardings on the cover boundary with almost every other ball. As the Gloucestershire batsman stroked the next delivery just wide of Andrews' left hand, Somerset's farmer-skipper inquired: 'Why didn't you stop it?'

Andrews, his normally bronzed Weston-super-Mare face already pallid with fear, may have had a stammer but his quick-witted repartee seldom let him down.

'Couldn't m-move skipper. I was so fascinated by Wally's backlift.'

White preferred flighting his left-arm slows to sharing a joke on the field. He didn't approve of Andrews' levity, or sloppy fielding. Maybe he was trying to sharpen the gangling Westonian's reflexes by pointedly putting him in the firing line to Hammond. 'I couldn't bring myself to go to J C White's funeral,' Bill told me in one of his many moments of extreme candour.

Hammond was the undisputed role-model for thousands of schoolboys. Len Hutton admitted that he was his, too. Maurice Leyland and Herbert Sutcliffe used to tell him that the Gloucestershire player was by far the most thrilling batsman in the country. Ironically, there is a solid esoteric school of thought that Hutton's overall technical qualities put him narrowly ahead. A few, swayed by geographical allegiance and a studied look at the comparative figures, even nominated Sutcliffe. Neither of these two great Yorkshiremen would, if asked, have considered themselves in the same class. Jack Hobbs is one to put, more realistically, alongside Hammond for those enthralling hours of inconclusive winter-evening argument. In the words of Hutton, Hammond was 'the most perfect batsman I'd ever seen, so much more enjoyable to watch than Sir Don'. He told many of his friends how much his career owed to Wally. It was a considerable compliment, and Hutton was not alone by any means.

Just very occasionally, when the pressure was off and the match was almost won, Hammond would unfurl a quaint variant from his normal well-defined repertoire and take a four with a tennis shot. It was so rare and unpredictable that spectators still remember it, shaking their heads in disbelief. The great batsman was essentially orthodox in everything he did. He didn't improvise or pull with an ungainly bat. He seemed incapable of playing an ugly shot.

His vast technical ability did, however, permit him just now and then to do things that lesser mortals would never have contemplated. He could place the ball delicately between fielders with the merest adjustment in the slant of the bat or magical twist of the wrists.

George Lambert may have been given a tough time by his captain. But he remained spellbound by the mastery that Hammond could assert over an opposing bowler when runs were badly needed and the spinners were on top. 'I remember him cutting a leg-side delivery between the stumps and short gully down to the third-man boundary . . . . And another trick of his was to whack the ball straight back at the bowler's feet on his follow-through. And sometimes, at the start of an innings he would hit the ball very hard to each of the off-side fielders in turn – to sting their fingers and unsettle them.'

His off drives may arguably have been unrivalled in the history of the game but his genius was most evident of all on fiendishly difficult wickets. His concentration was phenomenal. Gloucestershire team-mates used to say that his vision and intuition were so extraordinary that he could play the spinners off the wicket, once they had pitched. At a score of grounds, from Bridgetown, Barbados, to Brisbane, he defied nature's obstacle courses.

Three cricketers – Les Ames, Charlie Barnett and Andy Wilson, unaware of the others' choice – nominated the same unlikely match as Hammond's finest. It was a long way from an international stage. On a dusty, thoroughly bad Bristol wicket in 1939, against Kent, the ball was turning at proverbial right-angles. Goddard had no complaints on that score; he took 17 wickets in a day. Batsmen were in markedly less good humour.

The ball was spinning like a top. One would also keep wickedly low every couple of overs. In more modern times, the inspector of pitches would have been down on the next helicopter. Then, as the long line of protesters bemoaned the appalling state of the wicket and suggested it might be advisable to move the whole square to the adjoining uncut grounds of the Orphanage, Kent were left to lick their wounds and suffer an innings defeat.

Seventeen wickets in the time it took wife Flo to sell a line of lino should have been sufficient to earn the lugubrious Goddard any acclaim that was going from a farce of a match. But Hammond was just as much Kent's executioner. He took on Doug Wright, who with his brisk leg spinners was quite as deadly as Big Tom, and took 9-47.

Barnett himself had refused to be cowed. He saw no logic in hanging around as the wicket simply got worse; he gritted his teeth and went straightaway on to the front foot. It was what he did best, whatever the reputation of the bowler or caprices of nature. His 66 runs came from bold and fearless shots, though it was never going to last. Wright, jigging up to the wicket and delivering the ball at disconcerting medium pace, patiently teased away before pinning Barnett LBW.

I go to team-mate Wilson for his version of Hammond's contribution. 'What followed was a sheer delight for the purists. While the rest of the team pushed and prodded like old ladies at a jumble sale, Wally treated the pitch as if it were a perfect batting strip. I survived for no more than ten minutes but I never saw him edge a single ball. Everything was played with absolute confidence in the middle of the bat. It was a performance beyond belief and I would wish to cite nothing else to stress his genius. Almost every batsman in that match was made to look like a novice. But Wally showed complete mastery. He scored 153 and put us into our winning position.'

Throughout his career, virtually every ball was middled. He didn't edge shots and give the slips much hope. The appearance of the face of his bats, as we have already mentioned, was a constant topic of admiration as weary colleagues lounged on the benches of the dressing rooms at the close of play. Once I asked 'Roly' Jenkins, that clever leg-break trickster from Rainbow Hill, Worcester, what he remembered most about Hammond. The reply was instantaneous. 'It was the middle of the bat, every time.'

We have discussed his rejection of the hook shot. He could play it well enough, as once he had proved with unbridled bravado against the fiery Ted McDonald. The fact is he listened to advice from 'Plum' Warner and the other 'elders'. So did

Harold Gimblett when this farmer's son was initially touted as an England prospect on the strength of that glorious and furious onslaught against Essex on his debut at unfashionable Frome. Gimblett, a cussed individual, chose not to act on the counsel and believed his Test opportunities suffered because of it. Hammond was an altogether more pliable cricketer; he accepted that the hook was a dangerous, risky shot and cut it out. I return to Barnett: 'As a result of that aversion, his rule when he became captain was that no one else should go for the hook shot. If you'd been brought up to play it to the fast ball, as you should, then it tended to be difficult to find yourself with your bat in mid-air, thinking you mustn't hit that one. I'm afraid Wally had those dictatorial touches.'

Hammond could bring out the most perfectly coordinated on-drives, he could clip through mid-wicket and had a decidedly effective, personalised sweep. But no, his leg-side repertoire did not match the glittering armoury for his off-side aggression. Clarrie Grimmett, the Merlin, had found that out. 'Tiger' O'Reilly gave him more trouble than anyone. It looks perilously like nit-picking to pause in search of the technical chinks with which to criticise. So often, as at dusty Bristol in the summer before the war, his batting was beyond criticism; it belonged to a higher sphere than anything around him. Yet in an honest assessment it would be wrong to evade the suggestion, voiced in muttered asides or in some cases, more open public opinion, that he lacked the stomach to face the most hostile fast bowling.

We come back to Barnett and words of his in print: 'It was part of his make-up that he did not relish fast bowling, so if he had his way, which he normally did when he was batting, he took one run off the fast bowler and left his partner to get on with it and do the best he could. The last time I saw him really take on fast bowling was at Trent Bridge in 1932, the first occasion I opened for Gloucestershire. Harold Larwood was one of several in that match striving for a place on the boat for the winter tour of Australia. Wally played one of the most brilliant innings I ever saw from him. He stood up and cut the fast, rising ball for runs time and time again and it was a wonderful hundred he made. Sadly I never saw him do it like that again.'

As a 17-year-old, Hammond came up against Jack Gregory (McDonald's great partner in Australia's opening attack), and he didn't enjoy the experience. The towering physique and pounding run up to the wicket, rounded off by that famous leap, generated immediate apprehension in a boy batsman. 'Yes it's true I flinched away from it a bit – in common with many others'.

Hammond wrote in *Secret History* of a match against Essex when H D Read, the Essex amateur who played one Test Match in 1935, was bowling very fast indeed. He was digging in short and there was the challenge for Hammond to hook. But he chose not to and was criticised because of it; again the hints were that he didn't possess the necessary courage. 'It was simply that I did not think the possible profit worth the risk, either of getting out or being injured. As I got older, I virtually abandoned the hook. I do not care for it and Hutton is just one who agrees with me.'

At another point, he wrote significantly on the subject of intimidating bowling as it affected Hutton. 'I felt a great deal of responsibility when captaining the 1946-47 tour because Len Hutton was our best batsman and the Australians did not refrain from bouncing the ball at him. If anything serious had happened to his damaged arm, not only should I have felt guilty but resentment in England might have caused something like a new version of the trouble we had over the Bodyline affair. Len's arm was struck two or three times by very fast balls but luckily no serious injury resulted.'

The England captain commented on the noisy evidence, in one particular match, that memories of Larwood's aggression hadn't completely died. There had been barracking and a cry of 'How do you like it?' when balls from Ray Lindwall and Keith Miller reared past Hutton's head. Hutton, for his part, appreciated Hammond's protective attitude to him; he'd been visited in hospital when hit on the head during the 1938-39 series with South Africa.

'It seemed to me that Len had to face more bumpers in the 1946-47 tour than the rest of us put together', wrote Hammond, who had, in one kindly gesture that shouldn't be ignored, asked Hutton if he'd like a little respite by dropping down the order.

In the course of making that television documentary, *Walter Hammond, a Cricketing Great*, HTV gathered together a number of Hammond's famous contemporaries at the College ground in Cheltenham. What they said on camera was fascinating enough; what they added during their informal reminiscences was even more so. His loyal pal, Les Ames, pointed out that in England's outstanding 1928-29 series, Australia didn't really have a fast bowler. Jack Gregory was by then over the hill and soon broke down. Apart from the inexperienced Tim Wall, making his debut in the final Test, Australia had little more than Grimmett and some medium pacers. Ames continued: 'But when we came up against the West Indians, I did detect on Wally's part a slight weakness against the really quick, short stuff. Yes, of course, Martindale and Constantine worried him a bit.'

There was general assent that Hammond, who on occasion opened the batting, didn't much care for the new ball. As Wyatt put it: 'I'm sure he preferred going in further down. And anyway, it was a silly waste to risk him going in first. He did once open with me at Cape Town, where Bell was getting the ball to lift. Wally stayed mostly at the other end, chuckling at me every time I was hit on the ribs. He could have played it with ease, I'm sure, if he'd got down to it. I didn't hold that in any way against him – it was just a good-natured laugh at my expense.'

The annual fixtures between Gents and Players, now seen by many as nothing much more than a quirky anachronism, at times carried hard-eyed rivalry and manifestations of the class war. In 1939 Wyatt was left 'covered in bruises' after a thoroughly uncomfortable spell at the crease. Hammond was captaining the Gents and, according to Wyatt, virtually threw his wicket away. He was out for 20 in the first innings and 4 in the second. Copson and Bowes were in decidedly awkward form. Apart from the embattled Wyatt, Captain J W A Stephenson was a casualty.

Reg Sinfield would from time to time open the Gloucestershire innings with Hammond. 'He didn't like the new ball, not a bit. He used to tell me to take as much of the strike as I could until the shine had gone off the ball. And he'd give me that crafty look, reminding me I was more used to opening than he was!'

Now, what of his bowling? The run-up was smooth, the delivery effortless like most things he did on a cricket field. Fred Root used to say Hammond was almost as fast as Larwood for half a dozen overs. That is clearly an exaggeration but it does reflect one bowler's regard for another. There was a deceptive change of pace and, in humid conditions, discernible movement through the air. For most of the time he was slightly faster than Maurice Tate. If only he'd bowled more often, we could have evaluated him with greater accuracy.

Hutton may not yet have been, by any means, the sophisticated technician in the mid-30s. His early experience of facing Hammond at the Wagon Works in Gloucester lived with him in graphic, perplexing detail for years. 'Wally came on with the new ball and I went in first. For two or three overs I had no trouble at all. Then suddenly he unleashed a ball that knocked my middle stump out of the ground. I haven't a clue where the ball came from. It was too quick for me.'

Many players and knowledgeable spectators were in no doubt at all that he could, if he had wished, have done the double every year. That could have established, beyond question, that he was one of the greatest allrounders in the history of the game. He decided to conserve his energies and focus on the batting crease, and he may well have justified the logic. Some of us feel, however, that a contrary streak determined the number of overs he bowled.

He took 83 Test wickets and it should have been more, though England captains met with a more willing response than did Bev Lyon and Basil Allen, when his bowling was needed. In his biography of Gubby Allen, E W Swanton recalled the fourth Test at Adelaide during the 1936-37 series, when Voce and Allen were only half-fit. 'Gubby gave the new ball to Farnes and Hammond . . . . Hammond, using the cross wind at a brisk medium pace, rose to the occasion in the way he always could as a bowler when there was a real need.' Wally was easily the most effective bowler in Australia's second innings. In just over 15 overs, he took 5-57; it seems churlish to record that Bradman was 212 when he gave Hammond a return catch.

Jim Swanton is a wise judge and student of character. Yet his view that Hammond could be relied on to rise to the challenge whenever there was most need of him as a bowler is a romantic one. Lyon, Wally's drinking chum, used to say: 'I've taken a few risks and we've won rather a lot of matches. But we'd have won more if I could have pulled you out of the slips more often.' The reply would be that he was a specialist batsman – and there were others to take the new ball. Alas, over several seasons at Gloucestershire, there weren't.

In Yorkshireman Bill Bowes' opinion, Hammond was 'a grand bowler, who wouldn't take it seriously enough and would wangle out of it as much as he could'. He was capable, all the same, of testing a batsman with both in and out-swingers, not to mention a lovely off-break. 'Roly' Jenkins, always willing to acknowledge a good and cunning spinner, was unstinting in his praise for the adept and consistent manner Hammond kept turning the ball from the off on that remarkable day when he took nine wickets against Worcestershire at Cheltenham. The fact was that Hammond had acquired vast knowledge about the technique and 'wrinkles' of the game, to complement his innate ability. Younger team-mate Lambert reckoned that Wally could bowl the lot, from pacey in-swing to leg breaks – and he often did so in the nets. He liked to bamboozle the awkward Goddard or some of the trialists.

As a fielder, he had incomparably good hands and razor-sharp reflexes. Those who watched him regularly, dotingly for his county, say he never once dropped a catch. Well he put one down at first slip at Adelaide during the Bodyline tour. It was such an unthinkable occurrence that it made news, competing with the more controversial issues of the series. Latterly, he failed to get down to one or two, but that was the fibrositis and should be excused.

When he joined Gloucestershire first he darted around the covers with such athletic style that West Country supporters used to claim they went to watch him field as much as to bat. He had a deadly return to the wicket and would cut off boundaries after youthful sprints that made a mockery of the county's reputation for geriatric fielders. Parker may once have placed his hands on his hips and muttered 'There go my greyhounds' as Dipper, Mills and Dennett huffed and puffed at snail pace in pursuit of the same ball. Wally genuinely was a handsome greyhound, darting from his trap and flying across the outfield. You could put your money on him saving a four.

He had the safest hands in the team – and the county badly needed a reliable slip to capitalise on the craft of Parker. The pair were to work wonderfully in tandem. It was all done with the minimum of fuss. Hutton, close at hand in the Test matches, was also astonished at the matter-of-fact way Hammond held on to catches. 'It was like catching a tennis ball, no noise at all'.

Wicket-keeper Wilson says of him: 'Built like a heavyweight but able to move like a flyweight'. Wilson would boldly stand up to Lambert on a good Bristol wicket and if there was late movement, he'd deflect the ball. 'Wally would be going one way at slip but he'd recover and, in the same movement almost, swoop the other way to catch the ball and throw it back. It was all apparently so casual. He'd say nothing'.

In a Test match at Leeds, he was first slip and Wyatt was second. Ames committed himself and moved across to the leg-side in anticipation of a delivery which had slanted into the batsman. But the ball pitched and straightened – and the batsman got the finest of nicks on it. It would normally have been a straightforward catch for Ames if he had not been deceived into going across to leg. 'Wally somehow picked up the catch a couple of inches off the ground and two yards wide of him. He put the ball into his pocket and the batsman hadn't a clue where it was. Wally retained his balance and made it all look ridiculously easy.'

It is time now to discuss his captaincy, mainly in the context of England. His appointment brought resentment from many quarters, some of them blinkered and class-based. Typical of the latter was the odious comment that you couldn't have a car salesman leading your country. Another one was that he wouldn't know which fork to use at the official banquets. They are not worthy of further consideration.

I have retrieved a cutting from the *Bristol Evening World* from one of my treasured scrapbooks of nostalgic trivia. Age has turned it the colour of a battered *Wisden* left to wilt in the sun. The month is June 1938:

> Wally Hammond is to be England's captain in the Test matches against Australia. Today at Lord's, the captaincy was offered to him and he accepted the honour.
>
> This decision of the selectors follows closely upon the choice of Hammond to lead the England side in the Test trial which is now being played, and is a tribute to his brilliant handling of the bowling yesterday and again this morning.
>
> Gloucestershire followers of cricket will rejoice at the honour which has been paid to a member of their county side. There is no man more fit and although not entirely unexpected, in some quarters it was thought he might be passed over owing to the fact that before this season, he had played as a professional.
>
> The selectors are obviously convinced that the extra duties of captaincy will have no adverse effect upon his batting and other work in the Tests.
>
> R E S Wyatt will not be in the Test side. He informed the selectors today that he would not be available. As a matter of fact, he will be at the Tests but in a role of reporter.
>
> Hammond is the first player who was formerly professional to be chosen to lead his country. Since assuming amateur status last autumn, he has been considered as likely to succeed G O Allen.

The regional pride can't be disguised in the report. There follows a resumé of his career – and a tribute from the Lord Mayor of Bristol. Hammond was to captain England 20 times from 1938 to 1947. He led a winning team four times; the Australians came out on top three times when he was in charge. The remainder of the matches were drawn.

Opinions as to his merits as a skipper vary markedly. The Australians Ray Robinson and Jack Fingleton spoke well of him, and praise from that kind of authoritative source should not be under-valued. But it has to be said that reservations and outright criticism outweighed the praise. His detractors, some in high places and unmoved by Warner's undeviating support, couldn't wait for the first flaws to show. The snobs among them may have snorted at his social pedigree but they were soon targeting his tactical shortcomings, as they saw them. Did he know how to use his bowlers? It didn't look like it in the opening Test when Hedley Verity was seriously under-employed in the first innings.

He privately loathed the criticism of him, however fleeting it was. He would pounce on a stray sentence in a match report and never forgive the writer. He failed to accept that journalists were entitled to an opinion of their own. His dislike of the press was irrational, but it didn't soften. Hammond's inability to come to terms with the needs of public relations, even before the war, was a weakness that he did little to erase. Barracking also irritated him, but of course he was not alone in that. In the West Country and on the county circuit in the late 1920s and through the 1930s, the regard for him was almost reverential. If any supporter shouted at him, it was likely to be: 'Come on,Wally, give us a six.'

The raucous language emanating from The Hill at Sydney was very different; it was too caustic for his liking. Once, he admitted, he picked out the offending critic and aimed a six at him. 'Sorry to say I just missed,' he was to write. It reminds me of Viv Richards, years later. He had wonderful eye-sight and could recognise facial features deep in the crowd; he, too, was known to smash the ball high over the boundary fence as a venomous riposte. In Richards' case, he would also vault the fence, when fielding, to confront an unpleasant customer indulging in racist abuse.

Hammond had willed himself to become England's captain. He charted a single-minded course, though he did his best to hide his naked ambition for the job. After his appointment, some of the professionals at Gloucestershire said: 'Now we can see why he chose his friends so carefully.' He studied the approaches of Percy Fender and Walter Robins, Gubby Allen and Bob Wyatt. Bev Lyon taught him most of all and he only wished he had the temperament to emulate his methods and flair. In his books he wrote generously of many leaders, right up to Bill Edrich and Lindsay Hassett ('someone who was universally liked'). He often bracketed Fender with Lyon. 'It's all those Jewish brains', he used to say with real affection, making the same mistake as so many others about Percy's ethnic background.

Hammond lacked the flexibility and boundless imagination of the great captains. He could stick to his guns over Edrich's selection, without being especially dogmatic, and got on well with his selectors for the most part. They relied on him to win the toss – which he did eight times in a row using a lucky threepenny bit. The responsibilities were more onerous than he had anticipated. When a Test was coming up, he'd retreat and stay a few days with the Neales. Andy Wilson used to see him pacing the orchard at the farm, frowning and preoccupied. He left Phyl Neale to answer the door or the phone if it was reporters in search of nothing more than bland copy. In one letter written before the war, he wrote of 'feeling the strain'. But he had absolutely no wish to give up the duties.

We are all aware of the pressures, not solely to do with cricket, that bore down on him during the post-war Australian tour. Hutton sympathised in that he had a relatively weak side around him, especially inadequate in bowling apart from Alec Bedser and the erratic Doug Wright. It was strange, he said, that in all the time he had known Hammond he never once managed a prolonged and proper conversation with him. Nor, he would hurriedly add, did he have a cross word.

By 1946-47, whatever his introspection, Hammond had improved in self-confidence and speech-making. In his baptismal days as an England captain, he had been inclined to mumble his obligatory oratory. Fellow amateurs would scribble notes for him on the back of menus. In days when the wireless was still the king of communication and the magical mike had a glamour all its own, he paradoxically rather enjoyed being interviewed by the BBC or sending a taped message home at Christmas time from a distant cricket ground.

'At times you've got to be a martinet', Warner had told him. This wasn't easy if, only the other day, you had been another pro, without privilege or extra status. There were one or two abortive attempts to instil discipline. Self-consciously, during an away match, he suddenly stunned his Gloucestershire team-mates by telling them he wanted them in bed early because of the importance of the fixture. It was an uneasy moment. 'Several of them told him to get stuffed, or something that was equally pointed and dismissive. He didn't pursue the theme.'

Let us forget the last, sad Australian tour for the moment. Dressing rooms, when Wally was skipper, rarely throbbed with controversy. If he was curt with his orders and, according to Barnett, hardly ever said 'Please', such blemishes in human behaviour were not the obvious components for a row. He was a silent man, at times a brooder, and the dressing room tended to be influenced by that pervasive mood and presence. If Compton hustled in, perilously late, offering an engaging air of youthful innocence and zestful charm in apology, his captain conveyed any token reprimand in the mute eloquence of the glance.

Too many people saw Hammond's appointment to the highest level as a manufactured one. The way he turned amateur was all a little too neat and tidy, predetermined. Proletarian Britain, quietly taking on a new vigour in preparation for the unleashing of self-expression after the war, liked the idea of a pro from Bristol taking on the establishment. They conveniently forgot that he'd had to desert the paid ranks to do so. But, well, in any case, it was a start: he had never gone to a public school and, as we will later discuss, was in trade. Before too many years, those starchy divisions in cricket would have gone for good and English players would be led by a proper professional who didn't have to make any concession at all.

The fact was that Hammond was our best player, possessed a profound technical and tactical grasp of the game, had an intimate knowledge of international opponents and had, after all, led his county on occasions. It takes only the most cursory examination of all our Test captains in the history of first-class cricket to realise that Hammond had the most valid claims to the appointment.

But I must return to the conflicting viewpoints. Ames was an interested party in that no one ever heard him say a harsh word about Wally. There wasn't an instant rapport but the friendship grew. When Gloucestershire played in Kent, Hammond stayed with Ames. 'I found him a very good captain. He captained the team quite beautifully on the South Africa trip. We weren't defeated at all. I spent a lot of time with the Kent amateur, Bryan Valentine, on that tour. We found ourselves discussing Wally a great deal. And we couldn't find any serious faults at all.'

Gubby got on well with him by their second tour together in 1936-37. 'If he was a bit aloof – well, so was I in Australia, where I went off to see my relatives.' Alec Bedser told me that he found Hammond 'pretty ordinary' as a captain. He dwelt on it for a few seconds, adding, 'But we've got to remember he was an amateur by then and I was just starting out. I certainly didn't expect a pat on the back for doing well'.

From Bob Wyatt comes this typical thoughtful view of him: 'I think I'd rate him as a *lucky* captain. I wouldn't have said he was a great tactician. He often changed the bowling, which gives the impression of sharp tactics, of course. In the Test match at Lord's when he made that magnificent 240, Doug Wright had got an early wicket, a catch in the slips. In came Don, and Doug beat him three balls out of four. To my astonishment, at the end of the over Wally took Doug off and brought on Verity in his place. I just couldn't understand it. The wicket was plumb and if anybody was going to get turn, it would be a wrist-spinner. But, well, a few overs later, Don pulled a wide one from Verity onto his stumps . . . and it looked like brilliant captaincy. I met Don later and I told him I was surprised he'd got out to Verity like that. I was equally surprised Wright was taken off after bowling that tremendous over to him.' His reply was: 'I was very relieved.'

Of the 1946-47 tour, Jim Swanton was to write: 'I had seen Hammond as a touring captain in South Africa in 1938-39 and on the evidence of that tour was more than apprehensive how he would answer the considerably more rigorous demands of this one eight years later. Like other brilliant natural sportsmen to whom success has come easily, Hammond had little apparent understanding of the problems faced by less gifted mortals, nor did he seem to appreciate the value of the personal word of cheer and advice. He could be very good company when in the right vein but there were bleak, moody spells which were apt to coincide with his own failures and those of the side . . . .'

Reg Sinfield made his solitary, treasured Test appearance

against the Australians at Trent Bridge in 1938. Back in Bristol and Cheltenham, it had been Lyon or Basil Allen who set the fields for Reg. 'How many short legs do you want today?' 'I'd like three', he told Wally. That probably took everyone by surprise. He repeated his bold request a couple of times. His skipper and team-mate finally agreed to give him two, one forward and one backward. Sinfield's plea for an additional fielder, short and square, was turned down.

In came Stan McCabe, who almost at once popped the ball to where a square short-leg would have been. It should be added that McCabe went on to score 232 – in Bradman's view the finest innings he had ever seen.

Every one of my fruitful conversations with Reg, usually in his local village pub after he'd come back from coaching the boys at Colston's or from mending an elderly neighbour's roof when coming up to his late 80s himself, drifted inevitably to an appreciation of Wally. 'Oh yes, such a great player – and such a bad captain.' Andy Wilson had reservations, too. At the same time he remembered the brisk way Hammond marshalled his county players immediately after the war, showing renewed enthusiasm and supervising the training. 'We'd never been so fit – it was almost, it seemed to me, a Yorkshire-style approach.' But that enthusiasm couldn't be sustained. Too many things were crowding in on the Gloucestershire and England skipper. Within 12 months he would virtually have deserted the game for good. As he led the physical jerks in front of the pavilion, he was deluding himself as well as his players. The body was still pretty trim but the eyes were already weary; the muscles remained taut and his off-drives were as silky as ever; but he was looking prematurely an old man. By 1947 he'd gone and, coincidentally, Gloucestershire so nearly won the championship.

We come back to Wilson: 'The supporters were quite despondent and they didn't give us any chance without Wally.' The portents weren't good when they lost their first match, at Lord's, and put down half a dozen catches. It was even being said that they were the worst side anyone could wish to see. 'Basil Allen was our captain again now. He rallied us and we didn't lose again until we came to Cheltenham. The point I'm making is that they were different types of captains. Basil was a natural leader.'

How many more hundreds, how many more Test appearances would Hammond have made but for the war? Would he have had the wish, the temperament or, it must be asked, the tactical skills to go on captaining his country? How many more pages of cricket's scriptures would he have dominated?

PART IV

THE RIVALRIES

The Spectre of Bradman

It is time to study, at some length, the remark by an experienced psychiatrist, suggesting that Hammond would be upstaged by the emergent Bradman. Nothing could be more perspicacious. It was no spur-of-the-moment remark, and it is clear that the Australian's impact is central to any analysis of Hammond's complex-laden career. Through the 1930s and again immediately after the war, the Don's massive presence gnawed away at the surprisingly sensitive and fragile persona of Hammond.

Wally worked hard to convey an air of complete unconcern over the staggering statistics that Bradman amassed and the attention he commanded increasingly around the world. Yet those who knew him best – the relatively few who were privy to his confidential asides – sensed an attitude and state of mind at times not far removed from paranoia. When he assumed the captaincy of England and even before that, Hammond's message, voiced or unspoken, was: 'Let's get Bradman out, then we can think about beating the Aussies. He's the obstacle. Bradman . . . Bradman . . . Bradman . . . .' It enveloped and stifled any other tactical consideration.

Hammond was not a vain or conceited man. But it was natural enough for him privately to bask in the acclaim and status of celebrity that he had progressively acquired. Confirmation of his princely gifts came with his superb stroke-making in Australia during the 1928-29 series. The England party, under Percy Chapman, an enthusiastic leader ever ready to throw himself about spectacularly in the field, was a relaxed and happy one. And Hammond was the undisputed star.

It seemed that they'd hardly landed before he was taking a

hundred off South Australia and a double century off New South Wales. That was when he first came up against Bradman, a slight figure with strength in his forearms to mock the seemingly unimpressive physique. In the match at Sydney, Hammond played some beautiful, aggressive shots. Bradman's response was a hundred in his second innings; he hadn't been far short of one in the first. The Don was still a newcomer. No one was yet drawing comparisons or talking mischievously of rivalry.

The Gloucestershire man was sturdy in the shoulders, tapered at the waist. His athleticism impressed the Australia crowds. They drew breath and looked silently at each other whenever he was at the wicket; they suspected, with rational foresight, that here was a batsman who would be troubling them for years.

In the second Test, at Sydney, he scored 251 out of England's total of 636. It was his first Test century. Bradman had been dropped after failing in the first Test. Hammond went on to Melbourne – for another double century. The statistics alone are exceptional; the manner in which they were compiled, so brimming with sheer style, was even more so. His Test aggregate was 905 runs, with an average of 113. For the tour as a whole, he achieved an average of over 91.

By now the commentators were doting on him. Adjectives from the game's Golden Age were unwrapped and dusted-off. 'Plum' Warner and other lofty judges were positively lyrical in their songs of praise. The soldier's son was acclaimed as the finest batsman in the world, England's natural successor to Jack Hobbs: one Master taking over from another.

Yet, with cruel irony, Hammond had hardly achieved this apotheosis before Bradman entered a decisive challenge for supremacy. Just one year later, in 1930, the Don came to England and annihilated the records. 'Bloody Bradman!' Wally's county team-mates would hear when they eavesdropped on his occasional reveries that summer.

There were matches in the England series when Bradman appeared invincible. His detractors were less inclined now to sneer at the way he veered occasionally from the orthodox and cross-batted. They came to marvel at his timing, his mechanical precision, his rigidity when one landmark was passed: the ritual taking of a new guard on the way to a new hundred.

In five Test innings he scored 974 runs for an average of 139. The summer aggregate was just under 3,000 with an average of almost 99. At Test level, he simply kept going one better – as Hammond watched in silent eloquence and frustration from slip. Bradman scored 131 in the opening Test, 254 in the second, and 334 in the third. His failure to reach a hundred in the fourth was almost comically anti-climactic. But, ah well, he was back to form with 232 in the final match with England.

Bob Wyatt stood back to admire, yet still put Hobbs, with some sentimental regard, marginally ahead of the Don as a batsman. But this was what he wrote of Bradman's achievements in that golden summer of 1930: 'He was a genius of which, as run-making machine, the like had never been seen before. He was short and slimly built and didn't look particularly strong, although he had considerable stamina. Perhaps his greatest asset was his wonderful eye, able to judge the length of a ball exceptionally early in its flight. This allowed him to play strokes which other batsmen wouldn't even attempt.'

Wyatt, with vivid memory, described to me how Bradman would spot a ball just short of a length on the off and crack it effortlessly wide of mid-on. It wasn't what the coaching purists were used to. Hammond watched and realised the advantage Bradman had with that additional leg-side repertoire.

The rivalry between Wally and the Don can be precisely traced back to 1930. That was when Bradman, with grim-faced resolve, made his figurative statement of superiority. It was a psychological triumph, as if he had briefed himself to erase for ever the memory of Hammond's wondrous deeds on the previous series.

In England, while Bradman soared in brilliance, monopolising the crease with complete disdain for our bowlers, Hammond faltered by comparison. In 1930 his total of Test runs was no more than a third of those of his rival and his average more than a hundred less. The relative figures of the two were being paraded in the papers. This was painful to the England player who did his best, none too successfully, to obscure an obsession

– based in some measure at least on envy – that was beginning to plague him.

Fellow Test cricketers were aware of it. They did their best to bolster Hammond when he seemed at his most vulnerable. 'He's no better than you, Wally – he'll never be able to play the cover drive like you.'

Hammond was more pragmatic than that. He envied facets of the Australian's play – the unconventional drive, based on faultless timing which minimised risk, the unyielding concentration and, above all, that assertive scoring to leg. The Australians were ruthlessly conscious of the Englishman's minor weaknesses. That was why Grimmett and O'Reilly gave him more trouble than all the rest put together: they knew exactly where to pitch the ball.

Bradman and Hammond: that was the way, the order, that the pundits saw it. The styles were utterly dissimilar. It could be argued that Hammond's batting had more soul and more humanity, if you like. He always gave the bowler just that glimmer of hope. The Run-Machine, conversely, was programmed to stay, seemingly impervious to the spectrum of bowling wiles pitted against him. That sobriquet conveyed some kind of dehumanised aspect. Bradman didn't have much to say for himself; the relationship between him and Hammond was destined to be taciturn and formal.

Scholarship and common-sense judgment on matters where mere mortals hit cricket balls for a living don't always go together. Alan Gibson left a First in history at Oxford and some university lecturing behind to become for a time one of our best Test match commentators. His book, *The Cricket Captains of England*, was full of sage comment. This was what he had to say about that pertinent 1930 season:

> Bradman, in a display of flawless batting which has never been equalised, not even by himself, not even by Grace in 1876 or 1895, not even by Hobbs in 1925, not Trumper in 1902, broke Hammond's 1928-29 records for a Test series, in both aggregate and average . . . . For the rest of his career, Hammond was destined to be only the *second best* batsman in the world (possibly not even that, but we had

> not learned to take the West Indies and George Headley seriously then): and he was not, as far as his cricket went, a man content to be second-best. His cricketing life, thenceforth, was over- shadowed by Bradman.

A little later, Gibson mentions an untimely exit by Hammond, bowled by Fleetwood-Smith with the third ball of the day and George Duckworth's view that you would never have got rid of Bradman in the first over when the Ashes were at stake. The author concluded: 'This was Hammond's problem. It was not enough for him to do well. He had to do better than Bradman.'

Interestingly, our county players and the spectators in this country – some understandably influenced by nationalistic zeal – were divided in making considered comparisons between the two. Bill Bowes and Denis Compton were just two who put Bradman ahead. Fred Root, who accompanied Hammond on that ill-fated tour of the West Indies and had many early opportunities to study him at close quarters, took a different view.

He actually claimed that in style, temperament and natural ability, Hammond was more like Bradman than any other cricketer; he went on to make it clear that their personalities varied considerably off the field. Root maintained that Wally was quicker in making up his mind about the shot to play. The ease with which he handled the slow bowlers, often on a difficult wicket, brought this comment from Root: 'He went after the spinners with confidence, almost savouring of carelessness to the onlooker.' No one would have dared write that about Bradman, of course.

Fred couldn't resist a modicum of reflection on his own skilful use of leg-theory. 'Wally took some time to master it and didn't get too many runs against Worcestershire when the leg-trap was in operation'. But his unqualified regard for Hammond as the best in the world was not a lone voice. Root's enthusiasm was broadened to include all aspects of Wally's cricket. As a fielder, he put him ahead of the panther-like Constantine; as to his bowling, there was the match Root liked to recall against Gloucestershire. 'We actually got him out when he was going well. And Dickie Pearson said to me that that was the end of him. But then he went on and took nine wickets!'

The lugubrious Bill Bowes, who gave up bowling to become part of a Yorkshire press box which was about as animated as the devoutest religious order in Lent, was a likeable and astute man who could be persuaded to escape from those stifling confines of silence and to amble, with that distinctive stooping movement of his, in reminiscent mood round the boundary. That was when the dry observations and humour would surface through the dour exterior. He'd promise to show you his latest conjuring trick back at the hotel – or simply talk of Bradman. Bespectacled big Bill, even more owl-like in his later days, especially enjoyed his journalistic excursions to the West Country. He used to stay with Andy Wilson, the former Gloucestershire wicket-keeper, one of his many friends. His esteem for Bradman was expressed without reservation.

One of his favourite summaries of good-natured homage was: 'That man could bat better than anyone else on a corrugated iron roof'. He used to say that Bradman had no real weakness at all. 'I'm telling you, he was so much in charge that he could punch half-volleys wherever he wanted to, between third man and wide mid-on. All down to the way he could position himself so quickly. And he had no equal when it came to batting on a sticky wicket'. Now there, Bill's enthusiasm was unintentionally less than fair to Hammond. The evidence comes from at least half a dozen wonderful exhibitions of vigilance and defiance on the most evil of strips, when wickets were tumbling all around him. Is it unreasonable to suspect that Bowes was influenced a trifle by his own experiences, compounded from a distance of 22 yards? Only once was Bradman out first ball in a Test match. It happened at Melbourne during the Bodyline series – and the bowler was Bowes himself. The delivery was preceded by a fair amount of justifiable, old-fashioned duplicity of Elland vintage by Bill over the stage-managed field placing. Bradman misread the intentions and was left groping and was bowled.

There was never a more intense thinker about the art of bowling than Bowes. He and Hedley Verity, in tandem for Yorkshire, were the two cricket 'intellectuals' of their day. Team-mates would joke that they could hear Bill thinking as he took those big, ungainly strides back to his mark. He pondered even more than usual in a Test in Leeds. He was under orders from Hammond: 'Bradman's getting too many singles off the last ball of the over. Don't let him get away with it.'

This was the cerebral challenge that Bowes relished. He stood with hands on hips, encouraging the big native crowd – and Bradman – to wonder what he was going to do. Deliberately he withdrew a fielder to deep on the cover boundary. The Australian skipper assumed that here would be a ball wide down the off-side. Again Bradman was absolutely deceived. It was a yorker on the leg-stump. The great batsman, already bracing himself for a cut, had no time to revise his defences. The ball seamed away wickedly to take the middle stump out of the ground.

The Leeds crowd exploded in delight. Bradman offered a melancholy shrug. Then he walked down the wicket to the bowler. Bowes waited, with no idea what to expect. 'Well bowled, Bill – one up to you.' That courteous gesture was not forgotten.

Sir Len Hutton was a man of restraint; he didn't go in for sweeping judgments. When he said: 'I have a feeling somehow that neither Don nor Walter liked each other very much', it was the Pudsey diplomat plumbing the depths of controversy. Shortly before he died, Hutton was encouraged to ponder the relative merits of the pair. 'Do you know, I'm certain that Walter made 336 against New Zealand in a Test match simply because Don had made 334 against England at Leeds in 1930. To be honest I preferred to see just an hour of Walter Hammond to eight or ten hours of Don Bradman'. Wally could never have asked for a warmer compliment than that. Hutton went on to reflect on the 1946-47 tour of Australia. 'There was this feeling, this rivalry between the two captains. Neither was going to give the other anything at all. You have got to give a little bit when you are captain of England, and you hope the opposing captain will do the same'.

Bradman and Hammond both wrote about the other. The prose was more subdued than one might have imagined. They sustained a veneer of civilised regard – from their distant vantage points. They barely knew each other; conversation was virtually limited to the perfunctory exchanges on the stroll to the wicket before the start of play on the opening day of a test match. The Don did once or twice tell Wally a droll joke during the tea-interval; we know that from Hammond's books. It's unlikely this touch of jocularity was reciprocated. Wally couldn't tell jokes in any case. In their writings they took a few digs at each other; they didn't always disguise feelings of Cold War proportions.

As I prepared to write this book, I wrote to Sir Don. His reply was prompt and courteous. It was also brief. Here is an example of our laconic exchange:

DF: How much were you conscious of Wally's remoteness?

DB: I felt he was a reserved character.

DF: Had it always been so – or was it more obvious on the last '46-47 tour?

DB: Yes, always so – but accentuated in '46-47.

DF: How about your own dealings with him?

DB: My dealings with him were cordial and appeared to be no different in '46-47.

DF: Can I persuade you to say a word about the disputed catch at Brisbane?

DB: The disputed catch had nothing to do with him. An appeal was made and turned down – no more and no less than, say, an LBW appeal.

DF: Did you ever make contact again – letters or Christmas cards?

DB: No.

DF: Were there ever private dinners together, moments of genuine fellowship?

DB: No.

DF: What about his ability as a captain?

DB: He had no special attributes as a captain but seemed to be quite orthodox.

DF: Was there an element of fierce competition between the two of you?

DB: We were merely opposing captains.

DF: Were you surprised how much he had aged after the war?

DB: No more than anyone else.

DF: How much antagonism towards him was there in the Australian dressing-room?

DB: None.

DF: Did you detect a hint or two of snobbery in his make-up, in the way he became an amateur?

DB: No sign of it at all.

DF: Were you aware of the domestic complications which hovered over him during that final tour?

DB: No.

DF: Any personal memories, maybe even with a touch of humour?

DB: He had a quiet sense of humour but was inclined to be moody. The humour was deep-seated. I found him a reserved but warm and friendly person. But I think he became sad in 1946-47 that his previous great talents were failing him.

There were other monosyllabic answers. As an intended interview, conducted by air mail, it was for me disappointingly vapid. Yet Sir Don was not being deliberately unhelpful; he seemed reluctant to expand or regurgitate past differences or scraps of hackneyed folklore. I hoped in vain for a new insight or two. Sir Don's reply, however sparing in words, still appeared succinctly honest. At this distance, perhaps one should understand a reticence to express any view that might smack of malevolence. The letter and brief answers to my questions carried an engaging mellowness of nature. He was in no mood to criticise his old adversary.

A decade earlier he had told Gerald Howat, who was researching Wally's biography: 'I felt Hammond showed little imagination on that last tour and did not display the leadership and tact required of an overseas diplomat which international captains on overseas trips are required to do'.

Bradman and Hammond . . . . Their careers progressed roughly on parallel lines. They enriched the game of cricket by their presence. As Fred Root said they had much in common. He might have added that they were also introverts who often preferred their own company.

They could both have gone into League cricket in this country. Accrington were interested in Bradman and started to flutter a cheque which represented more than £1000 a year. Hammond admitted in his *Secret History* that for 24 hours he, too, was very tempted. He, also, was offered £1000 a year for limited appearances and commitments, a seductive invitation to a poorly paid pre-war pro cricketer. 'At the time,' wrote Hammond, 'I had high hopes of captaining my country against Australia and I preferred to go on and take my chance rather than turn out for a League side.'

In that same book, Wally got round to pondering the Don's mental make-up, a slightly cheeky exercise. He mentioned the early snubs that Bradman had suffered at home. This, Hammond felt, accounted for 'his defensive attitude . . . . Having his enthusiasm nipped hard when he was young, he retired permanently into a shell'. Well, now. Such psychological probing overflows with irony, however accurate the conclusion of the author. Hammond cited that day at Lord's in 1948 when the crowd called for Bradman to come out and say goodbye – but he refused. 'At the end of the most brilliant career in modern cricket, he was still feeling ill at ease because of the early snubs'.

The history of first-class cricket has been coloured, at times defaced, by controversy. It's part of the endless appeal of the human condition. Genius is often flawed. The great practitioners, Bradman and Hammond, tended to encourage criticism. They were both hard to understand and, maybe, to love. But time lends a mellowed charm. There is a generous heart that beats in Bradman's letter; he omits what he didn't like about his rival; he has gone to pains elsewhere, too, to remind us how much Hammond was suffering from fibrositis on that last, and in some ways ghastly, tour.

And here, on record, is a retrospective opinion from Hammond on Bradman's role when they first competed as captains in the 1938 series. When it came to the Oval, England piled up the runs with remorseless efficiency. 'Hardly less praise goes to the Australians. What other team would have stuck it through those hours and days and never let their fielding flag at all?' wrote Hammond. 'It was a fight every inch of the way and Bradman is to be congratulated on the magnificent way he heartened his men . . . . When Hutton passed Bradman's 334 record, Bradman was the first to slap him on the back . . . .' Australia lost heavily by an innings. The Don had been carried off with a fractured shin. There was surely a case for generosity of spirit.

Generosity, or even shades of hypocrisy – what does it really matter? The memory can become conveniently selective. But, of course, Jack Ikin's catch at Brisbane after the war can't be forgotten, either. Bradman had no wish at all to discuss it. But it made contentious headlines at the time and was documented in detail in a few hundred cricket books. I shall be unable to resist coming back to it in later pages. The almost universal view was that Bradman was out. He didn't walk, and the umpire ignored the appeal. Hammond swore audibly; his fielders were nonplussed. For years Hammond had been obsessed with the notion that the dismissal of Bradman was the prerequisite to any win over the Australians. And now, with both of them close to the end of their career and an elusive scent of conquest so near, he felt he'd been cheated. Bradman, then 28, went on to score 187, adding 276 in a third wicket stand with Lindsay Hassett. It would be an imperishable and sour farewell. The human chasm was never to be healed.

Envy is never far away in first-class sport. It is an understandable, if negative, quality. There are always fears of being displaced, of being victims of personal prejudice or politicking. Hammond suffered his share, to accompany his needless self-doubts. We've already mentioned Charlie Dacre, whose brash self-confidence and jaunty attitude towards going for his shots, not necessarily in the team's interest, led to a number of bellicose exchanges with Hammond. 'I just can't get on with that bloody Kiwi,' Wally would say. He bridled whenever Dacre's name was mentioned. Yet behind the saturnine expression of near-contempt lurked a misplaced layer of envy. Hammond would have liked just a little of that self-confidence, a little of the extrovert bravado that could command the attention of the dressing room's other occupants. The chirpy Charlie had a certain worldliness about him which, in those days, left the England batsman feeling and sounding jejune and bereft of positive language.

Bev Lyon was envied, but that was different. In his case, it was because of his sangfroid, the sophistication he oozed, his classless charm ('Come on, chaps, forget this defeat at the Oval – back to my pub for the evening.' The 'pub' was the

Dorchester Hotel; transport was his swish Roller.) Wally idolised Bev. The envy was invariably tinged with affection.

When it came to Dacre, there was no love at all. I went to Grahame Parker for confirmation of one much-related incident which had featured prominently in Gloucestershire mythology. But it happened, in the mid-1930s against Sussex. Parker had always savoured the humanity of the game, generating the chuckles – or occasionally sharp intakes of breath – with his charitable accounts of sport's absorbing *dramatis personae* alongside him in the England rugby XV and the endearingly rugged Gloucester RFC and Cambridge sides, county cricket or even – when he briefly and joyfully on teenage Saturday afternoons played at left-back with the semi-pros – at soccer. Now he chuckled again as he remembered that match with Sussex at Cheltenham. 'Bev had persuaded Wally to bowl and it was the first time I'd seen him really hurling them down. It was the second innings and we were looking forward to an early finish. But Maurice Tate and Jim Langridge were holding us up.'

Dacre was in effect Gloucestershire's third choice wicket-keeper. He had done the job often enough back in New Zealand and, in his rather flamboyant manner, was efficient and tidy when called on by the county. More often, he patrolled the covers in noisy commentary that could be seen as either cordiality or irritation. He liked to take the wicket-keeper's gloves; he had an intrepid approach and chose to stand up to the medium-pacers. Hammond, in one of his less subtle stage-whispers, was inclined to make it obvious that he'd feel happier if Harry Smith were behind the stumps.

'Oh dear, they really hated each other – they had nothing in common', Parker recalled. 'Wally had begun with a few off-breaks and cutters, rather than seam. But he suddenly let one go and it hit Charlie on the shoulder. It must have been very painful. Some cursing went on. Wally's response was to go back a yard or two – and the next ball flew past Dacre's head and went for four byes.

'Charlie wasn't having that, so he went back five yards himself. Before very long, Wally had retreated another ten yards and Charlie twenty or so. He was now more of a goalkeeper than a wicket-keeper. The ball was veering all over the place, very fast, almost impossible to keep to. He ended up with two important wickets – but Charlie conceded more than 40 byes.'

Hammond was making a point. In his own way, maybe small-minded but with some logic, he was saying to Dacre: 'Don't pretend you can stand up to me. I'm a *fast* bowler.'

The confrontation that day seemed alien to the customary cloistered calm of the College ground. Eyes blazed in mutual belligerence between bowler and keeper. The rest of the Gloucestershire fielders confined their inner glee to exchanged glances. At short leg, Lyon wiped his glasses on his sweater and smiled to himself. He didn't approve of the extras that were being accumulated as a result of such anger. Yet what a triumph it had been to goad Hammond into lengthening his run and steaming in like that.

In one of my many enthralling chats with Reg Sinfield, he said: 'At times I had to keep the peace, you know. Once I asked Charlie Dacre what was the idea of throwing his wicket away like he had. And he told me he wasn't going to bat with Wally and have to act as nothing much more than a runner. Charlie Barnett was just the same. Both of them could hit the ball as hard as Wally – and that was the problem, oh dear me, yes.'

We return to envy. Hammond was a reasonably intelligent man, no more. He had been an average scholar at the grammar school and would never have come top of his form. There were times when he told trusted acquaintances that he wished he was better educated. He envied the wide-ranging knowledge, mostly self-acquired, of Charlie Parker, the farm-labourer's son. Charlie would rhapsodise about left-wing politics. He had read all about the Russian revolution and believed that Britain was ready for radical socialism, too. He'd also hum a snatch from the classics or, as an alternative to the vituperative oaths that came in comic rotation from his lips, would throw in a Biblical text with unselfconscious ease to lend weight to one of his dogmatic assertions.

Hammond, on a good day, might whistle a Harry Roy rag-tune. He'd dance impeccably to the rhythm of Jack Payne. He could play golf, tennis or, on a wet day, cards. If he had any thought about politics, no one ever heard it. He listened to the compulsive monologues of Charlie – even if their opinions of 'Plum' Warner were so diametrically opposed – and envied him.

How he envied, too, even if subconsciously, the ordered domesticity of West Country team-mates like Alf Dipper, Bernie Bloodworth and that valued mentor of his, George Dennett, an unflurried Man of Dorset, with life very much in perspective. Hammond would see them gulping down their pints and then hurrying off home to families. Their family background had been different from his; they had sustained a regulated and contented home-loving lifestyle which had utterly eluded him.

Somewhere between envy and jealousy came a glimmer or two of resentment. We can think of both Keith Miller and Denis Compton. They were two glamorous figures, figures of heroism and romantic fiction. Their dashing good looks made them irresistible to women (and acquisitive advertisers). They were younger than Hammond and they made him aware of a midriff that had, particularly by the end of the war, become flaccid. They were to succeed him as monopolists of the back-page headlines.

Miller was the night-fighter who would come straight off duty, snatch his flannels and turn up at Lord's. He and Hammond were the stars of that glorious, almost surreal, symbol of release and celebration in the summer of 1945, the 'Victory Test' matches, and specifically the match between England and the Dominions at Lord's in August. Some still say it was the finest they ever saw. No doubt they were swayed by the sheer joyfulness of resumed peace, and why not? Every catch seemed to be one of swooping brilliance. The batting was daring and frequently sublime. Hammond scored a hundred in each innings. Yet the majority of those who watched the whole match went home talking of Miller. It wasn't just that he was so tall and handsome. He made 185, an innings that demanded immortality.

And Compton, the Brylcreem Boy. The hoardings, the tube subways, the full-page ads in the papers, the display stands in the barbers' shops all carried his familiar face (and, soon, Miller's too). A few years earlier, Wally would have been the obvious target for the advertising agencies. Denis, the elementary schoolboy and seller of scorecards to supplement his meagre earnings when on the Lord's groundstaff, made his first-class entry into the game with the innocence and poetry of athletic boyhood. Old pros were always inclined to sniff disparagingly at these baptismal flurries. Hammond wasn't even old. He was playing some of his best cricket, building on his reputation and devouring pages in the record books. Forgetting Bradman for the moment, he was still the icon of international cricket. And now, suddenly, Middlesex had come up with a new pretender.

They said that Compton was just as good at soccer. He was being groomed to chase down the left wing for Arsenal and, according to *The Star* and the *Evening Standard*, faithful chroniclers of sporting endeavour in London, he would play for England at both sports. And so he did, amid a national frisson of excitement. In his first Test against the Australians, at Trent Bridge in 1938, he scored a hundred. He went on to play in a dozen wartime internationals for his country at soccer, though he was never in the same class as his brother Leslie.

Hammond kept his thoughts to himself. He acknowledged Compton's precocious talents and sat on the players' balcony to lead the polite applause for boundaries, born often from an innate sense of adventure and entertainment. As for the football, Hammond as we have seen had been briefly a professional winger in the West Country. One coach had said he was the fastest and potentially one of the most skilful they had ever seen at Bristol's Eastville Stadium. There were no Highbury marble halls down there, of course, no Epstein busts of past managers. But Hammond knew his worth as a footballer. Running, beating his full back and crossing the ball came easily to him – just as it did to Compton, despite his saucy tendency to dally and outwit the same opponent three times. Wally tasted modest play down in the Third Division (South), proved to himself that he could do it, and got out. He decided to concentrate on one sport; and he wondered when the younger Compton might do the same.

As fellow England cricketers, before and after the war, they were never churlish enough to devalue the other's considerable contribution. They came from different regions, with different cultures. They both had a human weakness or two no doubt;

there was little rapport between them. Hammond always suspected that Compton had a low opinion of him as a captain – and he was right. He was seen as too negative, too reluctant to take a risk with field placing. Compo was a man of instinct; he acted on hunches. His Test skipper never did. Compo liked his captain, even if not quite one of the boys, to be accessible; not to be breezing off in comfort, from Aussie ground to ground, in a specially provided Jaguar. That rankled for years.

Theirs was a mutually wary relationship, but not an abrasive one. Some involving Hammond clearly were abrasive. One with Learie Constantine was a good deal more than frosty. Constantine was to claim that the feud went on for ten years. In the process he bowled Bodyline in a patent attempt to intimidate the Gloucestershire man. According to Constantine, whose riveting career as a cricketer was burdened by the political chips on his shoulder (some of them more than justified), his antagonistic feelings towards Hammond emanated from what he saw as a slight over the colour question. The incident happened in the West Indies, but was not fully articulated. 'I swore by all the gods to make him regret the day,' wrote Constantine later in seemingly histrionic language.

It appears that Hammond had arrived on tour and Constantine had made a special effort to meet him off the boat. He extended a welcome, and all he got in reply was a rebuff. 'We'd been good pals in England. Now I got the strong impression that though I was good enough for a morning's fun in England, things were not quite the same where the colour bar was more pronounced.'

Constantine certainly suffered some unforgivable insults because he was black. His intelligence and outstanding prowess as a cricketer often counted for nothing amid the social divisions and inequalities of the Caribbean. In England, too, he was subjected to the most demeaning of slights in hotels and public places. He remained hyper-sensitive to the question of racial discrimination. He'd see rebuffs where they didn't exist. That may have been what happened on the quayside in the West Indies on the day he said his words of welcome were ignored.

He wasn't one to bury a grievance, real or imagined. There were matches when he went out of his way with his bowling to attack Hammond. 'I had the ball whizzing round his ears,' he wrote. 'Wally didn't look happy so I sent down a few more, with my mind no doubt lingering on his frozen expression and the coldly casual rebuff to my eager greeting when he came off the boat . . . . He did his best to make my bowling look silly so I made the ball jump around and whisper in his ears'.

The Constantine version of that particular confrontation was that Hammond eventually appealed to his captain for some protection. This unpleasant vendetta still went on 'with too much acid'. If the aggressive Learie perceived it as some kind of political statement, he was probably a victim of his own compounded complexes. There is little, if any, evidence that Hammond was a bigot. He would have seen the long-standing feud more as a physical contest: here were two great players, the best in their respective countries, pitting their skills – muscle as well as grace – against each other. The Englishman didn't like balls that reared regularly towards his unprotected head. He used to see Constantine scowling and didn't take to him. It would have been understandable for words to be exchanged.

But the feud was to end, abruptly, during a match at Old Trafford in 1933. Hammond had been cut on the chin. He had plaster on his wound and may well have been feeling psychologically battered. Suddenly he left his crease and walked down the wicket to Constantine. 'Let's make peace, Learie'. He held out his hand. The West Indian later said it was something he would always admire.

That comes from Constantine's own book, *Cricketer's Carnival*. I'm sure that in essence it was true. If so, it does credit to both players. Their thoroughly bad-tempered differences, based on a misunderstanding, had gone on far too long. The acceptable rivalry continued, though never again tainted by spite and scorn. Grahame Parker recounted how the two had unofficial contests. They bowled the occasional bouncer at each other, in playful challenge and reprisal. 'Learie once took a catch behind his back. And they'd say that Wally would try to do it as well'.

By Hammond's own inhibited standards of intimacy, they became friends. They publicly regretted their past differences. Hammond heard from his companion poignant stories of talented young West Indians whose cricketing progress was ruined by lack of money and encouragement. There were numerous reactionaries within the game; he was not one of them. In his books and ghosted columns, he expressed sympathy about the frustrations and deprivations suffered by black players.

On one occasion he wrote: 'Constantine himself, on his first tour of England, had to stay in bed at hotels a good deal of the time because he simply had not got enough pocket-money . . . . But he did get to England and because cricket in his homeland would not support him, he had to stay here. I know he liked League cricket and League cricket loved him. But I can't help wondering how much higher the standard of West Indies cricket would have been if the two Constantines, George Headley and other West Indians who have gone into the League had been able to live at home and teach the young how to bowl and bat.'

That would have been sincere. Constantine read and approved. Slowly, the burdens on the shoulder lessened. From the intensity of rivalry, which had been interpreted wrongly as an ugly manifestation of racism, a discernible if restrained conviviality emerged. The pair were to share laughter about the cunning manner a quiet word from Learie to his batting partner once deceived Wally into not making a sensible bowling change during the last Test before the war. The pair even had a bet over which of them could hit the Long Room with a six in that bounteous match between England and the Dominions in 1945. Unlike Hammond, Constantine failed to make a century at Lord's, but in the second innings he hit the English bowlers for 42 in 14 minutes.

Charlie's Not My Darling

I could without any difficulty write a whole book about the relationship of Charlie Barnett and Hammond. They are both dead and there would be no laws of libel to temper the narrative. Yet I suspect that litigation would still not be too far away. I had two lengthy interviews with Barnett. He could be quite prickly and even pompous in his dealings with journalists, but we got on pretty well. Andy Wilson had, I remember, prepared the way for me.

In the dressing room at Bristol, Cheltenham or the Wagon Works, Barnett was known as The Guvnor. That was because he'd been to a public school, had a better voice and more authority than most of the committee, and usually won an argument when he went striding in – on behalf of fellow pros with a legitimate grievance – to take on the county club's management. He didn't have a great sense of humour and was inclined to be bumptious. Bob Wyatt and his wife, Molly, didn't take to him at all. 'I found him rather dull and he once went on and on so boringly that he nearly ruined a television programme in which we were both taking part.'

At my second meeting with him, Barnett appeared to have worked out what he wanted to say. I'd hardly got inside his house before, in just one graphic, rhetorical sentence – nothing, it should be said, to do with any illness contracted in a distant bed chamber – he offered a withering indictment of his former skipper and one-time friend. It so startled me that I spluttered: 'You just can't say that, Charles' (I had been briefed not to be sufficiently informal as to call him Charlie).

'Why can't I? It's true.'

He proceeded to give chapter and verse. It was about

something that had happened long ago. Barnett had no qualms about letting the public know. There was something approaching contempt in his voice. I talked to various other contemporaries and their memories were more blurred. In any case, they considered the incident, which had never become general knowledge in the West Country, should now be be discreetly forgotten.

I have no wish to make Charlie Barnett some kind of ogre. He was a Gloucestershire man of some social status who was not ashamed to play cricket as a professional. This he did with undisputed élan. He went after the bowling and took hundreds before lunch. He would drive eagerly off the front and back foot as handsomely as any opener around. His father and uncle had played for the county as amateurs. He was a well-built Cotswold resident who lived in a fine Georgian house, hunted twice a week with the Beauforts and the Berkeleys and didn't stand any nonsense from anyone. The other pros very much respected him; he was more popular than Wally.

Barnett was fired by a fierce integrity. He had his standards. He was straitlaced, not interested in gossip or the more sensual frivolities. Those who transgressed were roundly condemned. The condemnation he focused on Hammond bordered almost on cruelty in its unforgiving nature. Wally was older but they made their way together in the Gloucestershire team. There were several years when they lived only a few miles apart, at Chalford and Thrupp, near Stroud. They often travelled together. Their first wives were close friends; the two families would share the meal table on occasions. Wally told Charlie he would play for England one day – and so he did.

But then team-mates noticed them growing apart. Snide comments could be overheard. 'Do you still have Wally round for a meal, Charlie, when Dorothy is back in Yorkshire with her family?' The reply would be curt. 'No. Don't like his social graces.' And then after a pause: 'Don't like the way he behaves when his wife is away.'

It's true to say that the relationship drifted from rural friendliness, shared transport and occasional shared suppers at Chalford to grudging regard and then to unmitigated contempt on Barnett's part. It would be dishonest to couch his fast-diminishing affection for Hammond in more diplomatic language. Not many people knew Barnett better than Alan 'Ally' Phillips, a capable local club cricket captain, point-to-point jockey, groom and confidant of Charlie. Ally was once told over the late-night whisky: 'Wally said he could have done with me on that 1946-47 tour of Australia. My response was that really he had no time for me, nor I for him'.

Barnett would list some of the things that he disliked about his one-time co-driver. He was furious at the way Wally would encourage Tom Goddard and one or two others to take bets on whether they were in the Test 12. 'He was prepared to take a fiver off a team-mate,' Barnett would recall to Phillips. 'It was an absolute nonsense – after all, he was the captain and largely responsible for picking the side!' Barnett used to add: "He even tried it out on me. I'd tell him that if I was good enough, I'd be in. I certainly wasn't going to put any money into his pocket for that kind of bet.'

Not so long before his death, Barnett was taken along by Phillips as the guest of honour at a social evening arranged by one of the local cricket teams, Frocester C.C. He was a popular visitor and the good-natured questions from star-struck villagers came from all angles. It was a relaxed night and Charlie was enjoying himself. Suddenly someone, in all innocence, asked him about Wally. He clammed up; that was the end of the questions.

'The Guvnor' wasn't going to compromise. In its simplest terms, I think the irretrievable division can be attributed to two reasons – Hammond's womanising and his duplicity over Barnett's benefit match. He was appalled by the glib manner Hammond deceived or, just as bad, ignored his first wife Dorothy. Barnett was consumed with loyalty to her. He felt she was treated despicably by a husband who rarely seemed willing to hurry dutifully home to her after a match or maybe a northern tour.

'Her parents had bought her a lovely house just down the valley from my home. But when Wally dared to bring another woman to the same village, that for me was the end. When a wife has by then lost all her money and a husband is casual like that, it doesn't go down very well. In Gloucestershire we don't like that sort of thing.' It was the puritan and the snob coming out together. But many others in Barnett's hunting set had noticed it. And, no – they didn't like that sort of thing . . . .

The benefit match ended for ever any pretence at lingering affection between these two talented, attractive Gloucestershire and England batsmen. Charlie would bring the subject up during my visits to his home. He wrote in anger about it; he wanted people to know.

Barnett was given the home match with Yorkshire at the end of May 1947. Hammond had been home from Australia for seven weeks or so; he had a new bride on his arm; his intentions were to drift out of the first-class game. But in terms of Nevil Road, and a benefit match, he was still a vital ingredient for success. A telegram was sent from Bristol signed by the team, pleading with him to play.

I have in front of me a yellowing newspaper cutting from the Friday of that week. It carries a brief interview with him in London. 'I am absolutely unable to get away from London. I regret the fact very much indeed. I would very much have liked to play . . . . I wish Charlie all the luck in the world.' The newspaper commented: 'To the disappointment of players and public alike, he has had regretfully to decline. His presence would have added thousands to the gate.'

Barnett was livid. It was known that Hammond had a business career increasingly on his mind – and the attractive Sybil in tow – but everyone had expected him to support his experienced county colleague and near neighbour. The public were for the most part oblivious of the schism. At least the beneficiary had more luck with Yorkshire. He had written in advance to Len Hutton, saying how much he hoped he would be playing. The reply came back that Yorkshire had every intention of putting out their best team. Barnett invited Hutton and Bill Bowes to stay over the weekend with him at his home. Professionals liked the occasional opportunity to stay at a private house during their away games. 'I'll drive you out to a trout farm at Bibury on Sunday morning', the host promised.

They stopped at some kennels on the way, where Len, a dog-lover, had his eye on a golden retriever that was for sale. Charlie whispered to the kennel-owner; 'Don't give it away, not even to

Len. He's got plenty of money'. Hutton, with a reputation for watching his pennies, procrastinated and then turned down the sale. So on to the trout farm. It was there that the owner turned to Barnett and said: 'Had a friend of yours here yesterday. With a lady. They spread a cloth and had a picnic'. So Hammond hadn't been in London; he could have played for Charlie.

'I'd turned out in 20 or so matches for him – and this was how he was treating me. That was it as far as I was concerned,' said Barnett with a bitterness that was never to go away.

A former *Guardian* journalist, John Hudson, came west to edit an attractive glossy magazine, the *Gloucestershire and Avon Life*. He lived not far from Barnett, had a natural affection for cricket, and encouraged him to write several autobiographical articles. Some of the opinions were characteristically pungent. In discussing captains of Gloucestershire, he had this to say:

> Basil Allen was one of the considerate types who understand that half of the battle is to keep a settled and happy side. He was doing well when Wally Hammond was appointed as captain of England and it was soon felt that it would be something of an anomaly if he did not fill a similar role for Gloucestershire. So Basil Allen stood aside and Wally stepped in.
>
> It was not a happy period for he was not a good captain. I think it is a fact that you will get a lot more out of people if you ask them to do something. If you stand behind them and crack the whip, you might be all right on a parade ground as a sergeant-major but you will not get very far leading a cricket team.
>
> He had the advantage of two fast bowlers, which no other captain of Gloucestershire had in my time. But George Lambert and Colin Scott said quite frankly they just couldn't produce the goods with Wally standing at first slip glaring down at them as they launched into their run-up. They were both good prospects and it was a great pity. Some people have the knack of leading – and some haven't.

That reference to the sergeant-major is interesting. Barnett told me he had no idea that Hammond had come from an army background; but that had explained a good deal: 'His failure ever to say Please, his demanding instead of asking'.

In that same excellent erstwhile magazine, Barnett on another occasion returned to the subject of Hammond.

> I think his weakness as captain was that he wasn't prepared to ask advice from others. He gave orders and woe betide if they were not carried out. The one thing he didn't understand was that if you give an order politely everyone is willing to do his best.
>
> There was never any kindness in his captaincy. He would not go quietly to a bowler who was struggling and say 'Thank you very much but I think we'll give someone else a turn'. It was just a rough 'Put your sweater on'.

I did some preliminary research for HTV's documentary on Hammond, fronted by Peter West, a BBC exile. The programme carried interviews with many of the key figures, from Bradman and O'Reilly to Ames and Gubby Allen. There was some rare footage and it seemed to me remarkable, if not small-minded, that the network failed to take the programme, which finished up being restricted to the regions. There were engrossing insights, off and on camera, used in the programme or reluctantly consigned to the cutting-room floor. So many of the interviewees came up with the same conclusions. How could a person, built like a God, so instinctively gifted on the field, be so lacking in human qualities off it?

Maybe Barnett was justified in bearing his grudges. There was an occasion after the war when Hammond dropped him in the batting order to no. 5. Andy Wilson reflected: 'Wally knew that Charlie couldn't bear hanging around for his turn to bat. He was essentially an opener. That incident led to quite a dust-up. Charlie emerged the winner and promptly returned as the opening bat.'

What astonished me, during my preparations for this book, was the consistent potency of the criticism. There was no tendency to moderate the retrospective observation, no sheltering behind bland and anodyne phrases. Time hadn't assuaged the sentiments.

Hammond and Bradman . . . Hammond and Constantine . . . Hammond and Barnett. These threads of conflict ran through his playing career. Was he really so bad at human relationships? Where did rivalry, unadorned, start and finish? Is it just a little too facile to heap all the blame on Hammond?

PART V

THE WOMEN

Distractions of the Flesh

The two ruling passions of Wally Hammond's life, it was once said to me in all seriousness by a famous cricketer who might in retrospect prefer to remain nameless, were his cricket bat and his genitals. This was a neat assessment, not intended to be either glib or facile. The bat, as we have seen, was bejewelled with rare magic and touched the soul with its poetic language and beauty. Rather more prosaically, we should perhaps dally on Wally and his women.

At the end of his biography of Hammond, as he came to sum up his subject, Gerald Howat wrote: 'He had an eye for pretty women but was not promiscuous.' Mr Howat reached a number of sound, well-reasoned conclusions and understandably retreated from any sniff of sensationalism. Unfortunately, his sincerely held belief that Hammond's sexual activities were temperate and – by implication – influenced by a sense of loyalty is a long way from the truth.

It had all been innocent enough in schooldays. At Cirencester, the well-bred girls had ogled him from their upstairs classroom windows. Then in the summer evenings, they had walked, in awe, with him down to the marketplace. Wally alone was the attraction, not any of his noisier form mates. Those giggling pubescent girls, suddenly aware – as doubtless was Wally – of their bulging blouses, sought his attention not for what he said or even for his achievements on the sports field. The potent chemistry of the hormones was already at work.

Very soon after he left the grammar school, as he had his first pints in a public bar and accepted his first invitations to the tennis parties and Saturday night dances in Bristol and Bath, he discovered that a girl's company came easily. What did it matter if good looks apparently carried more social clout than mere personality? He began to part his hair in the middle; he made sure he had a clean shirt and that he had polished his shoes. Not yet out of his teens, he was becoming, with progressive pleasure, an addicted womaniser.

Around the barracks back in Malta, the ribaldry he had overheard meant little to him. Later, in all-male conclaves, whether in a school dormitory or at a black-tie sports dinner, he enjoyed and laughed at the raunchy stories. No one ever remembered him telling one himself. But he was never any kind of prude. He was cursed with a libido that, apart from enforced inactivity at the time of his illness, kept his loins burning.

Little Eddie Paynter, pride of Oswaldtwistle, was once asked for his abiding memory of Hammond. They had toured together, dined together, batted together. There had been scope to recapture in his spontaneous answer the infallibility of a great innings on a different wicket, or one of those illusory slip catches.

'Wally, well, yes – he liked a shag!' It takes an earthy Lancastrian to sort out the perspectives and arrive at that kind of honesty. In short, Hammond was promiscuous. He had many women friends and slept, I imagine, with a fair proportion of them. This went on inside and outside his first marriage. At times he carried on liaisons with two or three other women at the same time. The marriage to Dorothy had been a ghastly sham. He liked his women to be glamorous. 'Dot' wasn't attractive – but she had a wealthy father and a private allowance. That is, until the crash came. Then her father had nothing. Soon he was dead – dead as a marriage which, I suspect, was barely consummated.

Yet Hammond's natural sex-drive had become noticeable as far back as his winter months with Bristol Rovers, when he would turn up for training a little too ostentatiously in his first car. 'He's only got it to take them chorus girls out', the old pros used to say enviously.

His first regular companion was a long-legged soubrette called Grace James. Her family came from the area, quite proper and lower middle-class. Grace and her sister danced in revues and touring shows. Wally met them when they were appearing in

Bristol. It was Grace who decorously made eyes at him; he fancied her sister more. For six years he maintained a close, if intermittent, friendship with Grace. He got on well with her mother. Grace took him to dances after the curtain had come down. She was flattered to be taken out by a young professional sportsman who dressed and looked so good by the contemporary standards of a city in poverty. But the relationship was an odd one. It remained chaste and even unromantic. She was older than him, outward-going and quite stage-struck. She implied she'd have liked her boyfriend to be more gregarious, to laugh more. Grace told Gerald Howat that Wally sent her a cable from South Africa, where he had gone to complete his recovery from the Caribbean infections, proposing marriage.

According to Grace, she turned him down. She used to tell her fellow dancers that he was too shy for her – that he hardly kissed her in six years or so. Shy he may have been in the conventional social sense; there is not too much evidence that he was generally backward in carnal matters. The truth was that the world was opening up to him and he saw her as no more than a good friend. For all that mannered showbizzy vitality and baring of limbs in the chorus-line, there could also be a paradoxical asexuality about those who worked on the stage, once they were out of their costumes. If Hammond did propose to Grace James, it must be said that he could be liberal with such gestures. I came across at least a dozen names of girls, during my research, who were similarly invited to become his wife. Most of those proposals must have been offered impulsively, not always too seriously, without much thought for the responsibility involved – maybe when he was spiritually or physically frail and felt in need of a constant companion. The cable may well have been sent by him from South Africa. But at the time he was still painfully underweight, isolated and confused.

His mother certainly liked the idea of his marrying Grace. By now Marion Hammond was herself living in Bristol, settling into the maternal role that she had seemingly abandoned during Wally's schooldays. She would have been happy for her son to stay with her but he demanded independence. Mrs Hammond became friendly with Grace's mother and assumed that marriage within the families would follow. Her son was a cussed individual. He had no intention of allowing his mother to determine which young woman was to be his wife. If Grace did in the end reject him, he had no serious complaints. Life might indeed have been embarrassingly complicated if she hadn't.

It's a compliment to Grace's good nature that she stayed friendly with Wally and his mother over future years. He had reason to be grateful for the hours she spent at his bedside in the Bristol nursing home. If he really was sparing with his chaste kisses to her, it may have been because she dissuaded him firmly from more physical pursuits. His relationship with her, like that with Muriel Pannell, the daughter of his eventual best man, was platonic; but it should not be dismissed lightly because of that.

Mrs Hammond hadn't approved of the early digs which had been found for her son in Bristol. They were cheap and functional. She couldn't understand why he didn't want to stay with her; after all, a greater bond was now developing between them. Bert Williams' missus may have done his washing, but Marion made sure the shirts were ironed and that he wasn't going short of food. 'At least find somewhere nice to stay,' she nagged. She did not know him well enough to discern the clues that revealed he was already a bit of a snob, just like her. He was meeting affluent people in the city, ones who had had spacious homes in the more attractive suburbs. It didn't appeal to him to return to that tacky one room of his, dark and untidy, in a claustrophobic backstreet terrace.

His friends in Bath put him on to 'Auntie Chrissie' Stoneham. She possessed a jolly personality and what seemed to young Hammond to be a full and civilised lifestyle. She and her husband, Alf, ran a fish shop ('high-class, game, grouse, you know, that kind of thing . . . very popular among those who could afford it') at The Mall at Clifton, Bristol. The Stonehams were prepared to take him as a lodger. They had already met him socially. This was more like it. The Mall was comparatively up-market. It had a Georgian and early Victorian feel about it. The rich people were there; if you lived in Clifton, it meant something. If you were a greenhorn professional sportsman on two quid a week, it meant a great deal. As Bert Williams used to say to me: 'We'd look at each other and say "Bloody hell, young Wally's now gone and got a place for himself in Clifton – he's a bit different from the rest of us". We weren't sure whether he had enough money to pay the rent up there, mind you'.

Alf and Chrissie, in fact, charged him no more than a nominal amount. They treated him as one of the family. 'He'd have eaten well with all that good quality fish and game around. Auntie Chrissie was later to visit him in hospital,' I was told by a relative. He had a flat above the fish-and-game shop. In the morning he would pause on the pavement to light a cigarette before stepping into his car. He luxuriated in the ambience. Grace was occasionally brought back to the flat for coffee after the evening show. It was just as well, he reasoned, that the Stonehams felt his devotions were restricted to one girl. They, like his mother, Grace and the majority of his sporting associates, knew nothing of his simultaneous amours. They knew nothing, for instance, about Dorothy Oakey.

Dorothy had the necessary physical and social attributes. She was good looking and had a neat, slim figure. She lived at No 1 Bridge Road, Sharpness, a busy Severnside dock area, and in those days the third biggest timber port in the country. The docks there were invariably full of ships, at times with up to forty crews having noisy, happy evenings at the Railway Inn or 'The Shant' (Sharpness Hotel) as they waited for sailings. Dorothy's father, with his bushy grey moustache and inseparable trilby, was a docks manager at Sharpness. The dockers called him 'Sir'; so did all the village children who crowded the dockside to see the latest consignment of linseed, sugar or monkey nuts being unloaded. The timber ships came in from Canada and Scandinavia. There was still a railway bridge crossing the Severn to Lydney: it was an exciting place to live.

On his countless stays with the Neales at just a few miles down the road, Hammond would often walk to Sharpness to see the ships unloading. That was almost certainly where he met Dorothy's father. 'The Oakeys were very nice people but a trifle snobbish', I was told by Mrs Eileen Sims, one of the oldest local residents who as a 10-year-old would walk past the Oakeys' home on her way to deliver papers. That was when she noticed Dorothy sleeping in a hammock slung from two apple trees in the front garden.

That suggests both an unconventional and intrepid young woman. The dockside roads could be full of seamen into the early hours. There were many languages, but raucous good-natured oaths usually sound the same. Dorothy, in a light nightdress, slept through it all. Mrs Sims remembers: 'None of us bothered to lock our doors then. And this attractive girl was able to sleep without fear.'

Perhaps she went to sleep dreaming of Hammond. His blossoming friendship with her was no secret locally. But Sharpness and Berkeley could be tight communities, self-sufficient and socially incestuous. They were away from the main road between Bristol and Gloucester, and had no complaints on that score. What young Wally Hammond did in his spare time was no business of anyone else. His romance with Grace James was tepid in passion. The one with Dorothy Oakey was on a different emotional level. He made numerous visits to Bridge Road, ostensibly to be entertained by her father and to talk cricket, a topic Wally invariably recoiled from in normal conversation.

Cricket was taken seriously in the locality, however. Mr Oakey played for the village team. The children themselves, Mrs Sims among them, had regular improvised matches on The Green. 'There was a period when Wally was making up to four or five visits a week. He must have been amused at the way we played – we used a tin for stumps and tore up wood from old dockside crates for bats. The skipper of *The Salient*, which was holed up for some weeks at Sharpness, noticed our lack of equipment and actually bought the kids a full set of kit.

'It gave us a special thrill when we saw Wally looking over the fence at us. We encouraged him to join in and there were times when he did. When it rained, we moved to a timber shed.' Those days in the early 1920s, maybe at the end of the county season, also brought back a flood of memories to Cyril Savage, who used to work on the docks, like nearly everyone else in Sharpness.

'The rumour would get around that Wally was coming on the Sunday to see Dorothy Oakey. He'd turn up in his car, go in to see her father and, a bit later, emerge with a bat in his hand. I can remember the two of them playing with us on the concrete floor of the shed. It seemed pretty dangerous to me as Wally clouted the ball in all directions. Some of us used to cower by the door.'

A hard, rough ball skimming along a concrete outfield may well have been a terrifying spectacle. But this was doubtless offset by the sheer privilege of having him in their own comic minefield of an indoor net. It was just a token appearance to please them and to allow Mr Oakey to bowl at him. The father kept on his trilby. Wally would soon be buying his first.

Dorothy was always impatient to see him. She fidgeted while he had a glass of scotch with her father and while he playfully tapped a cricket ball to all corners of the shed. Then they went off for long walks, hand in hand. There were no prying eyes. She teased him a little, telling him how she slept in the open air outside the house. She was flirtatious, something he always enjoyed. In most of his dalliances, he preferred his women to be the instigators. Except when he was at the wicket, he was not a man of enterprise.

The romance, known to few beyond the banks of the Severn, lasted for several years. Then it suddenly petered out – at least on his part. There were other boundaries to conquer. This time Kitty Hall was emerging to lead the applause. Catherine Hall was the same age as Wally. She came from Kent and first met him when he stayed with the Gloucestershire team, for the Folkestone Festival, at Devonshire House, a hotel in Marine Parade run by her father. She was a self-assured young woman, a quality he appeared to need in his romantic friendships. She also had some kind of past, which she had told him about. This troubled her more than it did him.

Still in his early 20s, the headlines were beginning to fly for him. His presence was requested, especially by eligible and available young women. He could be selective, and not too many could say that. He was polishing his social graces and doing his best, a little tentatively, to improve his output of words and his confidence at the well-heeled gatherings.

The liaison with the comely Miss Hall was over by the summer of 1927. What is strikingly interesting about it is the way, quite apart from any physical affinity, he was encouraged to discard the irritating mask and to reveal something of himself for virtually the first time. Not too many extolled Hammond for his sensitivity. He could be cruel in that dismissive fashion, either for a passé girlfriend or a fellow cricketer. He had no obvious facility for the niceties of tact. But Kitty appears to have prompted self-analytical thoughts.

He may not have been a great talker but he was a conscientious letter-writer. At school he had written copious notes to the mother who seemed so far away. He wrote to congratulate his even more distant father when he was given a commission. There is evidence that he wrote to all his girlfriends, frequently in tones of mawkish, lovey-dovey triteness. Numerous letters surfaced and no doubt more will be offered for sale before too long. Successive generations of relatives have come to realise the historical and financial value of such penned intimacies. The letters, wonderfully authentic in their yellowing antiquity, have been emerging from attics and dog-eared family albums. He wrote scores of them, and many were retained. The correspondence involving Dot tends to make us feel intrusive and embarrassed, although unlike memories which have become soured, distorted, refined and often inaccurate, these letters provide rich and valuable insights.

Some of Kitty Hall's letters from Hammond came up for sale in 1994. The auctioneers were Vennett-Smith, of Nottingham. In one letter he writes about his private feelings for her. 'Don't worry about them for I am not in the habit of showing them anywhere. I don't seem to be made like that but I have plenty, believe me.'

Rather more lasciviously he tells her how nice it would be to be sleeping in the next room to her and have her tuck him in. 'I wonder if you want me as badly as I want you.' Not too much subtlety here. Nor was there, one could add, when he was staying with the Neales at Breadstone Farm and it was noticed that the tall wardrobe mirror in his bedroom was shifted to a different position each day.

Billy was told about it by the maid who came in to help with the cleaning. 'Why do you do that, Wally?' he asked. Hammond paused and laughed awkwardly. 'If I tilt it at the right angle, I can see your wife undressing.' Billy, not in any way a jealous man, just shrugged and smiled.

The powerful friendship with Kitty Hall had started the season before Hammond sailed on that personally chequered trip to the West Indies. It ended, in effect, in the late summer of 1927 when he wrote a vague, peculiar letter to her from the Waldorf Hotel in London. Are we entitled to conclude from the confused sentence construction that there was considerable angst or guilt involved?

'I do not know quite how to phrase this letter which I promised to write you . . . After yesterday I have made up my mind, and it is not unwise I think, not to think seriously of anyone for at least three years, as I am not in a position to do so.

I remain, as ever . . . . . Wal'

Ploughing our way through the triple negatives, it seems reasonable to assume that, without revealing the nature of his illness, he was trying to say that he believed celibacy was advisable for the time being.

Throughout the early part of the tour he had written to Kitty – from Trinidad, Jamaica and Barbados – saying how well everything was going, and that he would like to hear from her even more often. One letter, sent to her only a few days before he left England for the Caribbean, is – in the context of what was to happen to him – of particular interest. 'I've got the wind up,' he wrote. 'I have been and got an electric shock through my ring and burnt my hand. It has turned to blood poisoning and the doctor won't let me leave Bristol until the 15th December and even then may not release me.' Toxaemia, we discover, was in those days never too far away for him. He sailed with the bad blood: then came the mosquitoes and finally the ravages of mercury and other experimental treatment. The sturdy constitution, vibrant with anti-bodies, which had up to now served him so well, was suddenly ill-prepared to cope with the added complication of VD.

The correspondence that Wally and Kitty exchanged over the several years of their love-affair was flavoured by an aura of sexuality (especially in 1925), playful lovers' rebukes, affected jealousies, shows of impatience and recurrent needs for reassurance. He wrote in pen and pencil, from lonely hotel rooms, wherever the team was playing. When the affair was at its most impassioned, he would sign off 'With heaps of love and tons of kisses', followed by 'Wally' or simply 'Wal'. He addressed her as Kitty, Kit or C.

There were many cryptic references. Why did he once stay in a London pub under the name of King? Had he on that occasion waited in vain for her to turn up for a night's tryst? And what had he done to upset her parents? In a letter from Cape Town he asked whether her father had now forgiven him. Rather self-righteously, in that same note, he wrote: 'It may or may not interest you to know that I have been the perfect model of a good boy out here'. He must have felt the need to make a point.

Wally's mother figured prominently in the letters to Kitty. He implied that she was always hovering. 'For Gawd's sake be careful. Mother has made her presence very uncomfortable and I can't get rid of her. She is here now . . . . Sorry, love, and feel sorry for me.' It really is a significant sentence. Was he saying that, in matters of the heart or perhaps the groin, 'Ma' Hammond, sometimes referred to as The Dragon in the 1920s and 1930s, could be an irksome obstacle? Whatever maternal shortcomings there were during his schooldays, the influence of Mrs Hammond on her son should never for a moment be discounted. His regard for her was deferential. The psychiatrists must make of that what they can. We can only assume that she didn't, for some reason or other, approve of Kitty Hall. Possibly she still considered she was best placed to be the match-maker. She would have been horrified if she had known that her son could write like this to the Folkestone hotelier's daughter: 'Will it be possible for you to come to London and stay the night? You, of course, know what I mean'.

Frustratingly we remain in the dark about Kitty's so-called 'past'. She had confided about it to Hammond, and if it was a matter of some sexual experience, he was not in the least concerned. 'Please don't worry about your past for everyone has one of those, and I'll wager that there are millions who would be proud to be able to boast of one like yours.' A touch of unlikely chivalry.

Catherine Hall died in 1973. She had seldom talked to friends of her passionate evenings with Hammond – when she pleaded to see him more often, as she deftly evaded the formidable presence of 'Ma' Hammond.

Mrs Hammond had, all the same, grown perceptibly closer to him. She helped him with his diary and answered some of his business letters. She lent him money when he was over-spending. She often went with him when he bought new, fashionable clothes at his favourite tailors in Clifton. Everything points to a determination to become – perhaps a little late in the day – an indispensable part of Wally's life.

She had wanted him to marry Grace James. She had directed a withering eye at a score of 'unsuitable' potential partners as they vied artlessly for his attention at cricket functions. She would have liked to organise his private life. And he wasn't having that. Most of his amours were carried out surreptitiously. He was quite content for his mother to cherish the belief that he was loyal to just one, almost up to the time of his marriage. After his wedding the duplicity continued; and then there was every reason for discretion. 'Where is it tonight?' the other Gloucestershire players used to ask.

I went in search of Herbert Hampden Alpass, a name well known in Bristol's legal circles and formerly an outstanding schoolboy cricketer at Clifton. He was a slow left-arm bowler, who went on to captain Stinchcombe CC and to make seven appearances for Gloucestershire in the mid-1920s. He came from Berkeley, knew Hammond well and actually went on holiday with him.

> Billy Neale came, too. We took a caravan, two motor cars and a chauffeur supplied by Wally, and stayed in the New Forest. There was a tent which we attached to the caravan and that was where the chauffeur slept. Wally was pretty flush by then and his behaviour was interesting on that holiday.
>
> He'd go off on his own in the evenings to Bournemouth where he had a lady. It struck me forcibly what a lady's man he was. It also struck me how moody he could be – some days he'd hardly speak, and then he could be thoroughly charming. We would all go into Bournemouth in the day for a swim. When we stopped for a drink, Billy

and I had a beer. Wally had progressed to gin and French.

I became very conscious of how much he liked fast cars. On one journey back to the New Forest, he hit a pony which was all across the road. Afraid that was the end of him. Wally at the wheel could frighten the life out of me. Once he was driving me back from a match at Stinchcombe and we approached the BAC buildings on the outskirts of Bristol at more than 100mph. Remember that was in 1930 or even before that.

As usual he chose not to talk cricket very much. At the bar he often seemed preoccupied. It was that roving eye of his. We moved on to Surrey for our second week's holiday. All the time he took great care over his appearance.

Hampden Alpass shared many evenings with Hammond – as well as links with Bristol Rovers (he was chairman of the club for eleven years). 'There had been a spot of trouble with the Board of Trade. I joined the board at seven o'clock one evening and by half past I found myself chairman'.

For both of them, however, cricket was the greatest love. Hammond was choosing his male friends and drinking associates primarily from outside the game. He gravitated towards solicitors, like Hampden Alpass, and other professional men. The Gloucestershire pros observed the trend and resented it, believing he was consciously distancing himself from them.

Over the early years of Hammond's cricket career, Hampden Alpass proved quite a loyal companion, slightly less so as an opponent. He saw that fledgling performance by Wally, against the Australians while he was qualifying, when he was bowled by Jack Gregory. 'He was shaking like a leaf as he went in to bat with Alf Dipper. Dip did his best to reassure him. But his off stump was broken in half by the fast bowler.' Then when Hammond came back in 1927, after his illness, one of the first pre-season matches was at Tewkesbury. 'And, oh dear, I bowled him with a ball that kept very low. He made just four, I think. Not the match practice he badly needed. I felt a little sheepish about that wicket'.

In between those two fruitless games, Hammond's lawyer pal had been given his cap by Gloucestershire. He admitted to

Wally that no one was ever luckier. 'I'd had a match or two with the county and jokingly asked our captain, Harry Rowlands, when I was going to be awarded my cap. He told me to go off and get one.' The amateurs didn't apparently have to earn them in the 1920s. But everyone agreed that Rowlands, a Quaker, was a delightful chap. For once, the under-valued professionals didn't complain too vocally.

It will soon be time to take a considered view of Hammond's marriages and the family he eventually had. Before that we come to the case of his most long-lasting and perhaps most badly treated mistress. Ursula Wicks lived at Thornbury; the family were well off, with a fine Georgian house to show for it. They actively supported the county club and took Ursula to matches. She instantly fell in love with that innately graceful cricketer, already being dubbed 'The Prince' by some of the local sports writers.

I have in front of me a letter from the late Miss Wicks. It reads:

> I knew Wally Hammond from 1937-45 and for much of that time we hoped to marry. His wife had agreed to divorce him when he was sent abroad in 1940 but it was not possible in the case of a member of H.M. Forces while he was serving overseas.
>
> He stayed here many times with me at The Cedars and the first thing he did, on arriving in the Middle East, was to send a radio message to me. He wrote constantly while he was abroad saying in almost every letter that he longed to be with me. He came home in 1943 and telephoned saying he'd seen his mother and would be with me that night. He was here for four days and we could not stop kissing and hugging.
>
> He stayed six times in 1944, all recorded in my mother's visitors' book, and I was with him a great deal at cricket matches. He would never talk about cricket and could be moody and silent but, through it all, there was no doubt of his love for me.
>
> His remoteness was largely due to his longing for children, which his first wife would not have and, after our attachment, his worry over divorce. He never settled in

South Africa and should have stayed in England, married me and taken his proper place in the cricket world.

It has been said in print that our friendship withered and died after 1940. It was more than friendship and lasted a lot longer.

Ursula Wicks loved Hammond deeply. She had been conscious of him and his exceptional cricketing talents from her school days. She wrote about him in her diaries; she kept scrapbooks, full of cuttings about his best innings and Test exploits. She said he had already parted from Dorothy when they started seeing a great deal of each other. Several Gloucestershire players told me that she would always sit in the same place at the county ground, her dogs at her feet. Hammond, at the crease, would look in her direction and give a slight wave of the bat. That was enough for her.

The marriage had irretrievably broken down and for a time, up to the outbreak of the war, he was marginally less guarded in his public behaviour. Ursula would wait for him after the match and they would leave the ground together. Her father liked him to call in at The Cedars for a drink or two. She also accompanied him to some away grounds. In moments of intimacy they discussed the practicalities of his divorce. Dorothy was going to be stubborn but they would find, with patience, a way round that. He bought her jewellery and a ring, which he said she should keep for when they were married.

'He found time to visit us at The Cedars during the war. We would potter together. He was always happy to be here. My parents liked him and we were so pleased when he came. Sometimes he arrived by train and I'd rush to Temple Meads station to meet him. And he also came to see me by plane. Whenever there was a plane coming from one of his stations to Filton in Bristol, he'd be on it. I would get a telephone message to meet him.

'We had an Alsatian and a bull terrier and he loved the dogs. If he had enough petrol, we might go off for a ride. But usually he would then suggest we went home and walk the dogs.'

Their conversation was almost that of man and wife. They talked about where they were going to live, 'and one day he even said he had got some curtain material'. Yet was he being completely honest with her? As he cuddled Ursula in the summer of 1939 and allowed her to day-dream about a wedding to the most famous cricketer in England, he was writing affectionate letters to the strikingly attractive Sybil Ness-Harvey in South Africa.

We have to conclude that he was an incorrigibly fickle lover. Behind the façade of affection, he trifled with the emotions of others. He could move on to the next lady friend without too much remorse. It does appear, sadly, that Ursula Wicks' expectations were excessive. She was altogether too trusting. There was understandable bitterness in her voice when, years later, she said she was keen to put the record straight. She went on regional television and referred to Dot Hammond's unavailing journey to South Africa in 1939, a determined last-ditch attempt to save the teetering marriage.

'She went to try and patch it up. They could never make a go of it – and he asked her a lot of times if she would divorce him. She wouldn't, but eventually she said she would and would cite me. He wasn't having that. I thought his attitude was silly because we wanted to get married and might as well take that opportunity. Then in 1940 he went abroad and you couldn't divorce a Serviceman who was overseas during wartime.'

Ursula attributed the final parting to Sybil, who she felt had either written or cabled Wally, confirming romantic intentions. 'I think it was as much a shock to him as it was to his mother and me.' It is possible that Ursula, naïvely unswerving in her allegiance to him, hadn't known of the Natal beauty queen's existence; certainly she had no idea at all that Wally had sustained an intimate correspondence with her all through the war years.

Contrasting Wives

Wally Hammond's private life was littered with mistakes: in business, by listening to the wrong advice, in choosing at times unsuitable friends while rejecting some of the genuine ones, in being seduced by fleeting avarice. One of his biggest mistakes of all was in marrying Dorothy Lister, the daughter of a wealthy and influential textile merchant from Yorkshire in the late April of 1929. They had known each other, in a perfunctory and impersonal way, for less than two years, having met casually when he was playing in a festival match in the north. At a function in the evening he had been first introduced to her father, Joe, a bluff, loquacious man out of a Priestley novel. Joe Lister was forthcoming with his cricketing stories and in buying more than his round of shorts. Wally noted and was impressed by the fact that the father was surrounded by toadies. He was clearly a man of substance.

'And I want you to meet my lass, Wally.' The romance, if that is what it could be loosely called, took some sort of shape that evening. Only a blind man would have failed to sense it was destined for failure. Dorothy had a rich father but not much physical allure. She was biggish and inclined to gawkiness. She badly wanted a husband, yet was without the feminine sparkle to entrap one. Her voice was loud, like her father's, and her vowels flat. Conversely, she possessed some of the supposed virtues of her native county; she was generous and good-natured, a home-lover and capable cook, even though Joe had enough money to employ maids in the kitchen. In short, she really had nothing much in common with Wally. Cricket bored her on her obligatory annual visit with her father to the Scarborough Festival. He privately hoped that, with all those athletic young men around, she might find a husband there.

Hammond and Joe Lister got on well. There was always a room and a bed waiting for the cricketer if he was playing in Yorkshire. The textile merchant's home had the tang of freshly rubbed polish. The furniture was antique, the drinks cabinet was bulging. 'All by hard work, Wally. Ee, lad, but it may not last. I don't like what I'm hearing'. That was a vague reference to the Depression. It was already biting deep and mercilessly in some parts of the North Country. Joe was all right so far.

Wally and Dorothy didn't spend much time together before the wedding. They exchanged pleasant though prosaic letters and met only at cricket matches or when Hammond was invited to stay the weekend with them. Joe probably orchestrated the marriage out of the best of intentions. He was close to his likeable, gauche daughter and didn't want her left on the shelf. Hammond was a considerable catch. 'You know I'll look after you, lad. Nothing to worry about there.'

The wedding just happened. The Listers organised all the preparations. Wally was out in Australia and Joe wrote: 'Everything's in hand. Dorothy is getting excited. See you when you get back'. England's batting hero had barely stepped ashore before he was on his way to Bingley. It looked as though the whole of Yorkshire was there to greet him. The parish church had never staged a more fashionable wedding. Joe Lister's stature ensured that. He had asked the Bishop of Bradford to conduct the service. Sport, the wool trade and the cordially curious made up the pew-packed congregation.

In the street outside the church hundreds of people, stirred by the advance publicity and glamour of the occasion, inched closer hoping to glimpse the couple after the service. Herbert Sutcliffe was in the church as an usher, invited by Lister. But surprisingly, for the wedding of one of the country's most famous and princely cricketers, not many county players, from Gloucestershire or elsewhere, could be recognised in the congregation.

Hammond looked as handsome as any film star in his morning suit. Dorothy had a beautiful wedding dress and carried a huge bouquet of flowers. The bishop resonantly said his piece and eagerly revealed his knowledge of the first-class game.

Dozens of helmeted police struggled to make a path for the couple as they walked, stiffly, self-consciously, arm in arm, to the waiting wedding car. The reception was in Bradford, where the Masonic Hall had created a cricketing atmosphere, complete with bats, wickets and improvised scoreboard. The speeches were jovial; Prime Minister Stanley Baldwin's was among the many telegrams dutifully read out by the best man, Harry Pannell. Hammond had, rather oddly, chosen the older Mr Pannell, a family friend from Hampshire – indeed his first sponsor, who had discreetly given him some kit when Wally made his first tour to the West Indies – for those nuptial duties. Did that reflect long-standing loyalty to a substitute father figure, or the absence of sufficiently close friends among the players?

Hammond and his bride had a brief honeymoon and before long moved into their first home, a newly built bungalow in the village of Failand, over the Clifton suspension bridge from Bristol. Joe Lister had paid for it. In truth, Wally and Dot had looked an unlikely couple in church. By the time they were facing each other in the armchairs at Failand, any casual observer of the human scene might have forecast that the marriage was doomed. The husband, not yet 26, would bury his head in the sports pages; Dot cooked the meals with novice enthusiasm but found little about which to talk to her husband. The silences were already long – and they'd scarcely got the wedding presents out of their wrapping.

Male chauvinism was accepted then, of course. Wally would be playing cricket all through the summer, away from home for days on end. In the winter, when not on tour, he would often climb into the car and go off to Long Ashton for a round of golf. His free evenings were spent at the Failand Arms or the home of some of his acquaintances from the professions. Dot was seldom taken.

The other players at Bristol saw her from time to time. Some of them spoke of her warmly to me, their voices tinged with unease. Hammond's England team-mate and loyal defender Les Ames could still be objective enough to say: 'Dorothy was a Yorkshire lass in every way, very down to earth – not the type of girl you would have thought Wally would fall for and marry. But

I always felt she was a jolly nice girl. I was very fond of her and was terribly sad when their marriage broke up . . . . Yet, not too surprised.'

She didn't much enjoy going to watch Gloucestershire play. Maybe she should have worked harder to be a doting wife, taking her seat among the members whenever her husband walked out to bat. She was sparing in her compliments; Yorkshire folk never sprinkled them about like confetti in any case. 'Did you do all reet today?' was from her no more than a token inquiry. But she suffered not because she was inclined to be dour but because she wasn't pretty enough. Wally liked his girls to be sensual and coquettish. Dot was altogether too dreary.

She made an effort to please him. 'Invite some of your friends home and I'll prepare a nice meal for all of you'. Ames went; so did Bev Lyon and his blonde girlfriend. The house was always spotless, the food was wholesome, simple and plentiful. One old cricketer's wife remembered that Wally had 'a kind of valet' who did all sorts of domestic chores as well as laying out Hammond's clothes. Wally had seen how Joe Lister lived, with paid help around the house. In addition to his part-time valet, Hammond could call on a chauffeur for long journeys or to see him home after a heavy night. At the ground, Bernie Bloodworth, constantly affable although never too sure of first-team recognition, acted as his baggage-man. Bernie had been a brave rugby player for Cheltenham and was in no sense obsequious; yet he accepted it as a privilege to look after Wally's bats and lay out his flannels before a match.

Hammond liked things done for him. Liz Wilson, Andy's wife, a fair-minded woman, once told me how she helped Dot transfer the furniture and sort things out when the Hammonds moved from Failand to their next house. 'I'm afraid that between us we did most of the work. I can't remember Wally helping at all.'

I talked to several of the players and their wives who were asked back for an evening meal. 'Dot could be relied on to provide a good table. The places were always laid impeccably. A nice glass of sherry to begin with. But on a number of occasions, Wally just didn't turn up. We waited for a time and then started without him. Sometimes he'd arrive very late with an apologetic shrug.' Phyl Neale, Billy's wife, would find Dot in the kitchen, crying. 'She'd bravely wipe the tears away and say she'd be all right in a minute. I don't know how often that happened. She really was treated badly by him.'

There was virtual unanimity among her contemporaries in support of Dot. Yet is it fair to heap all the blame on Hammond? What about bluff Joe, the match-maker? And did the ill-chosen wife do herself a disservice by becoming more introvert, by not always choosing to socialise at some of those cricket gatherings where she had been invited? It is quite possible she had lost a great deal of self-confidence by then, was even a figure of fun to those insensitive souls who guessed that her famous husband was playing around behind her back.

What is beyond dispute was her gradual, sad acceptance that she had been in effect rejected. At their various homes she felt wretchedly isolated. She spent long days on her own. Some of the rumours were getting back to her. There was nothing much to do but reflect on what might have been – and to drink. By now her father had become a victim of the crash. He'd lost nearly everything. No more private income and generous Christmas boxes. The creature comforts made possible by Yorkshire largesse were over for ever. Joe himself died, and that saved his son-in-law the burden of too much marital guilt. From that point, life would be a constant financial strain for the Hammonds.

Dot skimmed the cricket reports and saw her husband's name in every headline. Again there was that puzzling dichotomy between the national idol, worshipped by the game's purists, by the poets and the cartoonists; and the brooding, uncommunicative partner who nominally shared her bed. There were no children to bring an element of joy, animation and fulfilment to the marriage. Had they wanted any? We shall never know for sure. Certainly there was too little love. Dot confided to other wives that she would have liked children. Wally, it was sometimes said, loved children. All one can conclude with certainty is that the Hammonds' home was – in terms of life itself – barren.

Deeply depressed, Dot surveyed their negligible bank balance and worried about the future. Her drinking increased. 'She would go along to Phyl Neale's to sober-up. They used to say she was tight half the time.' Someone who knew her well and liked her was Peggy Barnett, the second of Charlie's three wives. (He was her third husband: there was, it appears, no lack of marital activity, however proper, in the Berkeley Vale.) 'Dot's pleasant personality made up for any lack of looks,' in Peggy's view. 'But Wally was such a moody fellow. Just like Charlie, he'd tuck his head behind a paper and not acknowledge that anyone had come to see him. Yet I have to say there was something very likeable about him. In a way I felt sorry for him – Dot was very unhappy and on occasions I think she was deliberately difficult.

'When they were living at Knole Park, Almondsbury, after leaving Failand, Wally once phoned me and asked me to drop everything and go round to help him out. He was having visitors and he needed to keep Dot out of sight. She'd been drinking, of course. I went there and tactfully kept her upstairs with a bottle of gin. We had a few drinks together.'

Before Wally married, Peggy would often go dancing with him and a few friends to Gloucester or the Town Hall, Cheltenham. Some wondered if there had been a romance between them, another possible reason for the feud with Charlie Barnett. 'I can assure you we were friends, nothing more. But what a dancer! So wonderfully light on his feet.'

She paused and offered this poignant postscript: 'What appealed to him about this Berkeley and Sharpness area was that he could take those long, solitary walks. That told a lot about him. I don't think he particularly enjoyed his life.'

Poor Dorothy Hammond, once the contented, pampered daughter of an esteemed mill owner, rich until the wool prices went, was by now also beyond enjoying her life. With great personal courage and a spunky resolve few believed her capable of, she sailed to South Africa in 1939, when Wally was on tour in what turned out to be a futile rescue operation for the marriage. After that she more or less gave up. She counted her pennies, bought her gin and grew more dispirited. The last of the family homes was sold. She went to stay with various friends, spent several years on the Isle of Wight and then returned to the north of England, to live in Huddersfield. She applied to work in a dress shop and took other part-time jobs. One or two distressing stories filtered back to her erstwhile friends in Gloucestershire and Bristol.

Reg Sinfield was especially upset when he was told by Tom Goddard that Dot had been forced to do several menial jobs 'like scrubbing the floors in a hospital'. Reg, still a church sidesman when well into his eighties, treasured home life and the sanctity of marriage. 'I used to think Dot had plenty of charm and I also knew they'd lost all their money as a result of the crash. Tom told me she finished up absolutely penniless. A terrible end she came to. She deserved better than that. They both did'.

Let's take a charitable view – which would have pleased Reg, Big Tom Goddard and all the others whose affection for Dot and Wally survived the bad times and the rumour. I had also heard that Dot went through a spell doing some pretty undignified duties for the NAAFI. It is worth considering, at least hoping, that her work in the hospital and for the Services, was a voluntary wartime gesture on her part. For a time she was in the ambulance service, too; whatever the recurrent trials and frustrations of her life, she had a good and patriotic heart.

The unleashing of correspondence – more than 30 letters from Wally to Dot – at the Christie's sale in 1993, only confirms the insecurity of the marriage. The batch went for £2,400 to an unknown telephone bidder. Many who worried about such private thoughts coming into the public domain hoped that the purchaser was ensuring the letters would be returned to a state of permanent privacy. We must wait and see. From the restricted peeps potential buyers were allowed, Lot 33 was enticingly marketable. The genuine collectors and the ghouls converged; they had seen enough to know that the letters were laden with nuances, financial niggles and white lies. These together told infinitely more about Hammond than about his forlorn wife. They told, even by the words left out, the story of a marriage irretrievably in decline.

The years covered by the letters were from 1930 to the mid-1940s. In part his messages were sprinkled with terms of endearment and, in one case at least, garlanded with fourteen kisses. There were rare, almost homely asides in wishing relatives and mutual friends in the north well. It appears that he assumed the responsibility for the thank-you letters after the wedding. One, handwritten on Lister Ltd notepaper ('Wool, Tops, Noils, Laps, Waste, etc') from the firm's address in Crossland Street, Bradford, thanked a Miss Dighton for her 'very beautiful present'. A recurrent criticism of Hammond used to be that he lacked courtesy. His behaviour could be curt and dismissive, but I am not at all sure that the criticism is entirely fair. He sat down and wrote dozens of conscientiously composed notes, like the one to Miss Dighton, that revealed a more considerate man.

In their printed catalogue that incorporated the sale of the Hammond letters, Christie's assure surely incredulous readers that the relationship was very close, up to and beyond the point of their divorce. 'With their prolonged absences from one another, it is surprisingly Hammond who worries that the glamorous and more extrovert Dorothy might leave him for another man rather than vice versa – he is aware that both are capable of lapses but seems intensely affectionate if in some ways demanding of the creature comforts of home'.

Such conclusions must be based largely on the contents of some of those letters. But my instincts tell me they are a mockery of the truth. Dot may have been more outward-going than her husband; she was in no imaginable way glamorous. She was well aware that she lacked looks and presence. It even turned into something of a phobia as she shut herself away with her surfeit of gin. I also think it highly improbable that she ever had other male friends for whom her feelings were anything but platonic.

Wally teased her in his letters and hoped she was behaving herself. That was his Freudian way, I suspect, of excusing his own behaviour. He knew he could trust Dot, although maybe later, when thoughts of divorce preoccupied him, he wished she had been more free with her favours, to give him grounds for a permanent parting.

Less than a year after they were married, he wrote saying how much he was missing her. What followed was of far more interest. He said he wanted her to be more demonstrative with her affections, though preferably in a quiet corner. 'Will you, or don't you love me enough . . . . you must make a fuss of me everywhere and tick me off if I get annoyed.'

These were hidden repressions, demanding interpretation. Here were two young people, not long married and theoretically at their most tactile. Yet Hammond's words, carrying some kind of reprimand, suggested that she was far too frigid. It was simply not a letter than held out hopes of a lasting marriage.

By the early months of 1939, while he was playing and captaining in South Africa, money anxieties were surfacing. Writing from the Grand Hotel, Bela, Southern Rhodesia, he began in welcoming fashion, 'Darling .... It was grand to hear your voice again. I had begun to worry at not receiving a telegram to say that you had arrived safely. However, all is well now. How did you fare, did you stand the strain or did you have to retire *as is your usual custom?*' (a rather ungracious dig at her suspect sea-legs, we assume). He went on: 'I have been thinking over this proposed trip to Johannesburg and really, for the little I shall see you, it seems hardly worth while, as you say, spending all that money . . . .'

This was one of the first direct references to the Hammond's hazardous financial circumstances.

As a marriage-saving exercise, cloaked as it was under a veil of domestic harmony, Dot's visit to South Africa in early 1939 was abortive. Wally publicly made a fuss of her; in the privacy of their hotel room, they talked obsessively of money matters. Pictures of Hammond with Sybil, the beauty queen at an official reception in Durban, had found their way back to the English newspapers. Dot had seen them.

'But Dot, you know what it's like at these receptions. I'm the captain now and have to mix. She's just another woman with a double-barrelled name out here.' His wife was no more than half-convinced.

Various letters from Torquay, where he was stationed with the RAF in 1940, were less subtle. He made it clear he was irked by Dot's enclosures of unpaid bills. A few months later, he wrote: 'My dear, I am sorry to hear that you are disappointed with my efforts but it just cannot be helped. As to your doing a whole-time job, my dear, you must please yourself. There isn't much hope of your coming down here and I have a feeling that you would be much happier with something definite to do. Anyway, dear, you must do as you wish . . . . And you must also remember that if Marsham (Tyres) cracks, I shall be unable to allow you the same each month. Anyway, let us hope that doesn't happen for a while until I can get all the bills cleared up. Well dear, keep cheerful all of you. As always, Wal.'

All the bills. This was a household budget, complicated by separation and indeterminate emotions, getting hopelessly out of hand. The future of Marsham Tyres, his partial employers back in Bristol, was apparently not too rosy. According to that letter from Torquay, Dot was not pleased with his efforts. It does look as though she pleaded with him in vain to find the best method of settling the mounting number of invoices.

He was never a practical man in money matters. Torquay was a cushy number for a flight-lieutenant, recently promoted. But Service pay wasn't high and there were mess bills to think of. Social life was pretty good in wartime Torquay, all the same. There was, one detected, a hint of panic in his insistent riposte to his wife: 'There isn't much hope of your coming down here.' In any case, he was spending his free weekends hitching a lift to Filton to see Ursula Wicks.

Yet the marital deception persisted. In the April of 1941 – while carrying on an intimate correspondence with Miss Wicks, probably Sybil Ness-Harvey and no doubt one or two others – his playful sentiments of shared domesticity were quite untypical, thoughts perhaps influenced by a wariness about how things really were at home.

> I haven't had a letter of any description since the one from you dated January 4th. However keep living in hopes. Are you being a good girl – I hope so. How I should love to just walk in on you and give you the surprise of your life . . . . You would laugh if you could see all my clothes. All my socks without exception have holes, buttons off various places and a whole heap of odds and ends where the needle should be introduced, it's all so very funny . . . .
>
> When I get home, I promise to be just as lazy and rely upon you for everything. What a treat it would be. I just

> wet my hands when I think of tea in the morning and some food that has been properly cooked and which doesn't taste of paraffin or garlick [sic].

What are we to make of that? Is it possible that he was a more cunning psychologist than we gave him credit for? I prefer to think that, like so many Servicemen abroad, he was from time to time affected by waves of sentimentality. There could have been gratitude, mingled with remorse, in his nostalgic reference to the way Dot once did everything for him.

Within weeks he was writing again, apologising for a moody patch and sending what he called 'one of my silly letters'. He told her he missed her more than on any other trips. And in a strangely uninhibited sentence, he wrote: 'You can drape yourself over and around me, as much as you like, so get into training, my dear'. From a man who had earlier chided his wife for an absence of physical affection, this light-hearted challenge from the Middle East is hard to understand. Could he have been in his cups at the time? Was it part of the romantic pretences or wartime? Was it another strand of guilt?

Alas, so many of those 32 letters seem, at this distance, uncomfortably phoney. Why, we have to ask, did he continue to string Dot along? While he was stationed in Cairo, he actually fiddled a flight or two to the Cape. He did not go primarily to sample the wine. He had a brief posting in Kenya and then moved to South Africa. He began to stay at Sybil's home: and he sustained a façade of fidelity in his letters of oscillating moods, to his Yorkshire wife. Hammond had been a philanderer on the grand scale. That does not make him unique. There was surely additional excuse for sexual dalliances in wartime. He was a congenital fibber; his deceptions were equally on the grand scale. In fact, the marriage lasted after a fashion until November 1946. 'A decree was granted to Mrs Dorothy Hammond while her husband was leading England in Australia. Misconduct was alleged with a woman named Harvey with whom he had been said to be living as man and wife.'

A sad, succinct Press Association report stated that Mrs Hammond, of Bradford Road, Huddersfield, was the eldest daughter of the late Mr J B Lister, a Bradford wool textile manufacturer. She and Mr Hammond had lived happily until December 1940, when he joined the RAF and went to serve abroad. The report went on to say that in 1945 the husband wanted a divorce and there was no chance of a reconciliation. Later Mrs Hammond discovered there was a child on the way and she immediately instructed her solicitors to take proceedings. Mr Justice Pilcher was to grant a decree nisi with costs.

Hammond had met Sybil Ness-Harvey in December 1938 while captaining the England team in South Africa. She was considered the most beautiful girl in Durban and had picked up beauty awards in Natal. She had a privileged lifestyle and was a favoured escort at official receptions. 'We are going to sit you next to Walter Hammond, the captain of England', she was told. Sybil took even greater care than usual with her appearance. She wore a striking white evening dress: Wally noticed with approval how bronzed her bare shoulder blades were . . . .

The beauty queen had a sophisticated air, so different from the homely no-nonsense approach of Dot. She was flattered to have been placed next to a famous international sportsman, basking in the intimate attention he was giving her. By the end of the meal, they had exchanged addresses in South Africa – and he promised to see her again when the MCC team returned to Durban in the New Year.

Hammond was then 35, older than Sybil. Others at that initial reception, where Lord Nuffield was the guest of honour, were said to have nudged each other and implied that a romance might be on the way. Letters between them, discreetly written because Hammond was a public figure and married man after all, lent weight to the friendship. Then, of course, the war came. His posting to the Middle East led to ingenious logistical operations and wangled flights south. Before too long he was stationed in South Africa; leaves were plentiful, and he spent most of them with Sybil. Wally didn't have a bad war at all.

He told Sybil that his marriage was at an end. He would take her to England and she would be able to accompany him to all the county matches after the war. He was thinking of the late 1930s, when the country had come out of the Depression; there had been the best hotels and marvellous cuisine for the Test teams, the dances and the receptions. He would now have a beautiful young woman on his arm. The prospect excited her. She imagined that life in England would be even more privileged and glittering than it was in sunny South Africa.

Dutifully, eagerly she followed him back to England. It was not at all as she had thought it would be. There were shortages and a pervading austerity. She hated the climate and didn't make friends easily. Just like Valerie Compton, Denis's second wife, Sybil was thoroughly miserable here. Both of these unsettled wives had met their future husbands when they were on tour in South Africa.

Hammond had not expected England to be so drab after the war. The radio, back in Durban, had been full of effervescent dance music, so very different from the pleading voices of Attlee, Cripps and Shinwell. It was not at all what he had, in all good faith, promised Sybil. When he went out to Australia on the 1946-47 tour, he harboured nagging misgivings. He was leaving his wife-to-be behind in what she saw as an unfriendly country, and facing a chilly winter. He arranged for her to stay with his mother for company but it was never going to work, and they separated before long. 'Ma' Hammond was uneasy about the stories of Dot's financial plight and declining dignity that got back to her. She had also told Wally that she didn't approve of him living in sin. Hammond was in turmoil for so much of that last tour of his. The concern he felt for Sybil revealed a depth of feeling he had not demonstrated before in his life. He couldn't wait to return.

Wally and Sybil were married in April 1947 at Kingston Register Office. The bride was the daughter of Mrs E C Ness Harvey and the late Mr Ness Harvey, of Durban. By then, Sybil's name had already been changed to Hammond by deed poll. There were just four guests at the reception. Major Rupert Howard, who had been the tour manager in Australia, and Mrs Howard; Mr H E Pope, a fellow business director and his wife. Sybil wore a full-length fur coat over a turquoise blue dress, brown hat and veil. She was described in the local paper as 'tall, slim and fair-haired'. It was not the kind of wedding that her parents had once fervently wished for her.

Roger, the first of their three children, was born in 1948.

Their first proper home together was Thrupp House, near Stroud, in a commodious upstairs flat with enviable views of the Cotswold folds. For a time Hammond was positively domesticated; he fussed over his wife, he helped with the preparations for the birth. At last he was going to be a father.

PART VI

GRADUAL DECLINE

Not a Bad War

It was, in the language of the day, a relatively cushy war for Hammond. In October 1939 he went into the Royal Air Force and was rapidly commissioned. There was not too much real active service for him, apart from the frustrations and inconveniences suffered by so many. His sporting status and celebrity ensured a fair amount of privilege. He played a good deal of relaxed cricket and was rightly fêted in many an officers' mess. In the fatalistic spirit of war-time he sometimes drank excessively, though seldom with embarrassing results. One exception was when he took part in a match in Kenya.

Dickie Burrough, the Somerset amateur who was stationed out there, had organised the fixture and Hammond was the obvious attraction. He was flown down from Cairo to play. Burrough travelled to the airport to meet him and was horrified to note the famous guest player's state as he emerged from the plane. 'Oh, my God!' said Burrough. There was a big crowd excitedly waiting for Wally's entry. 'He was thoroughly pickled and I just couldn't see how he could possibly get through a match. Somehow or other, he sobered up miraculously – and actually scored a hundred. It was an extraordinary achievement.'

Much of Hammond's career in the RAF was involved with welfare work. Initially, when stationed in Sussex and Devon, he was given some duties as an instructor. These he carried out with a firm, slightly intimidating manner, causing 'sprog' airmen to mutter under their breaths and wilt under his fusillade of orders. He did nothing to court popularity and may well have lost the affection of a few unsuspecting hero-worshippers for ever.

That aggressive façade wasn't sustained. He had been told to give the new intakes a tough time; the authority that went with the pilot officer's uniform also appealed to him. Some of the trainees were 15 or more years younger and they needed to be knocked into shape. But, as he had revealed in his summers as a cricket captain, he was not a natural leader. The orders he issued lacked finesse in the art of psychology. 'That commission went to his head a bit,' a fellow officer told me.

Torquay was an early and envied posting. The lights may have been dimmed in some of the bigger hotels. There was, however, still a well-heeled social milieu to suggest that life on the 'English Riviera' wasn't yet too severely disrupted. It was also easy to make weekend visits back to Bristol or, more likely, to The Cedars, the family home of Ursula Wicks.

He played cricket for the RAF and for a few select teams in Devon. In one match, Leonard Crawley was among the players. Did they talk golf, the Walker Cup star and someone whose handicap was decreasing at a splendid rate when the war came? We can only wonder, too, whether they exchanged wry memories of the 1925-26 tour of the West Indies, when both were in the party.

There was Services cricket alongside Ames. Hammond could pull the strings and organise weekend passes for his cricketing pals. Edrich, soon to fly bombers, turned up for one of the matches in Torquay. They didn't bother too much with niceties like nets; Hammond simply batted from memory. He seldom tried too hard – and he seldom failed. The spectators were never let down.

At the end of 1940 he was posted to the RAF Middle East headquarters in Cairo. His work was to be administrative, covering both sporting facilities and, less so, entertainment for all the men serving in that expansive region. He was away from England for three years. There was much hitching of airborne lifts down to the Cape, for both official duties and hurriedly arranged cricket engagements. During this period he was promoted first to flight lieutenant and then to squadron-leader. There are photographs of him, reflecting his various levels of promotion; he wore his uniform with some pride and cut an impressive figure. The touch of arrogance that accompanied his days as a greenhorn instructor of pilot-officer rank lessened noticeably. He displayed useful organisational ability in overseeing the budgets for sports equipment and general recreational facilities for the airmen within the far-flung Middle East zone. When he was needed for a match, he delegated in the office with increasing skill.

Everyone agreed that, for officers, Cairo was an enviable posting. There was an elitist life among the commissioned Servicemen. The Gezira Club was the exclusive hub of sporting endeavour. Big crowds watched the regular Sunday fixtures there; famous cricketers other than Hammond also took part and savoured the exceptional hospitality. He scored several centuries in these games. In one, an umpire was Noel Thomas, later a well-known Gloucestershire member and habitué of the Cheltenham Festival. 'It struck me that Wally spent altogether too much time at the billiards table during the match'. Ah well, he was probably well on the way to a century-break there, too.

I once heard a careworn ex-private of the North African campaign bemoan the fact that while they had struggled to lift their spirits and find a new initiative to counter Rommel, 'just down the road in Cairo, all they seemed to do was play cricket.' It was a valid argument, yet the exploits of Hammond and other great players at the Gezira Club did offer their own kind of aid to morale for a vast concentration of combined services. Many weary troops, not just British, spent brief leaves in Cairo watching the cricket and pretending they were part of a civilised world once again.

Increasingly, he did lengthy spells of duty in South Africa. We can only speculate on how much this was the result of his own organisational prowess. It suited him admirably: the weather, the relaxed cricket matches, the leaves spend with Sybil in Durban. Their liaison, sustained since 1938 by correspondence and occasional cables, had been re-ignited. Back in Thornbury, Ursula Wicks was coming to terms with unrequited love; her letters weren't being answered, or only irregularly. As for Dorothy, now living on the Isle of Wight, the relationship with Wally had drifted into emotional oblivion.

He discussed with Sybil plans for a marriage and a new life in England after the war. She had read about the frightening air raids, on Bristol as well as on London. But he reassured her it would soon be over; she would go with him, from hotel to hotel, around the country as he played five or six more summers of county cricket. And there would be the opportunity to travel with him on some of the tours. And they would start a family. All of this was immensely appealing to a pretty, pampered, unworldly beauty queen , who knew nothing about cold winters, abject shortages of food and fuel, streets of wan and weary men in demob suits, and an overall aura of austerity. She would soon, of course – and she would hate it.

Hammond was posted back to England at the start of 1944. His office base was only a few boundary lengths from Lord's. The Air Ministry probably weren't too sure how to use him; in fact, like many, he found himself in effect marking time until the end of the war. His most valuable work was at the wicket in a succession of special games. Squadron Leader Hammond was in demand, though his back was beginning to trouble him more. He preferred playing to lecturing young aircrew members on aspects of RAF discipline and administration. In the evenings there were visits with other officers to some of the more sophisticated nightclubs that stayed open in London's West End. The eye roved less; Sybil by this time was an obsession, and he was showing virtues of loyalty that had been elusive in the past.

At the end of 1944, after a number of sorties to the RAF medical quarters and the resultant specialist reports on the fibrositis that seemed to strike him without warning and 'had him bent double at times', he was discharged. There was now work to think about: and, provided the back allowed, cricket.

Since he had returned from the Middle East, he had been astonished like so many, by the resurgence of interest in the game at the highest level then possible. The Royal Australian Air Force could assemble a strong and attractive side. In 1944 crowds of 26,000 and 28,000 were attracted to Lord's. There were the Victory Tests, with a lovely, nostalgic hundred by Hammond on a difficult wicket at Bramall Lane. Then, in a perfect construction of sheer theatre, symbolising the release from all the repression of the war, came the wonderful match against the Dominions. It contained every ingredient of glory: a hundred in each innings by Hammond: a stunning 185, fashioned for the occasion, by Keith Miller: a sparkling ton by New Zealander Martin Donnelly. Some still say it was the greatest match ever played at Lord's. That is fantasy: the bowling of both sides was weak. But no one who was there will forget it.

Gloucestershire were already in touch. 'Great form against the Dominions, Wally – can't wait to have you back for '46.'

'Feeling pretty good,' he fibbed, as he rubbed the prescribed liniment into his sore back. 'See you for pre-season. We want to win the championship.'

In fact, they dropped from third (in 1939) to fifth in 1946. Some appalling weather worked against them. Billy Neale's benefit match with Essex was ruined by rain. But Hammond simply carried on as before. The county *Year Book* tells us: 'Having been England's leading batsman for seven years preceding the war, W R Hammond headed the averages for the eighth time. After an interval of six years, it was a wonderful achievement and his average of over 100 for the county is a clear indication of the magnificent form he displayed.'

There were vague reports that he hadn't been 'in the best of health' towards the end of the summer. But nothing to suggest that he might soon be turning his back on the game. Hardly anyone, in truth, apart from one or two trusted Bristol confidants, had the remotest idea of how much pain he was going through every time he batted. His condition worsened considerably during that damp summer. He had started well enough, so much so that some of the older pros, back from the war with more cynical eyes and none too intent on personal fitness themselves, were staggered by what he apparently expected from them. He looked older, with small rolls of fat – which he did his best to hide – around the midriff. But, maybe influenced by some of the parade ground drills he had witnessed in the Services, he told his players he was placing a greater emphasis on fitness – and he'd be leading by example.

I recently came across something Andy Wilson wrote about that return to the county ground after the war:

> I played under him and could write a book about him. Opinions are sharply divided. But one view is probably

> unanimous – at the end of the war he was the most dominant personality in the game. What was his record on his return? He averaged 104 in 19 innings for Gloucestershire, scored five centuries and two double centuries.
>
> No county team in England trained harder than Gloucestershire in 1946. I can personally vouch for that. And I should add that no one trained harder than Walter Hammond himself. In fact, long spells of lapping round the track, seven-a-side soccer, P.T. and intensive net practice gave the county a North Country look when they took the field in May.
>
> The result was that we had the most efficient side for nearly 15 years. Players moved to positions quickly; fielding was excellent. Bowlers bowled to a set field and a well-planned attack. Hammond's wide experience was worth an extra player to the county. He studied every incoming batsman and changed the bowling according to the weakness of the individual. And his own personal example in the field was superb.

Stan Squires, the former Surrey player, was but one to notice the difference in the Gloucestershire attitude. 'It's like playing against Yorkshire', he said over a shared drink after a day's play at the Oval. We shall never know what was going on in Hammond's mind. Was he putting himself through the ultimate test of fitness to discover just how much his back could stand? More likely, I feel, was that he suspected his playing career was virtually over and he desperately wanted to conclude it with a championship pennant.

There were times during that 1946 season when he batted with as much panache as in the pre-war harvest time. He was last out for 134 at Gloucester when Dick Pollard was at his best. Over four and a half hours at Nevil Road, he scored an undefeated 211 against Notts. Not a chance given, not a bead of perspiration. Joe Hardstaff got a hundred in the same match, on his birthday, 'but we were always in a different class'. He went to Taunton and started hitting sixes off Arthur Wellard in an innings of 104; when Somerset came back to Bristol for the

August Bank Holiday fixture, he settled for 214. Who had been impudent enough to imply that the hiatus of the war had finished him? Who had suggested he was putting on too much weight?

The fact was that he was still the finest batsman in the country, even with Hutton and Compton at his shoulders. In the West, his devoted army of supporters watched in renewed awe as he figured in stands with Barnett, Crapp, Allen and Neale. They heard about a few uncharacteristic chances he had given to Charlie Knott down at Southampton but perhaps that was nothing more than a ruse, once he had scored 50, to leave his spinners, Goddard and Cook, time to bowl out Hampshire by the second evening.

Yet the more perspicacious might have detected rare indications of a technical weariness. Twice in that season, once against the Indians at Cheltenham, he was out 'hit wicket'; that would never have happened before. The instincts and the judgment had never let him down like that before. When the back was most troublesome and, as against Hampshire, he had dropped himself down the order, he could be snappy and irritable. One of the team asked him why he put George Emmett at No 6. 'Because he is a No 6,' was his curt reply. He chastised Emmett more than most, publicly rebuking him for a bad shot. Yet team-mates argued that he was less than fair to this small, attractive batsman, who possessed magical wrists and the sweetest of stroke-making facilities when the conditions were right and Wally wasn't breathing down his neck. The two should have had something in common – a military background, a slightly dour and authoritarian manner. When George later became captain, he took on the air of a martinet and frightened the life out of one or two of the young, carefree pros. Ironically, it was sometimes said of him by put-upon journeymen players: 'George can be almost as bad as Wally.'

Newcomers were always inhibited in the presence of Hammond. At the start of that 1946 season, an easy-going young bowler from Cotswold country, Sam Cook, came to Bristol on the bus and reported at the county ground. He had a nut-brown face, still bronzed from his posting in Rhodesia, and a pair of innocent eyes. He'd probably never been to Bristol before. Sam was pointed in the direction of the county skipper, standing imperiously at the side of the net. As a plumber by trade, Cook was used to knocking on doors and introducing himself as 'the chap come to mend the cistern'. In rather the same way, only a little more nervously, he coughed and waited for Hammond to look round.

'I'm Cook, from Tetbury.'

It meant nothing to the skipper. But it soon would: Cook was put straight into the team, took a wicket with his first ball at the expense of a double-barrelled Oxford batsman, and went on to take 133 wickets that summer. By July, after he had bowled Gloucestershire to victory against Leicestershire with 7-54 in just over 22 overs, Hammond turned to him and said: 'Cook of Tetbury, you'll do for me.'

At least a line of communication, however tenuous, had been forged. It was to last no more than one summer, still long enough for the essentially impractical captain to eavesdrop on a few esoteric short-cuts from the plumbers' union and secretly admire the newcomer's phlegmatic approach to life as well as cricket. Wasn't that the year when Gloucestershire were in all kinds of trouble against Yorkshire and heading for a nine-wicket defeat in a low-scoring match? Cook, last man in and imperturbable as ever, sauntered down the pitch to Wilson between overs. Could this be counsel from the dressing room that he was relaying, the defiant left-hander wondered?

Not quite: 'How are yer onions this year, Andy?'

Hammond couldn't openly laugh at such cameos. Yet, counter-balancing the remoteness and the division he quite consciously created, were moments of fleeting fellowship almost as if he wanted to purge some kind of guilt for distancing himself. He appeared to enjoy many of the relaxed benefit matches on club grounds. Still a year short of his unedifying rumpus with Barnett over the opener's official benefit match against Yorkshire, Hammond accepted the ritual of assisting less illustrious colleagues in the evening beer games. In that 1946 season he turned up for a benefit fixture at the YMCA ground in Golden Hill, Bristol. A schoolboy spectator remembered years later: 'The thrill was just to see him. He arrived by car and went in to bat almost straightaway. Wally hit a few sixes into the duck-pond at the ground and then retired. He didn't field or take any further part in the match. But the fact that he had come along was enough.'

Jack Britton, a local businessman, played cricket in Bristol for the St George club who were staging an evening benefit match, with several sporting celebrities including Wally taking part for charity. Britton was banking on Hammond's appearance and panicked when, in late afternoon, he received a message from the county ground that the skipper had had an onerous day in the field and would be grateful if he could miss the evening thrash. 'I jumped into my car and drove immediately to the county ground. Wally was just coming off the field, looking pretty tired, it is true. I virtually kidnapped him to make sure he'd be present for our game. And, yes, he made a hundred.'

Hammond looked forward to the annual fixtures at Badminton, where in turn he played for the county XI and then the Duke of Beaufort's side. This was country-house stuff, with as many shooting sticks as deckchairs on the boundary. Invitation cards to favoured guests carried an aristocratic, even royal, summons. Wally was invariably treated as a VIP; by now he had a voice to match the occasion.

The former Gloucestershire coach Graham Wiltshire – then 'just this raw young lad from Sodbury' – was playing for virtually the only time in the same match as Hammond. His duty was plain : to bowl for nearly two hours from one end, leaving him almost too shattered to stumble round the outfield in the late afternoon. Wally and the others had no more than a token gentle over or two from the other end.

'We all went back to the Hare and Hounds afterwards,' Wiltshire recalled. 'I'll never forget – Wally left with the rest of us at 3 o'clock in the morning and just couldn't find the handle of his car door. He still had to drive back to London. No motorways then, and fortunately no breathalysers.'

Wiltshire recalls one other incident from the match itself, reflecting favourably on the Gloucestershire idol. As 'Roly' Jenkins, a fine leg-spinner, walked out alongside Hammond for the Duke's XI, he nervously asked Hammond if he would take a studied look at the way he bowled. This was conscientiously done, with a brief, perceptive adjudication. How many county cricketers dared similarly to ask for advice like this? 'Roly', of course, went on to play for England.

One Tour Too Many

Should Hammond have been talked out of that last Test tour to Australia in the winter of 1946-47? Those closest to him in the West Country advised him, as tactfully as they could, not to go. They believed he was too old and not fit enough. They had admired so much what he had achieved and feared the visit might prove an inglorious exit for him; he deserved better than that. More relevant is the question: should England have undertaken the Test series so soon after a debilitating war? Were we, as a nation, anything like ready for such a demanding exercise?

Hammond was now 43; his eyes were tired and his teeth stained from nicotine. Some of the natural exuberance had gone from his exquisite stroke-play, even though he had just topped the first-class averages again (84.90) and at times batted quite beautifully in limited appearances for his county.

If England were going, then Hammond had to lead them. There was no realistic alternative and it would have been an unforgivable slur not to invite him to carry on from the duties of leadership suspended six years earlier. His high-profile cricket appearances in the latter stages of wartime gave a fillip to the nation. He was relaxed and threw out sporting challenges over declarations in the one-day matches. That was when he confided how much he looked forward 'to taking on those bloody Aussies again'. Now, with bottles of pain-killing aspirins rattling away in his luggage, a stack of stationery for letters to his future second wife, and fingers crossed, he was ready.

He wanted very much to go. There was an understandable element of vanity. He was confident that he could still handle the Australian attack as well as anyone; he harboured a desire to round off his Test career with an Ashes conquest. If he'd grown older and a little less sprightly because of the war, so had other players on both sides. Unlike Ames, who had gracefully withdrawn from international cricket, Hammond underestimated the ravages of war. He also badly overestimated the merits of the team that sailed from Southampton on the converted troopship *Stirling Castle* to Fremantle. As he was soon to discover, the England bowlers lacked pace – and the established batsmen couldn't score enough runs.

Bowes would, on his boundary walks years later, list the theoretical strengths of the England Test party and then sadly expose the fallibility of the reasoning. 'How wrong we were and how disappointing our performances. Wally Hammond, great batsman that he was, found to his cost that the coordination between hand and eye was not what it used to be. Time after time we would see him go adventurously up the wicket to the slow bowlers. A dozen times he might succeed, the thirteenth would find him with his left foot just a fraction behind. Colin McCool, with the type of bowling that Wally once revelled in, now had him troubled.'

But the collective shortcomings of the team, including those of Hammond himself, were not the half of it. Nor did the throbbing pain from the increasingly troublesome fibrositis tell the full story of his decline. Mentally he was in turmoil. The guilt of his divorce from Dot nagged at him. His wife-to-be, Sybil, had been left virtually on her own back in England. She felt isolated and thoroughly wretched. At one stage she phoned him in some distress. She wasn't getting on with his mother and she was even thinking of returning to South Africa. Such domestic complications were the last thing Wally needed; he took her message in the team hotel, retired immediately to his room and moped. He was much in love with Sybil and had made provisional plans for their marriage. Were those plans now in jeopardy? He accepted that leaving her amid the cold of an English winter for six months or more, was anything but an ideal prelude to a wedding which he had felt would at last provide him with domestic stability and help him to banish for ever the need for sexual dalliances.

Sybil wasn't only shivering in the severity of the winter. She was wondering whether she had made a monumental mistake in leaving the sunshine and privilege of life at home, too easily wooed by the fame of the man who said he wanted her as his wife. And what about those promises he had made, however unrealistic, about taking her around the world on tour with him?

Hammond wrote feverish, long letters to her from Australia. He pleaded for her patience; he dropped the first hints that he'd be launching into a new business career before many more months had passed. They would soon be living together in the loveliest part of Gloucestershire and he'd be taking her to all the cocktail parties. 'Just be patient, my darling Sybil, for a little longer . . . .'

Most of his team-mates were to comment on his moodiness. They resented the fact that he drove from match to match in a courtesy car, with the team manager Major Rupert Howard; they resented that he shut himself away in his room when he should have been making some effort to raise the morale of a disheartened party. He was missing entirely from the physical jerks and tone-up exercises that preceded one important Test.

Denis Compton wrote: 'I would have loved to share a dinner with Wally, just to soak up the aura of the great man, but in Australia on that tour, when the opportunity for some fraternisation was best, the only time I saw him off the field was at the pre-Test tactical talks. There can be no arguments that he knew the game inside out, but a captain has to offer more. The liaison never started. In fact, the tour got off to a terrible start because Hammond and Rupert Howard . . . travelled separately instead of being in the train – the most favoured mode of getting from place to place in those days. Norman Yardley [the vice-captain] looked after the team, which was met at the next destination by the captain and manager. Of the several tours I have made to Australia, South Africa and the West Indies, it was the worst example of mismanagement from the top I encountered. The players looked to the captain for guidance and it was not there. The only time we saw him was at the grounds.'

That was the inaccessibility of the man. Yet how much can we put down to the moods that dogged and tortured him: the moods, I am so convinced, that could be traced back, at least in part, to the effects of mercury poisoning 20 years earlier? At various stages of his cricketing life, at times seemingly without reason or pattern, he would start to brood and then withdraw from the presence of his colleagues. This kind of acute, incomprehensible behaviour surely had a far more deep-rooted cause than a run of bad form at the wicket, too many thick heads or a fatuous, short-sighted inclination to select his friends more on the basis of class than of true worth.

Paul Gibb, the Yorkshire wicket-keeper and in some ways an equally introspective person, didn't have a distinguished tour. He complemented his frustrations by keeping a diary. Like the best diaries it could be trenchantly subjective. As the tour was coming to an end, he wrote: 'I feel a new man, free perhaps from an ever-present awareness of my erstwhile skipper's presence, free from his unfathomable, quite unpredictable and rather untrustworthy moods. I wouldn't trust Wally Hammond any further than I can see him.' Gibb had made a bad start to the Tour, and no doubt incurred Hammond's displeasure, by making several crucial errors behind the stumps in the controversial first Test.

The England skipper had been positively friendly on the outward journey. He played deck-tennis with the other players and usually beat them. He enjoyed the jokes about the amount of food everyone was putting away, suddenly celebrating as they were after the deprivations of the war. 'Hey, Vocey, you're a size – got to shed some of that before the first game.' The ageing Bill wasn't the only member of the team to put on weight alarmingly. Occasionally Hammond invited other players to his quarters 'for a tonic water'. There, they discovered with unspoken chagrin that his cabin was infinitely more luxurious than the ones they were sharing. They discovered, too, that although the *Stirling Castle* was to their dismay a dry ship, Wally had made provisions. He retrieved from the depths of his personal luggage a welcome, potent accessory to the tonic water. Indeed at that point, team spirit was breezy and there were all the portents of a happy and successful tour.

Yet public relations were soon letting the captain down. Almost the first thing he did, consciously or carelessly, after disembarking was to antagonise an enterprising Australian writer who had turned up ahead of the field to welcome the team. That aspect of Hammond's duties didn't improve. By now the more hard-bitten of the Aussie journos had him in their unloving sights. Details of his divorce were splashed across many an Antipodean front page. Criticism of him as a captain, printed in the British papers, was eagerly regurgitated and embellished in Australia. He made no real effort at reconciliation. Hammond's knowledge of how the press worked or how to use it to relay a valid point of view was minimal. And hardly ever did he really try to understand or extend a hand of friendship.

Some of the criticism directed at him, fierce and personal, was almost self-induced by his apparent contempt for those who wrote about the game. It is possible he was influenced by the condescending manner of some of England's cricket captains who had done the job in the past. The Australians were never going to wear that attitude.

As to his form on that ill-fated tour, it started well enough. After a century in a minor fixture, he quickly stroked the Western Australian attack for 208. He was looking fit; the sports writers were generous in their praise, talking of vintage style, inevitably extolling the off-drives. Then came the first Test.

There was much talk that Bradman was close to retirement and that failure at Brisbane might finally persuade him. If he'd been out when he had made 28, would the great Don have reasoned it was time to go? We shall never know. What Jack Ikin and most of the England team, the majority of the press box and many of the spectators believed was that Bradman was clearly caught at slip by Ikin off Voce.

The Australian skipper had, by his own matchless standards, been scratching around and looking uncomfortable. Ikin's 'catch' had seemed so much beyond dispute that no one instantly appealed. The Don was expected to walk but didn't. When the appeal was made, it was turned down.

Thousands of words have been devoted to the polemics of that catch and this is no place to add to them. Bradman was entitled to wait for the umpire's decision. Hammond's stage-whisper at the end of the over of 'What a bloody way to start a series' was said to have been directed at the umpire rather than the batsman. What is significant is the fact that Bradman went on to score 187. Any thoughts of retirement were dismissed for the time being. He was to lead Australia when they returned triumphantly to England in 1948. And he would be awarded a knighthood, while Hammond missed out.

That Brisbane wicket malevolently turned against England, who lost by an innings. Hammond made 32 and 23, moulded meritoriously from unrelenting concentration. With the exception of Jack Hobbs, there was never a batsman better able to cope with hostile wickets. He was to make 188 at Adelaide against South Australia, in what turned out to be his final first-class hundred. It was suitably noble and enriching, as if an emperor was laying out his bejewelled garments to show his citizens before storing them away for ever.

From the innings defeats in the first two Tests and fast-diminishing hopes that England would pull back in some way to make it a truly competitive series, Hammond's own decline – in sport and demeanour – was gaining momentum. By the third Test, at Melbourne, he was being roundly criticised for his captaincy. 'He just seemed indifferent, unwilling to put the screw on when he had the chance – he let tailenders get too many runs. He was a jaded man.'

His absence for the brief tour of Tasmania just prior to his Adelaide ton caused a minor furore. Major Howard was called in to explain. He blustered a little and said, without too much authority or conviction, that the captain needed a rest. In truth, Hammond did need that – and a good deal more. He was in the most neurotic state of his life; he confided to friends at home, in later years, that he was near a breakdown. There were too many anxieties bearing down on him.

The record book tells us he made 40 in his last Test. The headlines were reserved for Compton and Australia's Arthur Morris, who both made a century in each innings. There was no result, although Hammond resuscitated the match with a challenging declaration. His challange wasn't accepted.

When it came to the fifth Test at Sydney, he delayed selection till the last moment and then left himself out. Some mischievously wondered aloud whether it had in honesty been caused by fibrositis. The rumour that he might have been persuaded to drop himself gained circulation for a few days. It should be discounted for ever. Pain alone kept him out, physical and not mental pain this time. He wasn't sleeping; he was taking pills all the time, even at the wicket.

He handed over to Norman Yardley, who led the side well and indeed had a good tour. Hammond went on to New Zealand for a final Test match. When he got to the wicket at Christchurch, the New Zealand players gathered round and gave him three farewell cheers. Some of the spectators spontaneously sang 'For he's a jolly good fellow'. It was a brief, moving scene; he touched his cap in visible gratitude and took Test guard for the last time. In a rain-ruined match, Hammond made 79.

And that was that. His mind was privately made up. There was speculation in the papers and the players talked among themselves. Most of them agreed that they should have done better. They admitted among friends that they were, in a way, given too much freedom, that their skipper should have been close at hand to instil added purpose when it was needed. For all his faults, they sympathised – though not to his face – over his extramural pressures. At Sydney, during the last Test, they were genuinely moved to see him sitting alone on the balcony, watching the play with unseeing eyes. They noticed a hitherto obscured air of resignation. The sparkle had gone; at least he had joined in the laughter on the boat during the outward voyage. In short, he now appeared to have lost interest in cricket itself.

With the tour over, the Australians interestingly took a slightly warmer view of him. They agreed he had been saddled with a modest side; they applauded his general absence of complaint over umpiring decisions – which tended to go against England – and poor wickets; they praised the way he kept going when clearly not fully fit. But by then, the series won, they could afford to be generous.

Some of their points were well worth making. Hammond was never, in the manner of recent and more abrasive times (let's forget Bodyline for once), a whinger. He registered his protest about the Ikin catch but didn't pursue it. Bradman was to say the ball came off the ground, up into the hands of second slip; so did at least one of the British press party. England had atrocious luck with the wicket on that tour. Hammond did no more than grimace when the rain came down at the wrong time; he strapped on his pads, and got on with it. He was quintessentially a good sportsman.

His social graces were cited as a deficiency in his leadership. I could name a score of other England skippers, certainly not just the pros, who were worse. On that tour, he said the right things at the Christmas receptions. His radio messages were diplomatically phrased. By the end his public words for the cricket writers were singularly non-combative. He was at his most dignified and sad.

Within 24 hours of his return to England, he'd married Sybil. To allay lingering fears that the tour hadn't exactly been the goodwill one that had been visualised, the president of MCC arranged for Hammond to go on the wireless and assure listeners that everyone had really had a fine time. Infinite care was taken over the script. Hammond delivered it admirably, as if auditioning for the Diplomatic Service. The broadcast was well received here and in Australia, even though the over-sensitive MCC had merely succeeded in drawing attention to the suggestion that relations between the two countries, on and off the field, hadn't been quite as harmonious as everyone would have liked.

Hammond's mother had saved the cuttings for him to read, even the most vituperative ones. His team-mates, on the rare occasions they were to meet him after that, said that he called Brian Sellers 'a bit of a Judas'. It was a justified, even restrained, comment. Sellers, although an England selector, had gone to Australia to report on the series for the *Yorkshire Evening Post*. If that posed a conflict and any tricky ethical territory for the writer to tread, Sellers ignored such considerations. As early as November he was weighing into Hammond. It's possible he saw it as constructive criticism, though that's doubtful in view of his reputation as an overbearing martinet. I view it very differently; the onslaught on the England captain was untimely and, coming from a selector, quite intolerable. He may have had some points to make – but it is debatable whether they should have come from him, and certainly not in the public prints. Sellers wrote:

> His captaincy in the Queensland match surprised me a great deal. If he gives another display like that, it would be of no use playing Tests because we shall lose them. I cannot understand his field placings. He chops and changes his men far too often for no apparent reason. I would like to see a bit more encouragement and I would like to see him smile.

That is just a sample. But it had Col. R S Rait Kerr, the secretary of MCC, wriggling uncomfortably in his chair at Lord's and saying rather weakly that he wasn't aware of Mr Sellers' words but, well, he wasn't out there as a representative of MCC.

Hammond himself must have squirmed just as much when he read the extent of the reservations about his captaincy and personality contained in reports cabled back to this country. At least young Godfrey Evans had had a good word or two to say about him: 'It would have been inconceivable had he not been made captain. I was young, uncritical and got on well with Wally'. Compton, despite that boyish smile, was in no mood to forgive the early reprimand in that pre-war Test. 'I was invited to dinner by Don Bradman and he gave me some useful advice'. We have already learned that Wally never extended such a paternal invitation.

There was so much to depress Hammond in those cuttings, diligently and impartially saved by 'Ma' Hammond. The great spinner Clarrie Grimmett, now retired, took a sideways swipe by writing: 'Quite the best cricket of the tour and the finest captaincy – by Yardley – seen in Australia this season, made memorable the third day in the final Test at Sydney . . . . Credit must be given to Yardley for the magnificent manner in which he handled the side. He managed his bowling and placed his fieldsmen with excellent judgment, and he did not allow his bowlers to stay on too long . . . . ' One could find a volume of implied criticism of Hammond in that paragraph. Bill O'Reilly also rubbed it in. He gave the clear impression he felt let down by the pallid form and the apathetic attitude of the waning star. 'I'd raved about him, from what I had seen before the war. Now he was out here – and the kids just couldn't understand why I had said he was so exceptional.'

Hammond glanced up at his mother and found her studying him. There was an eloquence in the silence. He had scored 781 runs at an average of 41 and had been subjected to some of the most venomous personal criticism that any England captain, apart from Jardine, had ever experienced. He was by now regretting that, in the spirit of national cordiality, England had agreed to undertake that tour with such indecent haste after the war, and that he had led it. This was something he never admitted in public.

Maybe those who arranged the series, however sound their intentions, should share some of the blame for the wretched climax to a great cricketer's career. Maybe he needed a firmer hand at his side than that given by the good-natured Major Howard. E W Swanton was one of those who had had forebodings from the moment the name of the manager had been announced. He wrote: 'Rupert Howard was a genial fellow who had teamed up admirably as Gubby Allen's manager in Australia ten years before; but had he the toughness to handle Hammond? Like Jack Holmes in South Africa, was he not too nice a chap? 'Plum' Warner could never believe that a man might be a fine cricketer and yet lack some of the important qualities needed in a captain, especially on a tour abroad.'

Despite his wary dealings with newspapermen, Hammond was on occasions prepared to confide in Jim Swanton. One morning, early in the tour, he sat down with him at breakfast in the hotel and said he couldn't choose between Gibb and Evans behind the wicket. It was a question of which one could keep most efficiently to Doug Wright. The man from the *Telegraph* wondered whether the leg-spinner might prefer Evans who of course was a colleague in the Kent side; but it was Gibb who retained his place.

There were other considerations altogether back in England. A renewed business career, more serious this time, was imminent. Equally serious was the business of marriage. It couldn't be allowed to fail a second time. He lavished his attentions on Sybil, rapidly shoring up bridges that had threatened to teeter and even collapse during his lengthy absence. He bought her presents, doted on her and discarded all his latent sexism. Ensconced for just under two years at Thrupp House on one of the verdant hills that fold their way round Stroud, he found perhaps the happiest period of a varied married life that encompassed two wives and countless bit players. Wally and Sybil motored round the honeyed Cotswold pubs in the evening; they went to dances at the Town Hall in Cheltenham; they shared dinner parties with friends. It was the perfect therapy.

'Now is the time to have a proper family life.'

'And you must start earning some money', said Sybil, who had enjoyed a good life in South Africa and had no wish at all for a repetition of the drab, chilly days of shortages and loneliness she'd gone through while he was in Australia.

One irretrievable decision had been made: he had finished with cricket. The joints wouldn't take any more. Technical flaws had shown up for really the first time during the tour. Those marvellous reflexes were beginning to let him down, whether he was moving to the pitch of the ball or swaying for a catch in the slips. He discussed his decision with Lord's, where in some quarters relief was evident. His county was far more reluctant to part company with him. His presence meant so much to them at the gate. He had written from Australia, saying he proposed to hand over to another captain but that he would be happy to go on playing, in the short term, under someone else. In his heart, he knew that could never be.

It was all over, in a kind of unexplained whimper. Many West Country supporters were convinced he would play for the county in 1947; they couldn't imagine a Gloucestershire side without him. He had given Nevil Road a radiance and magnetism that hadn't been seen since Dr Grace lifted his distinctive regal toe in that wondrously despotic reign of his.

Hammond made the break more easily than he had thought possible: the war had of course already disrupted the progression. In 1948 he signed a contract to write on the Australians' visit here, for the *Star.* His observations varied from the sagacious to the anodyne. He wasn't wholly at ease in the press boxes of the Test grounds and didn't have too much to say. Perhaps he came to appreciate some of the technical difficulties of the Fourth Estate at last. The *Star* had rigid deadlines to make, though Hammond was required to write only one piece a day, and that part-ghosted.

Leaving Thrupp House, the Hammonds moved to Esher, Surrey and then Cuffley, in Hertfordshire, to be nearer his work. He played the occasional match in club cricket, and enjoyed it. There was a six or two at Esher, though his days of smashing upstairs windows of adjoining houses were over. If he put down a catch in the slips, no one complained. He stayed for a drink afterwards and everyone liked to have him around. At the end of the 1950 season he was persuaded to play for MCC against Ireland in Dublin. He had hardly picked up a bat that year and didn't bother about a net. The bowling may not have been unfriendly but his second innings was the talk of those who came to watch. He made 92 not out. It was a pleasing and tiring performance and he was grateful for the glass of stout which awaited him at the end. John Warr played in that three-day match and benefited from one vintage catch in the slips by the ex-England captain. But he retains a more light-hearted memory of the Dublin visit. 'It was a slow pudding of a pitch with very little in it for me. Donald Carr was bowling his chinamen and googlies and 'Tim' Warr, a master from Harrow and a rugby international, was keeping wicket. He was also in all sorts of trouble reading Donald's bowling. At one point, Wally at first slip, told him: "You assume it's going to be a chinaman. If it's a googly, I'll take it!" ' One tongue-in-cheek comment in an Irish paper even suggested that Hammond kept wicket very well. Back in the hotel, John Warr played poker-dice with Wally for 'just a few quid, though I found him quite an intrepid gambler.'

Later that year Wally was back in Bristol, for Gloucestershire CCC's annual dinner at the Royal Hotel. It was a warm, memorable occasion and this was how my old paper, the *Bristol Evening World* reported it:

> The Duke of Beaufort stepped from his place and pulled aside the curtains hiding Gloucestershire's tribute to Wally Hammond – a portrait in oils of the great cricketer as we had so often seen him, pausing to adjust his batting gloves on the way to the wicket.

But after the large gathering of distinguished guests and members had raised their glasses to 'Wally', the man of the evening had a surprise of his own to spring. He had heard the tributes paid to him by the foremost names in the game. Yet he felt it should have been he who was giving something to the county club.

'I hope the solution I have found will be acceptable,' he said. And from outside the crowded room, a waiter brought a framed copy of Wally's own painting, to hang in the County Ground pavilion.

Just in front of Wally sat some of the colleagues of his early and greatest days. There was also Sir Pelham Warner, learned and dignified; MCC secretary Col. R S Rait Kerr, in earnest praise; and Bev Lyon, droll and intensely amusing.

Sir Pelham said: 'If cricket lasts a thousand years – and it undoubtedly will – Wally Hammond's name will always have a tremendous place in the game. Everything he did in cricket bore the hallmark of grace, power and perfect style.'

Col. Rait Kerr described Hammond as the most humble and approachable of mortals. 'His career is an example to all cricketers. He survived his handicaps – as other great players would have to do in the setbacks and disappointments of the early days.'

Mr Lyon: 'Do you know what it's like to sit with your pads on for hours and hours and hours, waiting to go in after a man named Hammond?'

He set the packed room roaring with his stories of the matches when he'd been captain and Wally played. 'I feel really entitled to say that in my opinion the greatest exponent of the art of the game of cricket, in its widest sphere, that I or anyone else has ever seen, is Wally Hammond.'

That is no more than a precis of the long, glowing report in the paper. Within the mood of the evening, we can forgive the Colonel's curious recollection of Hammond being the most approachable of mortals. Nor should we dwell in mischief on the fact that Charlie Parker was a conspicuous absentee among the former players. He was unavoidably kept away, according to the report. 'Plum's' appearance back in Bristol, the location for past near-fisticuffs between the two, was I fear, the true reason.

It is clear from the account that Hammond was moved by all the tributes paid him. He said it was one of the proudest moments of his life, and those were not glib after-dinner sentiments. Some who attended the dinner swear that they saw tears in his eyes. If that was so, such a show of emotion would have been rare indeed. His own speech was sincere rather than humorous. He went to pains to thank the many in Gloucestershire who had helped him. He didn't forget 'Tot' Hanham, the groundsman, or Bernie Bloodworth, who had been 'mother and father to the team, always a soul of discretion and kindness.' He apologised that he hadn't been able to watch more Gloucestershire matches; he had recently had an operation on his left foot, one of the reasons he gave up cricket when he did (something that came as a surprise to those present).

It seems right to pause and refer to that club dinner at some length because it was in effect Hammond's farewell to Gloucestershire. The evening was a happy one and deserved tributes were paid. If the atmosphere was slightly starchy, that was the way the county did things even as late as 1950. Lyon introduced informality and laughter; the old pros brought the right measure of cynical banter and authenticity, and made sure the wine waiters could find them pints of draught; and, most important of all, there was affection for Hammond. He wasn't going out on any kind of discordant note.

It is all the more regrettable that he agreed, in the interests of a membership drive, to take part in one final, completely unexpected, appearance for the county in 1951. He played in the August Bank Holiday match against Somerset in Bristol. It may have seemed like a good idea when dreamed up by committee members. There was a large, expectant and worshipful crowd. The gateman were kept busy counting the money. In every other sense it was a disaster.

George Emmett, ironically, made a hundred in the presence of the master who had held him in scant regard. Arthur Milton was another century-maker. But the match is remembered instead for the cruel drama of Hammond's appearance. Almost every spectator rose in homage as he made his way to the wicket. 'What did they expect – not a hundred from me, as well?' he asked later. There was no longer any majesty in his walk to the crease. The flannels were immaculate as ever but the limbs were weary, and it couldn't be hidden. Physically he appeared something of a shrunken figure; he was no longer dapper. He took guard and made seven runs in the most undistinguished fashion.

Somerset were as embarrassed as his own team-mates. Horace Hazell, who once used to walk four miles across Bristol to see Hammond play, actually wept as he recounted that Bank Holiday match. 'I was trying to give him half-volleys outside the off stick but he just couldn't connect. He'd lost it completely.' Hazell also claimed that a catch was deliberately put down. I can believe it; a freemasonry of goodwill existed among the professionals. And Wally had been one of them 'until he'd decided to become a toff'.

In the home dressing room, Tom Graveney said he couldn't bear to watch. 'Why, Wally, why . . . ?' they kept asking as he dabbed away and missed. The coordination, the timing, the joy of cricket had all gone. Milton, blond and boyish, nearly ran him out when they went for an easy single. Here were two football wingers (Milton played for Arsenal and England), but maybe he forgot the age difference. They had once played together in a benefit match, when Milton was still going to grammar school. Hammond liked the look of him. 'Don't interfere with the boy too much,' he told the county. A bad throw, perhaps deliberately so – even in a match between these West Country rivals – missed the stumps, and Milton was relieved. But Wally didn't stay much longer. He didn't bat again. It was the exit everyone did their best to erase from their memories.

No Head For Business

As a businessman, Hammond was naïve, unlucky and at times disastrously unsuccessful. He eventually lost money that he could ill-afford, though in truth – because of his normally limited resources in the bank – it wasn't a vast amount. Financial failure was not always his own fault. One or two of his business associates were singularly unreliable. Bob Wyatt put it rather more graphically to me: 'I got the impression that he suffered because of some of the spivs he attracted around him or had dealings with.'

It became clear to Hammond from the early 1930s that he needed more than a cricket pro's meagre pay-packet if he was to pursue the life of upward social mobility which appealed more and more to him. At those sherry parties, to which he was invited – and which took precedence over a pint of local Georges with his team-mates – he privately admired the quality of the cut-glass, the expensive dresses and the nicely tailored suits that symbolised good living for him. At golf club bars he gravitated towards the convivial, well-heeled business executives, eavesdropping on their boardroom language and the way they made their money. Some of them, it was true, were worrying aloud about the Depression – just like Joe Lister, back in Bradford. Yet, in a contradictory manner that Wally didn't bother to analyse, the nation's economic restraints seemed to make them all the more willing to live with a fatalistic vigour. 'Another round of Scotch, barman'. The club members fawned in his presence and wouldn't often let him buy. Hammond was not a sponger by nature. He wanted to be in a position to pay his round. He didn't want to feel inferior, or in debt.

At one of their confidential chats, 'Plum' Warner had said to him: 'You must get yourself fixed up in a good, remunerative job . . . one that would support you and enable you play your cricket as an amateur. How would you fancy that?'

'Plum' had broached the subject, in the most cursory way, once or twice before. Wally was well aware of the implications. The suggestion, impracticable as it might be at the moment, thrilled and flattered him. He smiled sheepishly, rather than openly acknowledge the nuances of the question.

But first, of course, he had to find a job outside cricket. There weren't many about. And what, apart from his growing celebrity status, did he have to offer? He had gone straight from school to the nets. He had no industrial aptitude, no trade. He knew nothing about book-keeping. There was one passion, however: cars. He'd bought a cheap one as soon as he joined Bristol Rovers, to the amusement and probably envy of his older blue and white-quartered colleagues. He drove with undisguised pride, his mother at his side, to the county ground. After a day's golf, his partners would allow him to drive them home in their big, fast cars. The bigger and faster, the better.

I have in front of me a cutting from a Bristol newspaper in 1930, headlined: HAMMOND BUYS AN ULSTER RACER. The report tells us:

> Mr Walter Hammond, the All-England and Gloucestershire cricketer, has bought a racing motor car, capable of travelling at more than 100 miles an hour.
>
> The machine is a special sports model and one of four constructed to take part in the Ulster Tourist Trophy race last year. It is identical with that driven by Malcolm Campbell. The car is a streamlined, low-slung model, painted grey.
>
> Mr Hammond drove the car from Bristol to Berkeley, where he has been staying with friends, and later to Bradford. In almost quicker time than it takes to tell, he disappeared in a puff of smoke.

There were no seat-belts and no breathalyser in those pre-war years. Wally certainly drove too fast, as we recalled earlier with that scary experience of solicitor Hampden Alpass, when the

England batsman hurtled through the then badly lit streets approaching Bristol at well over 100 mph after a night out. As for his drinking, he would doubtless at times have been 'over the top' by today's standards. So many would have been, of course. It should be mentioned that he was an excellent driver, with a good road sense and sound judgment. But how on earth could he afford to buy a racing car?

He wasn't exactly an expert on the internal combustion engine, but he liked to lift the bonnet and give an impression of mechanical expertise. If he was to find a decent job to augment his negligible bank balance, he decided, it would have to be in the car trade.

Dorothy used to sit at home, expressing with every right her fears about their parlous financial state. They could no longer count on a once rich Daddy. Briefly and uneasily, 'Dot' worked as an assistant in a dress shop. It was anything but the life she'd expected as the wife of England's most glamorous cricketer. She was at least placated when in the autumn of 1933 he told her: 'Our money worries may soon be over – I've been offered a job with Caters, the motor people. On the sales side.' She was to read about it in an 'exclusive' report the next day in the *Bristol Evening World*. He was being employed as sales promotion manager at a salary of more than £1,000 a year. There were early plans for him to be on Henly's stand at the Olympia Motor Show.

The chairman of Caters appeared to get quite carried away: 'Walter Hammond has had considerable experience of motor engineering and would be able to place this at the disposal of his friends. We are going to adopt a slogan: 'LET WALLY ADVISE YOU.'

Surely a rather extravagant view of Hammond's know-how among the purring motors. But the report became even more intriguing: 'It has not been decided yet whether we will develop an aeroplane side of the business. But if we do, he would also take that over, as he has had some experience of flying.' The Cater company was part of Henlys, the main Austin distributors. They had impressive showrooms in Bristol's Cheltenham Road, and exhibited a sense of public relations that was well ahead of their time. They immediately saw Hammond as a prized acquisition and proceeded to angle their publicity around him. The cricketing theme pervaded the showroom.

Colonel Bill Hooper was sales manager then. From his Droitwich home 60 years later he told me: 'I was advised by the Board in London that Wally was coming onto the sales staff. He was to be used as a "sales introducer". His arrival created a great deal of local interest. We had cardboard cut-outs of the whole Gloucestershire team and imitation grass was put down in the showroom. A genuine atmosphere of a cricket match was captured. The building also had a flat roof. We installed a screen and, having come to an arrangement with one of the local newspapers, we flashed up the latest county cricket score.'

When the Henlys operation was moved to a new Bristol depot not far from Temple Meads station, Hammond used his new-found influence to arrange for Malcolm Campbell's land-speed-record car Bluebird to be on show for the opening. Six thousand people competed in a special launch lottery, with a gleaming new Jaguar as the first prize. Wally made the presentation.

One of the savoured perks for him was to test-drive new cars. He would take different cars home to his Failand bungalow. In the way of many who are plagued by feelings of social inadequacy, he loved the ostentation afforded by the opulence of the latest car. He would sit behind the steering wheel, sink deep into the rich upholstery and luxuriate in the level of status that he'd achieved. He was socially on his way.

Bill Hooper was never quite sure of Wally's title. It was apparently enough for Henlys to have him around – and for the potential customers to see him there. He was given a flexible role which allowed him to go up and see Joe Lister's friends in Yorkshire for a few days. 'And he had so many contacts, through cricket, that he always seemed to come back with an order. His name was worth a lot to us. As far as I remember, it was invariably a "clean" sale – no part exchange involved. But, quite honestly, he appeared to come in when he felt like it.'

Henlys had more than 200 branches. Hammond would be moved about on special occasions to shake hands with VIPs. It didn't really matter that he lacked any of the customary persuasive eloquence of the efficient salesman. He was Wally

Hammond, Test cricketer, just back from the Bodyline tour, our answer to Bradman, idolised by a nation . . . . Bill and Wally got on well. The Hoopers would occasionally go to the Hammonds for supper, always followed by a game of darts for the men. 'He had a marvellous eye, even for that'. It was noticeable that Dorothy was less sociable, less relaxed over the meal table. Maybe, based on the experience relayed by other guests at Failand, she wasn't ever sure that her husband would turn up at a reasonable hour. The sales manager and the 'sales introducer' especially enjoyed their Saturday lunchtime ritual of going across the road from the showroom to a Victorian pub to play snooker and have a few pints. 'I never won a frame – and I was amazed how Wally could down five or six pints without it having the merest effect on him'.

It has to be said that, however satisfied Henlys were with his celebrated presence, he didn't go out of his way to learn the intimacies of the trade. He was apt to sit behind his desk, a handsome, familiar face, chain-smoking through a pleasant, indolent day. A contemporary from the motor industry in Bristol during the mid-thirties said perceptively but with some affection: 'He was never in any sense a grafter. He'd not have landed a sale by sheer persistence. His romantic view was that a deal could be concluded just as successfully over one of his gin and Frenches in the club house. And because he was Wally Hammond, it sometimes was.'

If an effective motor salesman ideally needs a ruthless streak, that quality lurked – if not always visibly – in Wally's persona. Andy Wilson chuckled, with no retrospective malice at all, when he told me of a proposed sale of a car by the landlord of the Prince of Wales pub at Berkeley Road on the A38 back in those distant thirties. The landlord, Paddy Hodgson, well-known to the Gloucestershire cricketers who often broke their journey for well-earned refreshment, was intent on negotiating with Andy over a second-hand Rover. The wicket-keeper went back to Billy Neale's farm, where Wally was staying. 'I think I'll definitely buy it tomorrow, Billy.'

Wally overheard the conversation. Early next morning, he made contact with Paddy Hodgson. 'Don't get rid of that Rover – I think I may be interested.' In the end, neither of the cricketers bought the car, but the incident provides a telling insight.

Thousands of cricket lovers, many of them schoolboys, doted on Hammond and this should not be forgotten. Some travelled all over England to watch him. They fantasised as they copied his off-drive. They talked among themselves of 'Wally', just as they did later of 'Denis', as if they were friends. Cricket, like no other game, lends intimacy to strangers. 'Nice chap, Wally, you know', they'd say, though they'd never met him. Because he was a national hero, they saw him subconsciously as a friend. Alas, in his case true friendship rarely came easily. His complexes made him far too selective.

Sir Percy Lister, West Country industrialist and pillar of Gloucestershire cricket, was a good and loyal friend. He was to be generous of spirit – and pocket – to Hammond in the years ahead. He lived grandly at Stinchcombe alongside a golf course. Wally played and joked with him. So he did with Bev Lyon, even if most of the joking came from Lyon. So he did with another successful industrialist, Jack Britton. When I was first a court reporter in Bristol, Britton was the chairman of the Bench. 'He knows Wally Hammond as well as anyone. Wally used to stay with him', I was told in hushed conspiratorial tones by a colleague. That sent a callow newspaperman's imagination scorching off to many a boundary fence when the mind should have been focused on the case for the prosecution.

Jack Britton's father was the founder of a shoe business on the outskirts of Bristol. The family were predominantly Methodist and Liberal, with aspirations to be represented at Westminster. Jack was described variously as austere, intimidating, irascible, congenitally impatient, cultivated, musical and kind-hearted. Those diverse descriptions came from half a dozen or more associates – from the magistracy, and the religious, sporting and business life of the city. His work-force in the shoe factory referred to him as 'Mr Jack'; he knew nearly all of them by their Christian names. At Oxford he'd put his athletics Blue before his studies, though he still came out with a reasonable degree. He played good-class club cricket in Bristol and was an excellent golfer. One of his proudest possessions at his home near Pucklechurch was a photograph taken on the day he and

Hammond had won the pairs championship at Knowle Golf Club, Bristol. Wally spent many evenings as Jack Britton's guest, sometimes staying overnight. Significantly, Dorothy seldom joined them. The industrialist, steeped in business experience, provided a free and willing education in the capricious ways of market forces to the most attentive of listeners.

Britton told Wally: 'You're not really getting anywhere at Henlys and I feel you can do better for yourself.' Others were thinking the same way. A little coterie from the environs of Lord's, headed by the unwaveringly loyal and effusive Warner, were busy sounding-out people they knew in the City. By now the intentions were more than a whisper. Hammond was close to bridging the great social divide, although such a radical bound was unthinkable to many and abhorrent to the game's intractable reactionaries.

In short, he was about to be made financially independent of cricket – as a prelude to being appointed captain of England. Marsham Tyres were to be his new employers. They'd been going, and flourishing, since just after the First World War. Soon they were opening branches all over the country, meeting a constant demand from the increasing number of motor vehicles on the roads. At the Bristol branch the sales staff sometimes met Hammond at the local pubs or at the Grand Hotel, where representatives of the motor trade used to gather after work. 'He's getting unsettled with Henlys – couldn't we make use of him?' they asked head office.

Of course they could. The managing director invited him to join the board and that was irresistible. In fact, their initial overture carried rather less clout and certainly no directorship. At Stinchcombe Golf Club, Hammond turned to an old chum, Gilbert Clutterbuck, who had once slept in the next bed to him at Cirencester Grammar School. 'If they want you badly enough, they'll take you on the board,' Wally was told. Similar advice was given him by his business mentor, Jack Britton. Marsham Tyres were well aware that they would probably soon have the England captain on their staff. It was a tingling commercial prospect.

The announcement was made with exceptional PR aplomb in

November 1937 at the Cheshire Cheese, conveniently close to the Fleet Street offices of the day. All the leading sports writers were present. Jack Coates, one of the sports editors in Bristol and an occasional confidant of the cricketer, took the train up to London but not before writing his first-edition story. It told readers that there was big news involving Hammond on the way, implying that they would do well to buy an afternoon edition.

Reporters had usually found Hammond hard going and unhelpfully taciturn. At first they had tried to trade jokes with him but ultimately they gave up. At the Cheshire Cheese, the scene of much Dickensian cordiality, Marsham's newest director readily smiled for the photographers. He made a neat and humorous little speech. He warmly shook the hand of columnists and feature writers whose words had at times over the years displeased him and caused him to withdraw from the most innocuous of interviews.

The press conference was extensively reported both here and indeed in Australia. Cryptically, the reporters were told: 'This opens up an exciting new future for the great cricketer'. Everyone knew what that meant: within a matter of months, cricket's worst-kept secret was officially out. A former professional cricketer would be leading his country.

He worked for Marsham's for less than two years before the war came. In that time he was frequently away playing cricket. The thriving tyre company placed no restraints on him: it simply basked in the acclaim he received on the field – and the number of his mentions in the newspapers and on the wireless. He was, in the modern idiom, a high-profile appointment; his picture, in a boardroom setting, was regularly seen in the papers. A fellow director, Bill Pope, became his closest friend in the company and was later to be the best man when he married Sybil: 'Wally's the finest thing that has happened to us – his countless contacts in sport have been invaluable.'

In terms of the business he brought in, this period must be viewed as Hammond's most successful. He dressed the part, enjoying the ambience and the civilised proximity to the drinks cabinet. All the time, he was acquiring greater social confidence: working on his accent, feeling increasingly at ease in the presence of the elite in the city. Back in Bristol, it wasn't only Jack Britton and Gilbert Clutterbuck who noticed it. 'I hear you're doing terribly well with Marsham's,' the Duke of Beaufort told him. 'You must bring your wife round for dinner at Badminton'. Hammond, business director, amateur cricketer and captain of England, was on the way up.

Not that he was oblivious of the murmur of discord. In many a London club, cantankerous old reactionaries from the shires rocked apoplectically in their leather chairs. The establishment didn't much like what they saw happening. 'My God! The fella's got no class. A professional cricketer! And now we're having him as captain of England?'

The Times was cautiously reserved in its congratulations. It quite liked the way he'd skippered the Players. Yet, well, would he be a better captain as an amateur than he was as a professional, they wondered? The Thunderer was, as always, unsubtle in its betrayal of class prejudice. Some other newspapers, including those with a radical bent, were enthusiastic. It was time to have the best man for the job, irrespective of social background. And hadn't he been surreptitiously groomed for the elevation? *Wisden,* however, was decidedly frosty about Hammond's appointment. It was altogether too much responsibility for him and he lacked the necessary 'experience', (another code word for class).

Hammond was well aware of these reactions and the wall of prejudice. He talked it over with 'Plum', who had done more than anyone to orchestrate Hammond's career to its highest point. 'Show them, Walter!'

In his own writings, Hammond appeared to take an ambivalent view of the amateur captain. In *Secret History* he wrote: 'The amateur has always been a vital and attractive figure in cricket . . . . I captained England after most of my life being a professional. I was the same man as before. Because I could change my label, all was well . . . . I submit this is illogical.' Elsewhere in the book, he wrote: 'I must admit that the best captains under whom I served were amateurs and they gained advantage from their amateur status. Jardine was perhaps the most effective of them all and in my opinion one of the finest Test captains in my time or since.' There follow words of understandable loyalty, reflecting infinite gratitude: 'One of the best under whom any of us had the privilege of playing was Sir Pelham Warner, on whose strategy and tactics Jardine based a good deal of his work.'

One also comes across clear hints of guilt over his decision to move away from his professional roots. A few who in later years persuaded him to talk of that watershed moment at the Cheshire Cheese claim he fidgeted without much comment. Perhaps he wanted to be seen again as 'one of the boys'. Writing of the sweeping social changes of the 1950s, he sympathised, too, with those amateur skippers, trying to play cricket and keep some kind of career going outside the game. He claimed there were no more than three amateur captains in English cricket then who understood the game in the same way as the professionals. 'I think a system should be devised whereby the amateur can take honourable pay and compete on equal terms with those who make a living from cricket.' Prophetic words, of course.

I am convinced that, whatever his unquestionable leanings towards snobbery, he remained uneasy and guilty about the radical evolution he had prescribed for himself. It is so often less difficult physically than mentally to tip-toe into rarefied social territory. He assured us, again in print, that he had little time for the cosmetic amateur. 'Young amateurs of Test or near-Test class are among the best fielders in England. There has been a tendency among the selectors to give them chances in representative games. But I would like to be sure that these young players take their cricket seriously. If they only mean to play in holiday times and if in any case they intend to give up their first-class cricket after a year or two, it would be sporting of them to say so and stand down from Test teams. It may be flattering to vanity to say they have played a couple of times for England . . . . Young professionals feel this keenly and it is time someone brought it into the open.'

Another example of Hammond standing up for the professionals he had deserted. On the other hand, such protestations cost him nothing – and the particular point he was making here was hardly controversial.

If we care to look for it, there's ample evidence of his inner confusion and discomfort over his calculated shift to amateur status. Many of the professionals had seen it coming. Fred Root had gone into print. At Nevil Road in Bristol, there had even been a proposal to give him some secretarial duties, maybe on a nod-and-a-wink initiative from a committee chum at Lord's. The trouble was that Gloucestershire had little spare cash, in the mid-1930s to make it a realistic proposition for the cricketer.

We come back to Warner's earnest, affectionate words to him about the cynics, in and out of the game, who disapproved of his going amateur as a prerequisite for the England captaincy: 'Show them, Walter – show them!' Membership of MCC, rare then for an ex-professional, was part of the process. Earl Baldwin proposed him and Sir F S Jackson seconded. Hammond had a round or two with Jackson, a scratch golfer, as he found himself moving in those exalted circles. Apart from treasured brandies with the Duke of Beaufort – how he'd have liked to ride to hounds with him like Charlie Barnett, how indeed he'd have liked to have gone to Wycliffe like Charlie – there were weekends at Stinchcombe Hill with Percy Lister and with other West Country industrialists and celebrities. He was also, as we have noted, a member of the Bristol Savages, an esoteric and predominantly artistic organisation in the city. He had been put up for membership in 1935, almost certainly at the instigation of the secretary, himself a prominent committee man at Gloucestershire CCC.

The Savages could boast a prestigious membership and there was always a waiting-list. Their splendid focal building was known as The Wigwam. Wally was enrolled as a 'Green Feather' member, which meant that he drank and enjoyed the civilised cordiality of the evenings rather than sketched. A surviving Savage of those days recalled: 'At the end of one evening, I had almost to carry him up the not inconsiderable flight of stairs from the Wigwam.' What was that I wrote about never showing any effects from his drinking?

At least he now had more money to buy his round. When he joined Marsham's his salary doubled in a stroke. Dorothy, who had been kept on a desperately tight budget with the housekeeping, had less cause to nag him. In the 20 months or so leading up to the war, he was more socially fulfilled than he'd ever been before. He enjoyed his business life, which was both pleasant and undemanding. His mother, who continued to fuss over him, said he'd never looked so relaxed. If there were complications in his private life, they didn't appear to trouble him too much.

By the time the war came, he had acquired a distinct taste for the good life. Some would say he had enjoyed a self-imposed apprenticeship for years. The difference was that he now had it by right. Marsham's continued to function usefully with the revised demands of war. Hammond was discharged from the RAF, because of his fibrositis, in time for Christmas in 1944. Soon he was back with the tyre firm, finding his old pal, Bill Pope, now the managing director. The pattern of his work changed, just as the markets changed. There were difficult months, as for so many companies, in austerity Britain. He augmented his earnings with some ghosted comments on the 1948 Test series against the Australians for the London evening paper, the *Star*. It was during this period that several books were written under his name.

Pope had hoped that Wally would remain for the rest of his working life with the tyre company. But he sensed that his enthusiasm was waning. Sybil was homesick and Hammond had admitted, after a business trip to South Africa, how much he liked it out there. It still came as a considerable surprise when he resigned – on the same day as the sales manager, Richard Wilkins. Hammond and Wilkins, who had become personal friends, worked out a somewhat airy-fairy plan to start a joint business in Durban. They met up out there, started looking for a location and rapidly came to the conclusion they were hopelessly under-capitalised. Hammond had gone on a naïve whim and was to suffer serious financial losses because of it. With a wife now hoping for a settled and successful life in her homeland, and with two small children in tow, he had cause for acute worry.

His fame, however, quickly brought him the fortuitous compensation of other employment. He was eagerly taken on as a general manager for a car firm, Denham Motors in Durban. It was all very different from those amiable days with Henlys back in Bristol, where there was always time for a chat about cricket and then off early for a frame or two of billiards or snooker. At Denham Motors the need was for aggressive selling. It was a hard, competitive grind.

Posthumous Charity

Towards the end of the 1950s word got back to England that Hammond wasn't much enjoying life at Denham Motors and that cars weren't selling as they used to. The company had in fact run into serious trouble and in 1959 it went out of business, leaving Hammond out of work. He appeared to be stranded in South Africa without any prospects. In the evenings he would go into his shell. Sybil coped valiantly with his moods while bringing up the children (there were three youngsters now). She would look at him, sunk silently into the armchair, and know what he was thinking.

England's most celebrated cricketer had utterly mismanaged his business life. He had left jobs at the wrong time, listened to fatuous advice and ended up with virtually nothing in the bank. In Britain the rumours began to circulate, gaining colour with each telling. After all, no tittle-tattle is quite so tasty as that of the fallen idol.

Fleet Street was by now asking its stringers in the Republic to do their best to get an interview out of him. Most of the papers were curtly turned away. The London *Sunday Express* at last came up with a few bland paragraphs about him, including this quote from him:

> 'I don't know what people have been saying about me but it's a fact that I got out of the motor industry at the start of the year and, since that, I've been quietly looking around. But I'm not hard up.'

Brave, resilient words: yet who was he kidding? According to the report, he had put on a show of well-being at his 'coral-pink bungalow as he sipped his gin and tonic'.

> 'I'm not in the least worried about being out of work. I'm not considering any return to England. I love this country too much and it's right for my kids. My wife is also Durban-born, after all.'

In affectedly casual tones, he added that he'd go on playing 'a bit of golf' and do some trout fishing.

The reality was rather different. He fretted in the armchair at home. His moods intensified and he would snap irritably at his wife. Sybil remained an attractive woman but her standard of living had been drastically lowered. It was in no sense the Durban homecoming that she would have wished.

Then, towards the end of the year, by miraculously good fortune, came the offer of another job. Hammond was invited to become sports administrator at Natal University. It was perhaps a slightly grandiose title, the subject of cynical speculation by the mean-spirited who heard about it vaguely at second-hand. 'Hey, Wally's ended up a bloody groundsman. He's out there cutting the grass at some university.'

He was in fact doing nothing of the sort. It was a newly created, proper post, which came Hammond's way on the kindly initiative of Professor Owen Horwood – a noted economist, future Cabinet minister and the most unwavering friend of a cricketer he'd idolised before the war – who wanted earnestly to introduce new sporting facilities for the university.

There had been an immediate affinity with Horwood, who had been a capable cricketer for Cape Town and was potty about the game. The great Test player would be called to the Professor's study ostensibly to discuss the painfully inadequate sports amenities at the university and the way they could be improved. Invariably, the two ended up on a nostalgic conversational ramble, incorporating memories of dozens of past matches and the sublime players who dominated them. Horwood had the charm to extract these reminiscences from Hammond – and not too many managed that. Then they would revert to the reason for Hammond's appointment. 'I've got real plans for this university and you are the man to spearhead them.

It needs someone of your reputation in the game.'

The new sporting complex wasn't solely devoted to cricket. There were to be full facilities for tennis, squash and other indoor sports. An athletics track was to be laid, which made the new administrator think back, with the suggestion of a smile, to those cold winter months at Bristol's Eastville, where he put on his spikes and invariably beat all his fellow footballers in improvised 100 yard sprints along the freezing touchline. It made him think, too, of the evening chats he used to have with Jack Britton, who had been such a talented athlete when at Trinity College, Cambridge that he put his running before his studies.

When the professor moved onto cricket, however, Hammond's eyes lit up. There was to be a new square, the envy of the region. And Wally was to supervise the whole operation. After all those cars and the tawdry aspect of hard-sell that so clearly conflicted with his temperament and nature, cricket was a blissful relief. He couldn't wait to begin. He studied the plans and talked to the groundsmen. And then, in February 1960 with sudden cruelty, just four months after he'd started, he was almost killed in a car crash. He was on his way to help with some coaching at Pietermaritzburg when he was in collision with a lorry near Camperdown. His car spun out of control across the road, went onto its roof a couple of times and became a complete wreck of tangled metal.

A police car, on its way to another crash, momentarily pulled in. The occupants made a superficial judgment that Hammond was dead and apparently went on their way to the other accident. If that was so, it was disgraceful incompetence on the part of the police officers. Everyone seemed to agree that Wally had been given up for dead. Only the fortuitous arrival of a doctor, who happened to be passing, saved Hammond's life. He was rushed to Grey's Hospital in Pietermaritzburg with serious head injuries. He was eventually identified and his condition was conveyed to inquiring reporters as 'fair'. In medic-speak, familiar to journalists, that was usually the most optimistic way of saying 'extremely serious'. The front-page story in the *Bristol Evening Post* had the melancholy air of a pre-obituary. Hammond's cricketing statistics were trotted out.

There was a tribute from the Gloucestershire secretary, Harold Thomas: 'He was the greatest allrounder England ever produced.' In what appeared like misplaced optimism, the secretary mentioned that Hammond had written to him, asking for a cap badge of all 17 counties. 'I shall be sending them off soon.'

All the sports editors, in England and Australia rapidly got to work on their 'obits'. Contemporaries and opponents, from Les Ames to Bill O'Reilly, were asked for their tributes. They stuck to the cricket; hardly anyone quite knew what Hammond had been doing since he emigrated to South Africa. But as it happened, these eulogistic paragraphs would not be needed for another six years.

In Grey's Hospital, he initially drifted in and out of unconsciousness. His head was shaved and he was operated on for his battered skull. The doctors did not give too much for his chances. Yet they had under-estimated the sheer physical strength of the man. We remember again the words of surgeons, at the time he fought for his life in 1926: 'He's the finest physical specimen we've ever seen.' Once more, he defied medical opinion. Within a month or so he was out of hospital. He returned to his home, to be nursed with infinite patience by Sybil. As his hair grew again, she supervised his physiotherapy and firmly shook him out of his blacker moods. She also looked at his markedly lined face, not wholly attributable to the scars of his accident. He'd become an old man.

It is too easy to see Sybil as a pampered ex-beauty queen who, over the years, was too ready to show her restlessness and unhappiness engendered by Hammond's naïvety and fecklessness in business matters. In fact, she encouraged him to think again of the job ahead of him at the university; she encouraged him to spend more time on the unlikely hobby of ship-modelling; she looked after the three children, building the sort of warm relationship with them that her husband never quite achieved. As part of his recovery-therapy, she used to place the stack of letters and telegrams from well-wishers in front of him. 'How can you say you're forgotten?'

Professor Horwood welcomed him back at the university three months after the accident. The following year (1961), at the age of 58, he was even persuaded to play for a team of ex-servicemen in an undemanding cricket match. The bowling was modest but not that bad. He scored a hundred, his last. There were five nonchalant sixes. The accident had not sapped his remaining strength. On the campus – despite the occasional misanthropic grunts from the more stuffy academics, who felt that at a seat of learning books were more important than playing fields – the sporting transformation went ahead. Hammond relished the smell of a newly mown outfield. It filled him with nostalgia. He never again wanted the scent of fresh automobile upholstery in his nostrils.

So he was happier, back in the open air for at least part of the time, and once more among cricketers, albeit young and raw ones. As for the university life around him, he remained a peripheral figure, and some of the senior staff were patronising. One student of the time was to say: 'He was more at home with us than with some of the academics. He was inclined to tread a lonely path around the sports field and shut himself away in his office for a fair amount of the time.'

I have in front of me the words of one student from those days. 'There were a number of people pushing at one stage for his removal. Now this might sound odd but some argued that he wasn't doing his job as well as he ought, that he didn't coach as hard as he should have done, that he wasn't a motivator . . . and I think I could recognise some of those criticisms as being pretty valid.'

Others, influenced by the romance of his career, took a far less critical view. I'm thinking of the journalist Marshall Lee, who had skippered the university team when Hammond was there. 'Wally was my hero,' he says unashamedly. In a 1964 article for the South African *Sunday Chronicle* he wrote:

> I was fortunate to enjoy a close relationship with him when he managed the university side, of which I was captain, at an inter-varsity cricket week in Johannesburg. Our confidence with Hammond behind us was strong and he happily confessed that for the first time in his career he had been so absorbed as to watch each ball bowled.
>
> It is enough to say that my early hero-worship suffered

no disillusionment. Instead it was reinforced by a more adult respect for the man.

For Hammond it was a modest enough honour to manage the side, but still, we can imagine, immensely gratifying to him. Not for a realistic moment had he seen himself taking charge of a cricket team again. Yet here he was: supervising the net session, assuming responsibility with Lee for team selection, advising whether to bat first. There couldn't have been a more timely balm for a tender ego.

Mr Lee, who was interviewed by Peter West in HTV's documentary, described how Hammond 'mothered' them. 'He was always there. Certainly he was a good adviser when I needed help. He never failed to come up with some sort of reasonable and authoritative comment.

'But he didn't push himself. I can't recall him saying do this or do that. He was extremely reserved, actually withdrawn, I would say, for most of the time . . . . One of the things that impressed me most was his incredible modesty, a remarkable humility he always showed. In comparison with him, we were nothing. Yet if we asked his opinion, his response would be to ask ours!'

Marshall Lee was one of several admirers surprised that the cricketing authorities in South Africa did not take the opportunity to enlist Hammond's experience. 'I was quite involved in the politics of local cricket and my recollection is that the top executives neglected him. Their neglect was based on a gigantic misunderstanding of the man. They actually thought he was arrogant, that he was unsociable and that he'd turned his back on them. So therefore he wasn't worth bothering with. But I know that these things hurt him.

'One would have thought that a man like Hammond would have been given free entry, given a free pass to whatever match was going on – say, at Kingsmead – for the rest of his life. I remember arguing with a number of these cricketing executives and other cricketers who just didn't come close to knowing the man at all. I'm proud that I did get to know him rather better than some others.'

Mr Lee's criticism is primarily levelled against the game's

administrators at relatively local level. But surely there was also a case for Wally's counsel to have been sought, even in the most unofficial sense, by the Test authorities in South Africa? Sadly, recognition in keeping with the majestic dominance of his illustrious years, drifted inexorably away from him. During his years in South Africa, he changed home three or four times. Some of his neighbours barely knew who he was. In England it seemed that he was almost forgotten. Sports editors who once phoned his Durban number for the occasional observation on a contentious matter of Test selection or a worrying tendency in cricket's politics, now no longer bothered. He'd been out of the game and the headlines only for a decade or so but already he was passé as a sports personality worth the cost of a phone call. It is the sort of psychological recession that some erstwhile sporting stars find hard to bear. Hammond merely shrugged and stepped back another pace into his shell. Whether there was private pain is another matter. I'm convinced there was.

Professor Horwood remained the most steadfast of friends. He it was who gave Hammond the sniff of linseed again. He it was who at Natal University assured Wally that he considered there was far more to life than a pile of tomes under an academic's arm as he set off for the next tutorial. In his biography, Gerald Howat captured the warmth of the Professor's regard after an evening spent with him: Horwood told him:

> Once he had one's confidence, Wally became a true friend. I relied on him completely. He was a man of some force of character, consistently charming and modest. The students had a high regard for him. He was unassuming with them yet gave an impression of authority when needed. I never heard him talk in derogatory terms of anyone. He invariably saw the best in people and had time to chat with them. He left a fine name in the university. What he did for cricket there and, by example, for South African University cricket and South African cricket as a whole, is immeasurable. From his 'nursery' came six Springbok Test players. My association with him was one of the most pleasant things of my university career. It was a privilege to know him.

I have quoted the passage in full, with the author's permission, because it happens to be perhaps the most generous tribute I have ever heard paid to Hammond. It was both wholly genuine, and fascinatingly subjective. One or two of Professor Horwood's judgments must have been affected by romantic memories of the game of cricket and the style with which Hammond once adorned it. There's nothing wrong with that. His assessment of the man may be at variance with that of others. But it has an equal right to be heard.

Hammond was unassuming. He didn't make a habit of indicting others. The cricket pitch and other sporting facilities at the university would long remain a worthy, if unostentatious, memorial to him. Students, too, benefited from his tuition at the nets. He was never the most intuitive of coaches but he quietly showed the way, and his pupils, in awe of him because of what their fathers had told them about him, learned by example.

Sybil, too, encouraged him to coach, away from the campus. He did private sessions for neighbours and others in a net which had been erected on the lawn at the side of his house. One of his pupils, briefly, was Barry Richards. He was sent along as a nine-year-old by his father. 'I was a bit in awe of him because of what my Dad had told me. Wally had his coaching place in his back yard, as it were. I think he did it professionally and because of the kind of person he was, I suspect he only took the best. He wouldn't want to waste too much time on people who he knew wouldn't succeed.'

Richards, one of the most glorious stroke-makers produced by South Africa, said he read later what a great off-side player Hammond had been. 'Perhaps something rubbed off on that eager little nine-year-old'.

There was some limited coaching for Wally's son Roger, who suffered from no intrusive pressures to become a cricketer. Wally's first child, Roger, had been born in 1948; then came Carolyn (1950) and Valerie (1952). Their relationship with their father was pleasantly ordinary rather than in any sense tactile. They were all too young to appreciate fully his feats as a cricketer. He volunteered little information, and no anecdote, as he sat at home.

Roger was a useful school cricketer, no more. In 1966, as an

18-year-old, when he was living temporarily with his mother and sisters in Gloucestershire (of which more later), he was invited to the nets at the county ground in Bristol. There was even talk that he might be taken on the professional staff. Sir Percy Lister, the county chairman, had phoned to say: 'I'm told he's pretty good. A left-hand bat. I feel he should be given a trial.' Alas, it didn't come to much. Sentimental notions that the son might be in the same imperious mould as his father were not fulfilled. Everyone expected far too much from Roger. Richard McCrudden, the Gloucestershire secretary at that time, was tact personified when I went along with a journalistic colleague, in misplaced hope of a story which had already written itself in our heads.

'He's very likeable and has the build of an athlete. We were delighted he came along to see us. Of course, we've never seen him play. He'll be coming back for some more nets and if he turns out to be a promising batsman, then we shall be interested in his future.'

In truth, it hadn't been much of an introduction for him to Gloucestershire cricket. The pitch was under water and the pre-season training sessions had been disrupted. But early impressions did not suggest that he was county material. It didn't help that the TV cameras were there, lending unreasonable expectations to the occasion. During those improvised batting sessions in the nets at the side of the house back in Durban, Wally had probably made the same private judgment on his son. No doubt if he had been a different sort of person, he would have devoted more time to his three children. As it was, they were fed, clothed and educated pretty well. His darker moods, which they like Sybil came to accept, were seldom at their expense.

Hammond flew to England in March 1962, on the initiative of Sir Percy Lister, who had maintained a fairly regular correspondence with Wally during the South Africa years. One day, Lister rang Frank Twiselton, newly elected to the management committee and someone who had worshipped Hammond from his autograph-collecting summers. 'I queued up with all the other boys at the back of the Wagon Works ground pavilion. When it was my turn, he signed 'W

Hammond'. I looked at my score card and saw he was down as 'W R Hammond'. So I queued up a second time and politely asked for his signature in full. 'He gave me a funny look. Then he grinned and said that for my cheek, he would!'

Twiselton, later to be chairman of Gloucestershire CCC, proved himself an enterprising fellow, going on to run the International Wanderers, becoming assistant manager to Richie Benaud in South Africa in 1976 and taking on various other administrative roles. But back to that phone call from Sir Percy.

'You know, I've got this idea of having a series of dinners around the county to recruit new members. Wally's keen to come back and get involved again with maybe a bit of coaching if we can sort out some kind of income for him.'

It was to be a carefully planned public-relations exercise for the three weeks Hammond had planned to stay in England. Lister's idea was for Hammond to be the main speaker at each dinner. Lister would pay for him to come over and would accommodate him. Frank was to meet Hammond at Heathrow, but that was only his initial brief. At that time, Twistleton's outside-cricket job was sales director of West Country Breweries at Cheltenham. His task now was to draw up a list of good-class pubs in the area. The idea was to offer to install Hammond as manager of one of these pubs, and thereby to tempt him to return to England permanently.

Twistleton recalled: 'I was rather nervous about meeting him at Heathrow, having heard what an arrogant so-and-so he was supposed to be. In fact, I found him to be a friendly, diffident person – any former signs of stardom had long gone. It took us only a few hours to get to know each other. After a few days he was pulling my leg about who'd buy the next drink. I remember taking him to lunch at the Grand Hotel, in Bristol. We were having a drink at the bar, when several blokes nudged each other and then apprehensively asked Wally if he'd sign their menus. He turned to me and said with a moving simplicity: 'And after all these years.' Another day, our bowler Sam Cook lined up with all the others just to shake Wally's hand.' Again there was a revealing expression of gratitude, tinged with surprise. 'Did you see who that was, Frank? Fancy old Cook being so pleased to see me – wasn't that nice.'

Hammond and Twiselton built up a firm friendship. 'I used to go round to Percy's home at Stinchcombe each morning to pick Wally up. We did the rounds and there was never a suggestion that he drank excessively. Another impression I formed was that he was very proper in his language. I don't ever remember hearing him really swear.'

The daily routine was for Hammond to be driven to selected pubs and then to go in to obtain a feel of the place. To avoid any suspicion, brewery director Twiselton stayed out in the car some way from the inn. Wally would have his first drink at 11.30am and leave at about one o'clock. He liked the look of the Huntsman on the A38 between Gloucester and Bristol; but his favourite was without doubt the Talbot Hotel at Tetbury, with its men-only bar, tweedy farmers who'd long finished the milking, its skittle alley, dozen bedrooms and well-heeled clientele.

'This is the place,' Hammond would enthuse. 'Sybil's interested in catering. These farmers seem to have plenty of money to spend. And Percy's talking about me coaching the youngsters at Bristol and looking after the 2nd XI.'

There was a snag. The Talbot was already run by a young, capable couple who showed no inclination to leave. By now, Gloucestershire was rapidly becoming Hammond's spiritual home once again. He could see the chance of making some money and he wished fervently he'd never left. In the evenings he made his sincere, formal, rather humourless speeches to large companies of diners at Cheltenham, the Forest of Dean, Stroud, Gloucester and Bristol. He went down well; membership went up. Percy Lister's little PR plan appeared to be working, at least for the county.

Hammond returned to South Africa with some reluctance at the end of three weeks. Old acquaintances had made a fuss of him. Old players had shaken his hand again. From comparative obscurity in Durban, where some of those academics took a condescending view of his presence and had probably never heard of him as a great cricketer, he was acclaimed once again. But he'd have to convince Sybil. There were the children, now adolescents, to think of. And he wasn't entirely taken with some of the pubs which had vacancies for a landlord. The Talbot, now, that was different . . . .

'Think about it, Wally. This is where you belong. We'll work out something,' Sir Percy had said as they shook hands.

They never did, alas. Two or three years later, the couple who managed the Talbot moved to Dorset to own their own pub. The Talbot was on the market for a new couple to run it. Frank Twiselton immediately wrote to Wally. 'How about it?' The newcomers needed to put up some cash of their own to buy fixtures and fittings. Hammond's reply made it clear that the enthusiasm had passed. He had absolutely no money to spare for a new venture back in England. 'Thanks, Frank, it was a nice idea. Three years ago I could just about have managed it.'

His daughter, Carolyn, sees it a little differently. 'I gained the impression that he'd really have loved to go home, as it were. Mum had no wish to do so and she dug her heels in.'

By the summer of 1965, Twiselton was an executive for Whitbread's living in Devon. On 2 July he turned on the 7 o'clock morning news and heard that Wally Hammond had died from a heart attack. Less than an hour later, the post arrived. It contained an airmail letter from Wally, posted only two or three days before. 'It was like a letter from the grave. It was so upsetting. I just sat there with the tears rolling down my cheeks. I should think it was the last letter he ever wrote.'

The funeral was held on 6 July in Durban. Ex-South African Test captains Dudley Nourse and Alan Melville as well as Roy McLean, Trevor Goddard, Eric Dalton and Bob Williams attended. The family mourners were headed by Sybil, her son Roger and daughter Carolyn, Wally's mother-in-law Mrs Ness Harvey and her brother. A contemporary report appended a final paragraph: 'Seven non-Europeans attended the service. They were groundsmen from the Athletic Union of the University of Natal, who worked under Mr Hammond.'

Sir Percy Lister had been a generous friend to Wally. Now he was to be to be equally generous to his family as they were brought over and found a house at Uley, near Dursley. Roger was given a job at Lister's. He played some cricket for Stinchcombe Stragglers. Everyone commented on how attractive the two daughters were.

It was an especially difficult time for Sybil. She had precious little spare cash and was surrounded by strangers in a country she'd never really taken to on her earlier stay. Frank Twiselton found her 'quite tough and self-possessed, someone who knew what she wanted from life. There was a kind of resolve about her which said that now Wally had gone, she had the kids to think about and must get on with it.'

I heard it said by a number who sensitively monitored Sybil's days at Uley that she didn't like it in the area and some of the local people failed to get on with her. 'Wally's past may have partly worked against her. She wasn't taken-up locally', I was told somewhat enigmatically. She may well have discussed her unhappiness with Lister who rang Andy Wilson and asked if Mrs Hammond could go over and spend the evening with them. 'Liz, my wife, and I made her very welcome and we got on well. But we felt she was very lonely, that the family had fallen on hard times.'

Tom Goddard didn't long survive Hammond. He, along with his faithful wife, Flo, attended the memorial service for Wally at Bristol Cathedral on 16 July, 1965. It was a solemn, rather low-key event with an address by Viscount Cobham. The tributes he paid were sincere and serious. Bev Lyon, who sat with Hammond's mother, would have invested the homage with a gentler, more anecdotal touch. Yet insightful anecdotes don't tumble joyfully out of the mind when we think of W R H.

I sat in a side aisle and, a trifle shamefully, found myself spotting famous faces in the congregation. There was R H Twining and 'Billy' Griffith, president and secretary of MCC, in addition to old team-mates who acted as ushers. The formidable line-up from Gloucestershire CCC included the president, the Duke of Beaufort, who read the lesson, Sir Foster Robinson – Wally's first skipper when he arrived in Bristol – Sir William Grant and Sir Percy Lister. Other captains there were Lyon, George Emmett, Ken Graveney, Basil Allen and John Mortimore. There, too, bronzed as ever and almost unrecognisable without his battered brown trilby was Wally's 'faithful retainer' Bernie Bloodworth.

Hammond's devoted pal Les Ames, silent and dignified as ever, was in his place, along with Alec Bedser, Maurice Hallam and Tom Dollery. 'Bunty' Longrigg headed the Somerset contingent. Nearly everyone who had links with Nevil Road, from Ashman Olive – who had once motored off to Portsmouth to persuade Mrs Hammond to part with her son – to the groundstaff lads, had gone to the service, which was conducted by the Bishop of Malmesbury. A newspaper editor from Cheltenham, Cyril Hollinshead, who made a solitary appearance for Gloucestershire under Hammond the year after the war (and indeed was still playing cricket occasionally at the age of 90) was in the row in front of me. He had a hymnal and a notebook in his hands, and used them in alternation. They seemed equally relevant to me.

Bristol Rovers had remembered their fledgling winger and were represented. Bristol City's outstanding if autocratic chairman, Harry Dolman, was present. The leading local golf clubs sent their officials to mourn; there were unidentified, attractive, whey-faced middle-aged women, sitting alone, dressed in black. Ageing sportsmen, faces still leathery and nutbrown from August summers in the Cheltenham outfield, stopped later to chat in hushed voices on the steps of the cathedral porch. The craggy cricketers had a few minutes earlier been singing 'To be a Pilgrim' with throaty sincerity and many a tear in the eye. I recall vividly one of Gloucestershire's former players, turning to another while struggling for articulation: 'Greatest cricketer we'll ever see – but a funny bugger'. The succinct appraisal was in no way irreverent.

The obituaries had been uniformly glowing. Just a hint here and there of his moodiness, his difficulty or unwillingness to communicate with other players. The words, hurriedly penned by famous contemporaries at the time of his hideous accident, were now retrieved from the newspaper libraries.

Cardus referred again to the match at Bristol 'on a dreadful wicket' when Gloucestershire were put out for 31 in their first innings, before Hammond won the game with an undefeated 174 in the second. 'One could feel sorry for the bowlers when he was in this awe-inspiring form . . . bowlers were rendered his slaves, as fetchers and carriers . . . .' Swanton considered the comprehensive technical qualities of the man. He assessed the bowling at 'about the pace of Tate' and mentioned the means by which 'Tiger' O'Reilly had tried to curb Hammond's freedom by bowling at his legs. O'Reilly himself was warm in praise, though understandably he harked back to the 1930s. 'Australians then stoutly declared that they had never seen a better cricketer. Nor did they know him ever fail to give them their money's worth. He was in every sense a natural.'

In the local papers, Bev Lyon described Hammond as the greatest cricketer he had ever seen. Sir Foster Robinson added humanity to the tributes by recalling that early 'trial' invitation to play against the Free Foresters at Clifton College. 'He forgot his flannels but we managed to kit him out. I said at the time he'd become a second Jack Hobbs and was determined to retain his services for Gloucestershire despite Lord Harris's stubborn attitude.'

After all the column inches of eulogy, after we had all walked away from the cathedral in Bristol's College Green, it was not long before worrying reports were filtering back from South Africa. Wally had left no money. He'd made absolutely no provision for his family. They, for their part, probably hadn't been aware just how badly off he was. All his life he'd hated talking about money; when he had it he simply spent it – at the bar or the tailor's. His family didn't go short but there were latterly few luxuries for them.

Well-meaning friends back in the West Country made discreet calls to bank managers in Durban and spoke in confidence again to Sybil. They had quickly heard enough. A number of meetings were held, one with the Duke of Beaufort at Badminton House.

Barely three months after Hammond's death the Memorial Fund was set up. From the county ground went out a letter to all members and known friends. It was signed by the Dukes of Beaufort and Norfolk, both of them past presidents of MCC, as well as by Gubby Allen, Foster Robinson, Bev Lyon, Basil Allen, Jack Clarke, the current chairman of the county, Percy Lister, and Frank Twiselton. Part of the letter read:

> The cricketing world was shaken to hear in July of the premature death of Wally Hammond from an illness due, in great part, to injuries suffered in a motor accident.
>
> We have since heard that his widow and young family are

in financial distress. His elder daughter is training to be a secretary; his son, aged 17, should remain at school for another year, and his younger daughter is only 13. His widow has a job that is not highly paid, and she cannot feed, clothe, educate and maintain a home from her slender earnings without assistance.

When Wally Hammond settled in South Africa, he invested all his savings in the motor trade which has been the ruin of others with far more experience than he had. In a few years his capital had vanished and he was glad to be employed as coach-groundsman at Natal University.

We think that there must be many cricket lovers to whom, between 1923 and 1947, he gave such exquisite pleasure and rare entertainment, that they would wish to help to alleviate the misfortune of his widow and children.

Urgent contributions were requested, to be sent to Lloyds Bank in St James's Street, London. Seven-year covenants were recommended. In addition, specially printed leaflets and posters were distributed to cricket clubs and to any vacant notice board. It was no time for false pride. Hammond had never once asked for material help; now it was urgently required for his dependents.

Sir Don Bradman, it should be noted, sent a cable which was reprinted in the posters and leaflets. 'During his era Wally was undoubtedly England's greatest cricketer. I am very distressed to hear of the need for the Memorial Appeal Fund and feel sure cricket lovers will generously respond.' It was reinforced by persuasive quotes from Lyon ('PLEASE remember Wally Hammond') and Denis Compton.

We are left to lament that such desperate, unvarnished pleas for charity were necessary. Hammond's financial plight wasn't unique; it could be argued that it was partly self-induced. It is a matter of regret that he wasn't able to find a way of returning permanently to England to pursue the safe and solid career in the pub or hotel trade, that Lister, Twiselton or one of the other well-intentioned West Country associates were trying so hard to create for him.

The Memorial Fund raised something like £3,500 and was

never going far. In a few years' time, Sybil, increasingly pragmatic and not by nature a sentimentalist in cricketing matters, was making plans to sell most of her late husband's trophies and mementoes. It caused Ursula Wicks, spurned in love though imbued with a passionate regard for the game and its history, to say in anguish: 'Sybil's action has enraged so many old Gloucestershire friends.'

During her brief stay in England, Sybil and Roger were taken to Tom Goddard's funeral. There was a reserved block of pews for ex-Gloucestershire players. Rather poignantly, the wise, good-hearted Reg Sinfield beckoned to young Roger and put him in the middle of his late father's team-mates. 'Your dad liked Tom and he'd have wanted you to be here to represent him,' said Reg.

Sybil, however, had soon had enough of Uley and she went back to Durban after two years, taking her daughters with her.

Carolyn, Wally's older daughter, left a marketing post in South Africa to return to England in 1997 and make her home here. She admits she and her sister had little idea how famous her father had been and just how much he'd achieved. She saw, without as a child bothering to analyse, his signs of moody isolation and that preoccupied look as he sat on the veranda. 'Mum would quietly tell us to leave him alone. "Go off and play," she would say as she got on with her knitting. We had a strict upbringing. Good table manners, to speak only when we were spoken to. I was never allowed to wear skirts above the knees. I had to be home from parties by 10 o'clock. Dad insisted on things like that.

'As a family, we weren't good at showing our feelings. I don't remember ever being hugged by Dad. I was keen on sport and he always wanted me to be a winner. Once I had a swollen ankle and had to take off my spikes for a hurdle race. Because I didn't come first, Dad said nothing at all. There was no sympathy. He had love for us all without showing it demonstratively. It was so ironic that he was as close as he had ever been on the day he died. He drove us into the country to see the snow which had been falling at Kokstad up in the hills.

'We all had a snow fight and a lovely time. Maybe the sight of snow reminded him of happy schooldays in England long ago.

He died that night. The childen had gone to bed and I heard Mum on the phone to the doctor. Whatever his lack of emotions, family life *was* important to him. He loved his Sunday lunch – the ritual of roast beef and Yorkshire pudding. He sat at the head of the table. As for the children, they had to eat what was on the plate. We would try to hide the Brussels sprouts under our knives and forks. Often the vegetables had been grown in the garden by Mum. There were also the Saturday nights when, as a family, we went to a drive-in cinema, sitting in the car and watching the enormous screen. We'd take a picnic basket and make it a real family outing. Dad enjoyed that, especially the peanut-brittle which, I fancy, he insisted on keeping for himself. We weren't allowed that particular treat. He so obviously enjoyed going to the drive-up. And, of course, he was relaxed when coaching Barry Richards and others in the nets at the side of our house. He never lost his love of cricket, however much he seemed to have been marginalized by circumstances.

'Yet I have to say, latterly he was in some ways a broken man. It's even more evident to me at this distance. He must have been so lonely, so forgotten in the sporting sense. Once I had observed how charismatic he could still be, when we had friends round for drinks. Now the remaining self-confidence had gone, even the self-esteem. For someone who had for most of his life been so fastidious, he was now altogether less concerned about the way he looked. I remain very sad.'

Redressing the Balance

As I made clear at the start, this book was going to be more an examination of Hammond the man than of the cricketer. Hammond's thousands of devotees may feel displeased at what they see as an imbalance in my treatment. There is perhaps not enough chapter and verse of those exquisite innings at Auckland, Bridgetown and Tunbridge Wells for their liking; not enough superlatives about a player considered by many to be more princely than Ranji.

My self-imposed brief has been a consistently difficult one, bedevilled by rumour and suspect information. I have gone to infinite pains to check and, where necessary, to discount. No, he wasn't, despite the circulated innuendoes 'an incorrigible lush who drank away the family fortune'. The family never had any, alas. He may have been inclined to imbibe rather more than was good for either his pocket or his liver, but it was never a serious problem. Nor – while we are rejecting myths – was he a Freemason.

From a number of sources, inside and outside of the Gloucestershire dressing room, I was told that a high proportion of his associates in the business life of Bristol were Freemasons and it appealed to Wally to join them. At least some of his team-mates assumed that, after the close of play, he was hopping off to Lodge meetings. Knowing his hunger for status and for friendship among the influential, I decided to research this generally accepted claim. I wrote to the United Grand Lodge of England. They went through their records and assured me he'd never been a Freemason. So much for that.

More warily we now ponder the contentious question of his genes. There has been a good deal of ethnic speculation in the case of Hammond and we cannot ignore it completely. Many of his contemporaries, at both county and Test level, were well aware of the suggestion. Some compromised and accepted that he probably had some gypsy blood in him, just like swarthy Tom Richardson, one of the stars of the great Surrey sides of the 1890s. Only a few weeks before writing these words, a reputable figure in cricket coincidentally said: 'Funny temperament Wally, of course – but then, as you know, he was a Romany.'

Others went a great deal further in their theories of ethology. Joe Hardstaff told a colleague of mine: 'Standing near him in the field, you were aware of a certain nigger-sweat. When he ran, it seemed that he had no bones'. Such a description, seemingly callous, condescending and indelicate of language, causes us to fidget uneasily. Hardstaff was not a bigot; he was using, albeit insensitively, the rough-and-ready terms of his day.

Nearer home, Hammond's county team-mate and psychological adversary, Charlie Barnett, was equally suspicious. 'You had only to take a look at Wally's finger-nails. They were a giveaway,' he told me. It constitutes a mischievous line of argument. How many of us truly know our roots? And what business is it of others? In the puzzling world of genetics, traits are apt to surface intermittently through the generation sequence. From genealogical exploration available to me I found absolutely no evidence to support these theories about the cricketer in any case.

Yet one Gloucestershire colleague of Hammond, now dead, had confided to me: 'Everyone appeared to have heard those whispered rumours. Of course, we made sure we never even hinted at them when he was anywhere around. All the same, I'm sure he was aware of them. And although he'd have kept his feelings to himself, I know how angry he would have been.'

It is important to reflect again on the extent of the mental burdens that weighed him down. If he became almost paranoid on occasions, imagining that team-mates and opponents were engaged in their whispering campaigns – about past illness and even the colour of his skin – we should not be too surprised. The gossips never let him forget the miseries of his Caribbean illness. For his part, did he, I wonder, ever try to work out why he was subject to so many black moods, unpredictable bouts of depression and an inclination to withdraw from those around him? Did he ever consider the possibility, as we now can dispassionately at this distance, that he may well have suffered lasting damage from the toxic chemicals introduced as medication to his ailing system?

In an earlier chapter I attempted to justify my seeming obsession with his illness. It has nothing to do with prurience. I see it as an undeniable factor in his unstable temperament which, as all the evidence reveals, took effect from the late 1920s onwards. As my final word on the subject, I can only hope that the petty and the pious don't take a censorious view of the great cricketer on this account. If they condemn him, I have failed. Captain James Cook, a farm labourer's son, was no less a hero of exploration because he contracted venereal disease on his travels. Charles Baudelaire, extolled by Hugo and Flaubert, was no less a great poet because of the venereal demons that ravaged his body.

Those who had contact with Hammond in his last years came to a unanimous conclusion: he'd become a nicer person. Several, including John Woodcock, formerly cricket correspondent of *The Times*, wondered if the change might be attributable to the head injuries he received in that dreadful road accident. It wasn't an isolated opinion, so I discussed the possible effects with an experienced neurologist. He said that such brain injuries *could* lead to intellectual and personality change and, in some cases, to a loss of inhibition.

Woodcock met Hammond during the MCC's 1964-65 tour of South Africa. 'I'd thought back to my days at prep school at Oxford, when I asked for his autograph and was aware of his reputation as being difficult. Now here he was coming across as a most generous person. It could have been another man altogether. He arranged a wonderful fishing trip for me. We all became very fond of him.'

The renewed, unscheduled link with Wally was the inspired idea of the late Ron Roberts, cricket writer and friend of so many players. He had already been out to South Africa managing a private tour. 'Why not invite Wally over to join us for the day? He doesn't live so far away. Maybe it'll give him a lift'. Donald Carr was given the job of ringing him. The two had met briefly before, initially during the Victory Tests. 'Funny thing happened, then. We all went to a banquet and dog meeting at the White City on the Saturday. I'd never been greyhound racing before. By wartime standards, it was a pretty good meal. Wally sat at the head of the table with one of the White City directors, and he was being given tips. I was sitting with Luke White and John Dewes. Wally would lean across to Luke and ask him to put a few bob on Trap 2. Down it went. Then he wanted John to put something on another trap for the next race. When it came to the third race, it was my turn – and the dog came up. I was sent off to collect the money but didn't really know how to set about it. Eventually I returned to the table with our winnings . . . just 7s-6d. Wally gave me sixpence, I remember, for my troubles!'

Now, in 1964, he was on the phone to Hammond, asking him if he'd like to join the MCC players for a day's cricket and a drink or two. The reaction was as revealing as it was poignant. 'My recollection,' said Carr, 'was that he felt no one really wanted to see him – some of the present players would hardly have heard of him. I reassured him and told him that the team would love to have him along. He hesitated for a long time and finally agreed to call in the following evening just for a quiet drink with the captain, Mike Smith and myself. It went well. Mike was lovely with him. We sensed that he had enjoyed the visit, though I must say he was also very quiet and looked pretty worn-out. The first Test at Durban was coming up and we said the boys would love to have him there with them in the dressing room. He just couldn't believe it. He had to be persuaded. We tried to make him part of the team. He remained very private but seemed touched by the fuss we were making of him.'

England won by an innings, the only result in the five-match series. South Africa had rashly taken the grass off and prepared a turner. David Allen took seven wickets and Fred Titmus six. Hammond, self-conscious and not completely at ease, still enjoyed himself immensely. He had been involved again at a time when his phobias were telling him he had been rejected permanently by cricket's establishment. It left him in some confusion, as well as private pleasure. When it came to the final match, at Port Elizabeth, there was a general feeling in the England party that Wally would again be a welcome addition to the team's inner sanctum. 'We realised that he was in poorish circumstances. So we had a whip-round to pay for his journey and hotel.'

Within the variegated and at times upsetting life story of Hammond, the spontaneous gesture by a group of good-natured touring cricketers, with love in their hearts for a former idol, is a touching example of fellowship and goodwill, to be cherished.

David Allen had as a Bristol schoolboy seen Hammond score his double hundred against Somerset the year after the war. He and his wife had sat on the top table with the taciturn ex-England captain during one of those carefully orchestrated recruitment dinners when he was flown over from South Africa in the service of Gloucestershire. Now here he was in the England dressing room. 'He would arrive at 10.30 every morning and hang his coat on the same peg. Then he'd shake hands with all of us as he left in the evening. In his way he was so obviously enjoying himself.'

Even during his playing career Hammond had seldom offered a strong view about another player. At Durban, Allen overheard a stray comment that M J K Smith was someone he liked the look of. He couldn't apparently make up his mind about Ted Dexter! During that 1964-65 tour Hammond put on his flannels one last time. We can only imagine it was the persuasions of Ron Roberts again. Hammond, to almost everyone's surprise, turned out for a Durban Press team in a relaxed match at Richmond. Carr and Compton both played; so did Roberts and Woodcock. The Thunderer's man out there told me: 'It was so good of him to agree to play. He turned out because he wanted to. He got a few runs. And he fielded at first slip. The hard, new ball once went straight into his hands and came out again. Who worried?'

The flannels had been as usual pristine-white and freshly ironed. But the eyes were weary and watery; he would never hit a cricket ball again. Might we be allowed to interpret, albeit playfully, that by his final appearance, he was making his overdue peace with the newspapers? In a matter of months he would be dead. The way the England players had welcomed him caused him pleasure, at least superficially. It also made him ill at ease once again with the lack of fulfilment in his life. Guilt resurfaced to consume him. He would shut himself in his little office at the university sports ground, give the groundsmen their jobs for the day, and then allow his conscience to lacerate him. He thought again of the aridity of his first marriage and knew he should have worked harder and less selfishly to make it succeed. He thought of Sybil and the false dreams which had seduced her into following him to England. He thought of the mistresses he had successively discarded. Why had he always mismanaged his business affairs, leaving him now with empty pockets?

These were grievous regrets. His instincts had unfailingly urged him to yield to grandiose rather than commonsense advice. He had been indolent by nature and believed that he could by-pass the shopfloor and effortlessly occupy the manager's office. He had yielded too readily, he could see now, to snobbery. And how he had bristled when once he overheard a team-mate say: 'The trouble with Wally is that he's got bags of class at the crease – but not much of it off the field.'

His stage-managed route to the England captaincy was, in its way, a flawless operation. Pelham Warner was his campaign manager: he helped smooth the rougher edges and pointed Hammond in the right directions. Those who studied 'Plum' and observed how he nurtured his protégés said they detected a perceptible shifting of emphasis as Gubby Allen gave way to Wally in those paternal favours.

In matters of single-minded ambition, it is possible to make out a comparison between Hammond and Edrich. They had nothing at all in common in physique, batsmanship or even innate courage. What bracketed them was the modest roots from which they aspired, the posh accents they strove to acquire, their penchant for full bottles and pretty women and, above all, their conscious decision to turn amateur in pursuit of England's leadership. Edrich maintained that he found Hammond kind and often amusing. This, it must be said again, wasn't a generally held opinion, certainly not by Compton who wrote: 'I was never at ease with him . . . he rarely discussed tactics with his side and hardly ever congratulated players on a good performance.' Edrich, conversely, 'forged a strong friendship with Hammond and I felt we shared a common attitude to life. ' There is unmistakable evidence of the latter.

I have often discovered other examples of comparable traits in professional sport. For instance, I think of Somerset's Gimblett in the same breath as Hammond. Gimblett was a Methodist who rarely drank and probably remained faithful to Rita all his married life. But he could also bat quite beautifully, was said – by M M Walford among other respected judges and team-mates – to have an off drive of Hammond quality, and developed all sorts of social complexes. Like Hammond, he disappeared from cricket. He went to live in a mobile home, miles from the Taunton ground where successive generations of schoolboys once came after lessons to pay homage. In his last, sad years, he came to hate the game and with almost feverish resolve, refused to be drawn into a discussion of any of his personal feats, for England or his county.

How often did Hammond talk about his performances? He would turn the conversation whenever an acquaintance tried to reminisce on those lines. It occurs to me that he may have seen South Africa as some kind of refuge from the past. He had bade that sour farewell to English cricket after the acrid exchanges that accompanied his final, misguided tour to Australia. Was he too embarrassed to stay around for long after that? In opting, as perhaps he saw it then, for a new career in Durban, was he in the mood psychologically to turn his back for ever on the game he had graced with such felicity?

One could find no incident more melancholy than this, recounted to me by Eric Hill, the former Somerset cricketer who went on to become the elder statesman of the Taunton press box. He went out to South Africa to cover the 1956-57 Peter May tour. After play one evening, he went into a bar with Peter Loader and Brian Statham. The occupants made a great fuss understandably of the two England bowlers. 'As we left, "Scrubber" Loader turned to me and pointed to a solitary figure at the other end of the bar. "Here we are getting all this attention and there, drinking on his own, is one of the greatest cricketers we ever produced. It doesn't seem right." Eric hadn't recognised Hammond but it left him feeling uneasy. Before the war, as a schoolboy on his holidays in Taunton, he had nervously approached him and asked for his autograph. 'As he signed, some cigarette ash dropped onto my book – and I faithfully kept that ash for years!'

Hammond went through life with a relatively small number of intimate friends. That was increasingly evident to him during his varyingly optimistic and vexatious years in South Africa. At times he was thoroughly anti-social, and knew he could do nothing about it. He wished he had more friends: and then, in evenings of tormented reverie, he accepted that maybe he had not deserved more.

Although he'd never been openly splenetic, he remembered, no doubt with painful remorse, how disparagingly he had treated that other soldier's son, George Emmett, back in the West Country; how unforgivably brutal he had been in dismissing Eric Hollies' merits by savaging him in the nets during the West Indies tour (Wyatt saw what was going on and rapped out in rebuke: 'Stop that, Wally'); maybe he also recalled a benefit match at Wickwar, near Chipping Sodbury, in 1938, when young Frank Twiselton, youngest on the field, swung at Colin Scott and hit Basil Allen, three yards away at short leg, on the ankle. The boy-batsman dropped his bat and rushed to help. 'Oh dear, I'm sorry, Mr Allen.'

All the time Hammond stood impassively, arms folded, in the slips. He said to Twiselton; 'Don't worry, son. He's got a pair of hands.' There is a cruel edge to the uncharacteristic words, and we can only conclude that they conveyed a minimum of affection, one man for the other. I think again of Basil Allen's searing character assessment of Wally on the Lord's balcony when 'Plum' Warner asked what he thought of Wally as a man. Yet, for reasons I can't wholly explain, I have come to like Hammond more than when I set out to write this book. At the risk of sounding presumptuous and patronising, I have also felt desperately sorry for the way life treated him.

Let us gather up at random some of his most endearing qualities. Did anyone ever hear him boast? Did he ever seem querulous or peevish? Forget those little indulgences like the blue-silk handkerchief, the made-to-measure worsted suits or the plus-fours he paraded on the golf course: he was not a narcissistic man in any irritating sense. There were no extravagant flourishes of the bat; he didn't preen himself at the crease like one or two other famous players we can all think of. He wasn't maybe everyone's idea of the quintessential team man, in that he chose not to bowl when Gloucestershire were palpably short of seamers. Yet, looking at the county's records through the 1920s and 1930s, how can we say he didn't valiantly and willingly carry Gloucestershire on his broad shoulders? Hammond willed himself to excel and act as a magnet to boost the crowds for the benefit matches of both Sinfield and Goddard. Team-mates had much for which to thank him. So had the county treasurer.

I came across a yellowing newspaper cutting of a speech made by the Gloucestershire secretary at a club cricket dinner near Bristol. His praise for Hammond was unstinting and I quote verbatim from those references: 'I was associated with him when he was a professional, captain of his county and his country and he was 100 per cent loyal to Gloucestershire. In 1936, for example, when our finances were not bright, there was a question whether we could maintain the rate of talent money to the players. Wally came up to me and asked if it would make any difference if he went without his. I said that of course it would. He willingly went without his share for the benefit of others. It gives some idea of his great loyalty to the county and his teammates.'

Some saw him as a curmudgeon. Yet he could laugh with the others over a light- hearted game of deck-tennis during a sea voyage to Australia, or when he met the eccentric actor and ex-cricketer Sir C Aubrey Smith, as well as Binnie Barnes and Ronald Colman, during the team's brief stop at Hollywood on the way home. I have always liked the E W Swanton account, in his biography of Gubby Allen, of that much-discussed 13-ball over during the third Test against Australia at Old Trafford in 1934. Gubby tried to explain it by saying he was weary after a long innings in the stifling heat, and then having to cope with Bill O'Reilly's mammoth footholes at the Warwick Road end. Hammond had persuaded him to drink a whisky and soda before going out to bowl. It was the only time, according to Allen that he ever took a drink, surreptitiously or otherwise, before the close of play. We can only imagine what Hammond and some of his England team-mates said in jest, perhaps out of the corner of their mouth, as three wides and four no-balls were signalled by the umpire.

I pluck stray examples of Hammond's days with Gloucestershire, demonstrating that he could break into a grin. As we have seen, he was rather taken by Sam Cook, the Tetbury Plumber, and secretly admired his insistence that he preferred a quick pint down the road to the customary lunchtime mug of tea from Bernie Bloodworth's big brown enamel teapot. Once, teasingly, in the 1946 season Hammond lined the players up at the nets in early afternoon and asked Cook what he could smell on his breath. He went through the motions of a tongue-in-cheek reprimand.

In that same year, the famous skipper made a sizeable bet with the county secretary, Colonel Henson, that 'Cooky', this easy-going newcomer with the bronzed face and country ways, would take 100 wickets in his first season. Henson accepted the wager with alacrity – and had to pay up. Hammond was a fine judge of a new player. As in the case of Arthur Milton, he told the coaches not to interfere with Cook.

In that rather off-hand manner of his, Hammond admired Sam's unflagging accuracy, though Cook himself was quite indifferent about his natural ability. Cooky seemed as contented with an evening pint in his artisan hands as with five hard-earned wickets. Hammond was at the same time quietly pushing the slow bowler's Test claims. 'I was chosen for a Test trial at Canterbury and Wally was non-playing captain. He wanted me to do well and I think he was quite keen for me to go to Australia. I'd already put my wedding to Daisy off a couple of times and now I was actually in the middle of my honeymoon. Oh dear, I bowled badly and during lunch, Wally came up to me and said he knew it was my honeymoon but was I, perhaps, having too many nights in the saddle?' A rare flicker of humour from a man they all claimed hardly ever laughed.

Wally's first hundred for Gloucestershire had been against Surrey at Bristol. It was a boiling day and he opened with Alf Dipper, never the most elegant or athletic of cricketers. Bill Hitch was bowling well – and the heat was getting at Hammond. Dipper saw him wiping his brow and looking quite faint. He even went down the wicket to inquire if his partner was fit to continue.

The 19-year-old, proud of his normal physical condition and slightly embarrassed to be asked about his fitness by someone he saw as nearly twice his age, said he was fine. Old Alf, full of rustic cunning, decided to put his partner's less than convincing insistence to the test. He started calling for short singles, to the amusement of colleagues, well aware of his own uncoordinated style between the wickets. Hammond saw what was happening, half-smiled, and accepted the challenge. He outstayed Dipper and went on to a hundred. When he returned to the pavilion, modest Apperley's most celebrated resident was stretched out on the bench, exhausted.

'What's up, Mr Dipper? The sun got to you then?'

In his slow, wicked manner, the old pro looked up. 'Well done, me son. Not a bad knock. You've got a future. But, mind you, I'd like to see 'ee go for a few more quick 'uns. Upset the fielders, they do.'

It was the unlikeliest lesson Hammond ever had on physical prowess and mobility. This was a favourite story of his and it always caused him to laugh, however fleetingly the lips puckered.

Claude Reddy was a sugar merchant in Bristol. He played cricket for historic Lansdown and golf with Wally. Generations of the Reddy family had been life-members of Gloucestershire CCC. Claude's daughter, Yvonne, would go, as a child, with him to watch the county. Hammond was 'Uncle Wally' to her. 'At Cheltenham, in the mid 1930s, he once took me by the hand and led me round the ground to buy an ice-cream. He was courteous and kind – and I still get annoyed when people say how aloof he was.'

In the same warm vein was the experience of a schoolboy called Ralph Domican, whose grandfather, a Victorian figure with a bristling moustache, had played cricket with WG on Bedminster's ancient Clanage ground in Bristol. 'One day my grandfather announced it was time for me to be introduced to Gloucestershire cricket. I was brushed and scrubbed for the visit to the county ground. During the interval, my grandfather returned with a gentleman in white. I stood up immediately as was the custom.

'"I want you, my boy, to meet someone who is already a legend. Wherever you may be in the future, you can say you have met Mr Walter Hammond."

'He shook me by the hand. It was my birthday and the great cricketer presented me with a photograph, signed W R Hammond. I felt I was in the presence of God.'

Mr Domican was severely injured in the Bristol blitz, as a 19 year-old. His face had to be completely restructured and he needed 150 operations. He gradually conquered his inevitable complexes and returned to the county ground after the war. 'I was standing on the boundary when I was conscious of this cricketer near me. It was Hammond. He'd been in the RAF, of course, and must have noticed my face. I hesitated and then spoke, reminding him of our previous meeting. And I told him how sorry I'd been to lose his picture in the blitz. He went back to the pavilion and returned with another print. He signed it this time: "To Ralph. Nice to meet you again. Best wishes for the future . . . W R Hammond." Yes, I've heard all the stories about him. As far as I'm concerned, my experience only increased my hero-worship.'

Equally endearing is the memory of Mrs Iris Hutchings, whose father, a postman, delivered the letters to Mr and Mrs Hammond when they lived at Failand in the early years of their marriage. Wages were low and there were six children for the postman to feed and clothe in those difficult days. 'We used to look forward so much to Dad struggling home on his bike, his postal bag loaded with Victoria plums. Wally had them waiting for Dad when he'd finished his round. Not much you might think – but they were a godsend to us in those bleak 1930s. There were also mince pies for us at Christmas. We assumed Mrs Hammond had baked them. And Dad wasn't even a cricket fan. I, too, have read the nasty things about Wally. But from our experiences, he wasn't like that at all.'

So there was generosity in his nature, even if at times it seemed reluctant to surface. In South Africa, for instance, one neighbour of Hammond was Jack Cardew. They got on well and cricket was their conversational meeting point. 'Would you like one of my England caps?' Wally casually asked. The neighbour accepted it with much gratitude and immediately placed it in a glass case The great cricketer's treasures were never ostentatiously on view. Many of them were bundled away in a cupboard. Some were passed on to a museum but Wally's children were sadly left with few mementos to cherish. What happened to them? 'Maybe Mum had a bonfire,' is daughter Carolyn's wry conclusion.

The Cornish publisher Michael Williams has long been a Gloucestershire member. 'For me there is a tremendous sense of awe when I stand in front of the famous portrait in the Hammond room in Bristol. I never go to the county ground without doing that. The charisma, the colour and the complexity are all there. No ordinary man.'

Mr Williams is a Hammond connoisseur, aware of the weaknesses and the flaws, yet unyielding in his admiration. His treasured possessions include a specially commissioned framed drawing of the cricketer and three autographs. 'Interestingly, the signature changed. The older Hammond wrote with greater flourish and style. You wouldn't have thought they had been written by the same man.'

Just another riddle in the life of Walter Reginald Hammond. In terms of personality, he remained without any easily defined shape or purpose. He was never cerebral. Instead he was wonderfully physical – and when the body finally let him down, there wasn't too much left to sustain a fragile morale. The report of his memorial service, even in Bristol, was confined to the obscurity of page 11 in the local paper.

Recurrently I have gone back in my own mind to the question of parentage. To what extent would his stifling complexes – offset by the facade of assurance as manifested by the superficiality of his womanising – have varied if his father had come back from the war? Much of his childhood had been nomadic and then he found himself removed, by mysterious circumstances, already discussed, from the necessary proximity of his mother.

Yet Marion Hammond remains, in my conclusions, as a pivotal element in the story of her son. Quite by chance, the other day I came across a confidential aside that he once wrote: 'She has always been my inspiration and my wiser self'. It was a sweeping statement of affection and unrivalled regard. Those atypical sentiments of his, revealed at just about the time he was going into his second marriage, would appear to place his mother on a pedestal as the major influence of his life: ahead of the tragic Dorothy and probably Sybil, too.

I talked to Mrs Margaret Sealey, first cousin of Wally's boyhood friend, Billy Neale, and in effect the last surviving member of the Neale 'dynasty'. She was convinced that Wally's personality had been moulded by being an only child; she had noticed the considerable bond that existed between him and his mother. 'Ma' Hammond was indeed there to comfort him on that windswept Avonmouth quayside in April 1926. She had agonised over and then acquiesced, in the decision that he should become a county cricketer. She proudly went with him to the home matches; and she wept at his memorial service.

In her heart she didn't approve of the way he made a new home in South Africa. Gloucestershire's Sir Percy Lister was prepared to fly her out to see him, but she turned the offer down. The brief relationship with Sybil in austerity Britain had not prospered. Marion later came across from the Isle of Wight once a year to watch Gloucestershire. She knowledgeably applauded the off-drives but knew they fell short of greatness. Through glazed eyes, she looked in vain for Wally, the elegant, nonchalant, now-absent prince.

Did sport for Hammond, as for some other exceptional practitioners, come too easily for him? He played every game he essayed with a quite stunning prowess. He might have had a distinguished amateur career at golf and reached county level at tennis if he had treated either as more than pastimes. At cricket, he looked almost bored as he stood in mid-afternoon languor, hands on hips, at first slip. The reflexes did not fail him. As if to ease the monotony of the ordered ritual of a match, he had been known to take the wicket-keeper's gloves. This he did, proficiently as ever, for MCC against Victoria during the 1928-29 tour, when Leslie Ames was having treatment for a broken finger. Reports suggested that he performed with a natural poise, showing all the anticipation and intuition that served him so flawlessly at slip.

Once, at Southampton soon after the war, Hampshire's Jim

Bailey was proving annoyingly obdurate. Neither Lambert nor Cook were troubling him. By then, of course, Hammond was troubled by his fibrositis and well past his days as a (reluctant) seamer.

'Here, I suppose I'd better have an over,' he said to everyone's surprise.

He hardly bothered to pace out a run-up, but simply took a couple of steps and sent down a leg-break. Bailey was immediately caught at mid-on. At the end of the over, Hammond returned to the slips.

'It was remarkable. As if he still needed to show us how. But it was all done without fuss,' Cook remembered with transparent admiration. He had also taken the catch.

'Tiger' Smith had been playing first-class cricket since the year after Hammond was born. When the pair toured together in the West Indies, in 1925-26, 'Tiger' surveyed the lithe, balanced skills of the fledgling and said: 'You make me feel like a carthorse.' It was the effect he had on so many of his contemporaries.

It can be a perplexing business, when we choose to evaluate our heroes by picking our way through a labyrinth of private ambiguity, oscillating mood and penurious inhibition. Dr E K Scott, the England rugby centre three-quarter and captain, Cornish cricketer and superb cover point, played twice for Gloucestershire in 1937, still long enough for a teenager bereft of encouragement to form a distinct judgment. 'Hammond struck me as a disgruntled genius.' In the course of writing this book, I have been offered a plethora of infinitely less complimentary descriptions. Hammond must have deserved some of them. But then my spirit has been uplifted by the words and sepia memories of those who have seen and wondered at the shimmering beauty of his batting.

As Cardus put it: 'His cricket was, I think, his only way of self-realisation.'

Some years ago a well-known international sportsman was principal guest at the dinner of a leading cricket club. He had been liberally and imprudently wined before and during the meal. When it was his turn to speak, he staggered to his feet, utterly unable to summon up sufficient composure to recall what he had prepared.

'Gentle-um-men,' he began and then searched frantically for an opening thought or two. After an interminable delay, his face lit up. 'Gentlemen. I've got som'ing to shay to you.' Another long pause. 'Wally Hammond was one of the greatest cricketers who ever lived . . . . Yes, he bloody well was.' With that he slumped unconscious onto his seat. He probably hadn't even intended to mention Hammond. But the name simply rose unbidden from his befuddled memory, and his alcoholically blurred sentence said it all.

Let us drink to that.

Facts at a Glance

Walter Reginald Hammond was born at Buckland, Dover, Kent, on 19 June 1903; he died on July 1965 in South Africa.

Schools: Portsmouth Grammar School, Cirencester Grammar School

Played 405 matches for Gloucestershire, 1920-51

Made 85 Test appearances for England (20 as captain) from 1927-28 and 1946-47

Career record:	50,551 runs (av. 56.11) including 167 centuries
	732 wickets (av. 30.59)
	819 catches
Test record:	7249 runs (av. 58.45), including 22 centuries
	83 wickets (av. 37.80)
	110 catches

From 1933 he headed the national batting averages for eight summers in succession, a record that has never been equalled.

He scored more than 1000 runs in a season 17 times in England, and 5 times overseas. He went on to exceed 2000 runs on 12 occasions, and 3000 runs on 3. Three of his triple hundreds were for Gloucestershire; his highest score was 336 not out, in a Test match against New Zealand at Auckland in 1932-33.

He scored a hundred in each innings in seven matches.

He best bowling analysis was 9 for 23 against Worcestershire at Cheltenham, 1928.

Became an amateur in 1938.

Analysis of Test record:

Opponents	Matches	Innings	N.O.	H.S.	Runs	Average	100s	50s
Australia	33	58	3	251	2852	51.85	9	7
South Africa	24	42	7	181	2188	62.51	6	14
West Indies	13	20	2	138	639	35.50	1	1
New Zealand	9	11	2	336*	1015	112.77	4	1
India	6	9	2	217	555	79.28	2	1
TOTAL	85	140	16	336*	7249	58.45	22	24

Bibliography

Walter R Hammond, *Cricket My Destiny* (Stanley Paul, 1946)
Walter R Hammond, *Cricket My World* (Stanley Paul, 1948)
Walter R Hammond, *Cricket's Secret History* (Stanley Paul, 1952)
Gerald Howat, *Walter Hammond* (Allen & Unwin, 1984)
Ronald Mason, *Walter Hammond* (Hollis & Carter, 1962)
R E S Wyatt, *Three Straight Sticks* (Stanley Paul, 1951)
Alan Gibson, *The Cricket Captains of England* (Cassell, 1979)
Grahame Parker, *Gloucestershire Road* (Pelham Books, 1983)
E W Swanton, *Sort of a Cricket Person* (Collins, 1972)
E W Swanton, *Follow On* (Collins, 1977)
E W Swanton, *Gubby Allen* (Hutchinson/Stanley Paul, 1985)
Patrick Murphy, *'Tiger' Smith* (Lutterworth, 1981)
Ben Travers, *94 Declared* (Elm Tree Books/Hamish Hamilton, 1981)
Bill Bowes, *Express Deliveries* (Stanley Paul, 1949)
Tim Heald, *Dennis Compton* (Pavilion Books, 1994)
Bill Andrews, *The Hand that Bowled Bradman* (Macdonald, 1973)
Learie Constantine, *Cricketers' Carnival* (Stanley Paul, 1948)
Fred Root, *A Cricket Pro's Lot* (Edward Arnold, 1937)
Denis Compton, *Compton on Cricketers Past and Present* (Cassell, 1980)
Denis Compton and Bill Edrich, *Cricket and All That* (Pelham Books, 1978)
Denis Compton, *End of an Innings* (Oldbourne, 1958)
E M Wellings, *Vintage Cricketers* (Allen & Unwin, 1983)
Ian Peebles, *Talking of Cricket* (Museum Press, 1953)

Derek Lodge, *The Test Match Career of Walter Hammond* (Nutshell Publishing, 1990)

Godfrey Evans, *The Gloves Are Off* (Hodder & Stoughton, 1960)

Roger L Williams, *The Horror of Life* (Weidenfeld & Nicolson, 1981)

K C P Smith and M J Apter, *A Theory of Psychological Reversals* (Picton Publishing, 1975)

Wisden Cricket Almanack
Western Daily Press
Bristol Evening World
Bristol Evening Post
Bristol Times and Mirror
Bristol Evening News
The Times
The Daily Telegraph
Manchester Guardian
Gloucestershire & Avon Life
Journal of the Royal Society of Medicine

Index

Abel, Bobby, 39
Alexander VI, 44
Allen, Basil, 101, 130, 138, 165, 209, 253, 255, 266
Allen, David, 261, 262
Allen, Sir G O B (Gubby), 50, 85, 114, 116, 121, 122,130, 133, 134, 137, 166, 222, 264, 267
Alpass, H J Hampden, 51, 102, 181, 182, 229
Altham, H S, 101
Ames, Les, 9, 97, 119, 122, 125, 129, 132, 136, 166, 188, 189, 204, 214, 244, 253, 271
Andrews, Bill, 11, 12, 29, 123, 124
Apter, Michael, 54
Astill, Ewart, 27, 28, 32
Attlee, Clement, 198
Avery, Bert, 39

Bailey, Jim, 272, 273
Baker, George, 96
Baldwin, Sir Stanley, 188
Barnes, Binnie, 265
Barnett, C J, 10, 92, 116, 125, 126, 127, 136, 155, 161, 162, 163, 164, 165, 166, 167, 191, 209, 210, 238, 260
Barnett, C S, 162
Barnett, E P, 162
Barnett, 'Peggy', 191
Bartlett, Hugh, 120
Beaufort, Duke of, 211, 224, 236, 238, 253, 255
Bedser, A, 7, 135, 137, 253
Bedser, E, 4
Bell, A J, 129
Benaud, Richie, 250
Bloodworth, Bernie, 39, 42, 156, 189, 226, 253, 267
Boswell, James, 44
Botham, Ian, 123
Bowes, Bill, 121, 129, 131, 147, 148, 149, 164, 214
Bradford, Bishop of, 187
Bradman, Sir Don, 10, 56, 93, 111, 112, 113, 114, 115, 116, 118, 121, 124, 130, 137, 138, 143, 144, 145, 146, 147, 148, 149, 150, 151, 152, 153, 166, 167, 217, 218, 219, 221, 256
Britton, Jack, 211, 233, 234, 236, 243
Brodhurst, A H, 101
Brown, J T, 68
Brown, Ken, 105
Bubb, Tony, 63
Burrough, H D, 203

Buswell, W A, 92
Byron, Lord, 44

Calthorpe, Hon F S G, 18, 19, 25, 26, 27, 30, 34
Capone, Al, 44
Cardew, Jack, 270
Cardus, Sir Neville, 8, 25, 87, 88, 254, 273
Carr, Donald, 224, 262, 263
Chapman, Percy, 108, 111, 143
Churchill, Lord Randolph, 44
Clarke, Jack, 255
Clarke, Richard 55
Clay, J C, 105
Close, Brian, 85
Clutterbuck, Gilbert, 234, 236
Coates, Jack, 235
Cobham, Viscount, 253
Coleman, W L A, 70
Collins, A E J, 65
Collins, Betty, 81
Collins, George, 27
Colman, Ronald, 266
Columbus, Christopher, 45
Compton, Denis, 10, 53, 113, 116, 136, 147, 156, 157, 158, 209, 215, 218, 221, 256, 263, 264
Compton, Leslie, 157
Compton, Valerie, 198
Constantine, Sir Learie, 7, 10, 115, 120, 129, 147, 158, 159, 160, 167
Cook, Captain James, 260
Cook, Sam, 209, 210, 250, 266, 267, 273
Cooper, Henry, 17
Copson, Bill, 129
Crapp, Jack, 53, 55, 209
Crawley, Eustace, 30
Crawley, L G, 29, 30, 204
Creed, Len, 98
Cripps, Sir Stafford, 198
Curtis, Bill, 106

Dacre, Charlie, 10, 102, 153, 154, 155
Daniell, John, 78
Darling, Len, 117
Davis, Edgar, 81
Davis, Marjorie, 80, 81
Dawson, Eddie, 110
Delius, Frederick, 44
Dennett, George, 64, 68, 69, 80, 86, 131, 156
Dewes, J G, 263
Dexter, Ted, 263
Dipper, Alf, 24, 25, 40, 68, 70, 88, 131, 156,182, 268
Dollery, Tom, 253
Dolman, Harry, 254
Domican, Ralph, 269
Donnelly, Martin, 207
Douglas, J W H T, 103
Duckworth, George, 147
Durstan, Jack, 33

Eager, Desmond, 102
Eastman, Laurie, 103
Edrich, Bill, 9, 119, 134, 135, 204, 264
Edward VII, 43
Emmett, George, 51, 209, 226, 253, 265
Evans, Godfrey, 10, 221, 222

Farnes, Ken,104, 105, 116, 118, 130
Farson, Dan, 44
Fender, Percy, 39, 134
Fingleton, Jack, 133
Flaubert, Gustave, 44, 261
Fleetwood-Smith, Leslie O'Brien, 117, 147
Flexen, Ernie, 78, 79

Fowler, Robert St Leger, 26
Fox, Roy, 120
Franklin, Dr C J G, OBE, 46
Fraser, 'Pat', 64, 65, 67
Freeman, 'Tich', 97
Fry, C B, 51, 77

Geary, George, 109
Gibb, Paul, 216, 222
Gibson, Alan, 22, 50, 146, 147
Gilligan, Arthur, 25, 42
Gimblett, Harold, 11, 127, 265
Goddard, Tom, 6, 7, 10, 50, 91, 92, 93, 94, 99, 100, 106, 125, 126, 131, 163, 192, 209, 253, 257
Gough, Miss E M, 62
Grace, W G, 15, 23, 40, 89, 97, 98, 123, 146, 223, 269
Grant, Sir William, 253
Graveney, Ken, 52, 253
Graveney, Tom, 12, 51, 55, 227
Greenwood, Frank, 94
Gregory, Jack, 70, 87, 128, 129, 182
Griffith, S C (Billy), 253
Grimmett, C V, 93, 113, 114, 127, 129, 146, 221
Guest, Norah, 80

Hall, Catherine, 177-80
Hallam, Maurice, 253
Hammond, Carolyn (daughter) 248, 252, 257, 258
Hammond, Dorothy (first wife), 55, 162, 163, 172, 178, 184, 185, 186, 187, 188, 189, 190, 191, 192, 193, 194, 195, 196, 197, 198, 205, 230, 234, 238, 270, 271
Hammond, Marion (mother), 13, 18, 19, 20, 48, 49, 53, 59, 61, 63, 65, 66, 71, 86, 173, 174, 180, 181, 198, 220, 221, 222, 239, 253, 270, 271
Hammond, Roger (son), 198, 248, 252, 257
Hammond, Sybil (second wife), 15, 16, 17, 164, 185, 194-8, 205, 206, 214, 215, 220, 222, 223, 235, 239, 241, 242, 244, 248, 249, 251, 252, 253, 255-7, 264, 271
Hammond, (Gaureschi), Valerie (daughter), 17, 248
Hammond, William Walter (father), 13, 47, 48, 59, 61, 63
Hanham, 'Tot', 226
Hardinge, H T, 97
Hardstaff, Joe, 118, 208, 260
Harris, Lord, 29, 50 69, 72, 73, 255
Hassett, Lindsay, 134, 153
Hawke, Lord, 110
Hazell, Horace, 227
Headley, George, 115, 147, 160
Hendren, Patsy, 15, 74, 108
Henry VIII, 43
Henson, Col. Hugh, 50, 57, 266
Hill, Eric, 265
Hipkin, Joe, 103
Hitch, Bill, 268
Hobbs, Sir Jack, 15, 23, 106, 108, 124, 144, 145, 146, 218, 255
Hodgson, 'Paddy', 232
Hollies, Eric, 53, 265
Hollinshead, Cyril, 254
Holmes, A J, 222
Holmes, Percy, 27, 32
Hooper, Col. Bill, 231, 232

Hornibrook, P M, 92
Howard, Major Rupert, 52, 198, 215, 218, 222
Horwood, Prof Owen, 242, 244, 247, 248
Howat, Gerald, 3, 151, 171, 173, 247
Hudson, John, 165
Hugo, Victor Marie, 261
Hutchings, Iris, 270
Hutton, Sir Leonard, 5, 52, 87, 110, 118, 124, 128, 130, 132, 135, 149, 152, 164, 165, 209

Ibsen, Henrik, 45
Ikin, Jack, 153, 217, 219

Jackson, Sir F S, 122, 238
James, Grace, 172-6, 181
Jameson, Tommy, 32, 33
Jardine, Douglas, 15, 112, 115, 117, 118, 121, 122, 222, 236, 237
Jenkins, Roly, 126, 131, 211, 212
Jessop, Gilbert, 42, 123
Joel, S B, 33

Keats, John, 44
Kennedy, Ray, 17
Kilner, Roy, 18, 19, 27, 28
Kippax, A F, 93
Knott, Alan, 209

Lacey, Sir Francis, 39
Lambert, George, 4, 52, 105, 106, 125, 131, 132, 165, 271
Langridge, Jim, 154
Larwood, Harold, 15, 102, 103, 105, 109, 121, 127, 128, 130
Lee, Marshall, 245, 246
Lenin, Vladimir Ilyich, 44
Leo XI, 44
Leyland, Maurice, 15, 124
Lindwall, Ray, 128
Lister, Joe, 172, 186, 187, 189, 190, 196, 228
Lister, Sir Percy, 233, 238, 249, 250, 251, 252, 253, 255, 256, 272
Longrigg, E F, 253
Lowry, Tom, 114
Lyon, Bev, 3, 6, 10, 90-94, 103, 131, 134, 138, 153, 155, 189, 225, 226, 233, 253
Lyon, Dar, 11, 85

McCabe, Stan, 10, 93, 121, 138
McCool, Colin, 214
McCormick, Ernie, 118
McCrudden, Richard, 249
McDonald, Ted, 24, 25, 87, 88, 105, 126, 128
McLean, Roy, 252
Mailey, Arthur, 70
Malmesbury, Bishop of, 253
Martindale, E A, 10, 109, 115, 129
Maslin, Alec, 78, 80
Mason, Ronald, 3, 21, 51
Maupassant, Guy de, 44
Melville, Alan, 119, 120, 252
Mercer, Jack, 97
Meyer, R J O, 85
Miller, Keith, 128, 156, 207
Miller, Max, 119
Mills family, 63
Mills, Percy, 40, 42, 66, 131
Milton, Arthur, 226, 227, 267
Mitchell, Tommy, 89
Morris, Arthur, 218
Mortimore, John, 253
Munday, Mrs G, 60

Neale, Billy, 5, 8, 42, 46, 48, 63, 64, 65, 66, 77-9, 175, 178, 181, 207, 209, 232, 271
Neale, Hastings, 77

Neale, Maurice, 77
Neale, Phyllis, 135, 190, 191
Neale, 'Tiny', 77
Ness Harvey, Mrs E C, 198, 252
Norfolk, Duke of, 255
Nourse, Dudley, 252
Nuffield, Lord William, 197

Oakey, Dorothy, 175-7
Olive, Leonard, 66
O'Reilly, Bill, 127, 146, 166, 221, 244, 254, 267
O'Shea, J G, 45

Paish, Arthur, 99
Pannell, Harry, 188
Pannell, Muriel, 174
Parker, Charlie, 6, 24, 38, 42, 51, 52, 67, 68, 73, 74, 85, 90-94, 131, 132, 155, 156, 225, 226
Parker, Grahame, 24, 25, 90, 95, 154, 159
Payne, Jack, 155
Paynter, Eddie, 52, 118, 172
Pearce, Walter, 66
Pearson, Dickie, 147
Peebles, Ian, 33
Phillips, 'Ally', 163
Pilcher, Mr Justice, 197
Pollard, Dick, 208
Ponsford, W H, 93
Pope, H E, 198, 235, 239

Rait Kerr, Col. R S, 221, 225
Ranjitsinhji, Kumar Shri, 259
Reddy, Claude, 269
Richards, Barry, 248
Richards, Viv, 134
Richardson, Tom 260
Richardson, V Y, 93
Roberts, Fred, 40
Roberts, Ron, 261, 263
Robertson-Glasgow, R C, 51
Robins, Walter, 134
Robinson, D C, 23, 38
Robinson, Sir Foster, 23, 67, 70, 71, 253, 255
Robinson, Percy, 71
Robinson, Ray, 133
Root, Fred, 21, 27, 31, 130, 147, 151, 238
Roslyn, H E, 70, 72
Rowlands, W H, 183
Roy, Harry, 155

Sassoon, George, 17
Savage, Cyril, 176
Schubert, Franz, 44
Scott, Colin, 4, 165, 266
Scott, E K, 273
Sealey, Margaret, 271
Sellers, Brian, 220, 221
Shaw, George Bernard, 90
Shinwell, Emmanuel, 198
Sims, Eileen, 175, 176
Sinfield, Reg, 11, 22, 39, 51, 52, 92, 95, 98, 102-4, 129, 137, 138, 155, 192, 257, 266
Singh, Amar, 95
Smith, Sir Charles Aubrey, 266
Smith, E J 'Tiger', 18, 21, 27, 32, 273
Smith, Harry, 68, 74, 87, 92, 154
Smith, Jim, 116
Smith, K C P, 54-6
Smith, M J K, 262
Spencer, R W, 100
Squires, Stan, 208
Stephens, Dickie, 111
Stephenson, Capt. J W A, 129
Stoker, Bram, 44
Stone, Lew, 120
Stoneham family, 174, 175
Sutcliffe, Herbert, 124, 187
Swanton, E W, 29, 120, 130, 137, 222, 254, 267

Tate, Harry, 42
Tate, Maurice, 23, 42, 108, 130, 154, 254

Tennyson, Hon. Lionel, 25, 26, 27, 28, 30
Thomas, Harold, 244
Thomas, Noel, 205
Titmus, Fred, 262
Toulouse-Lautrec, Henri, 44
Travers, Ben, 112, 113
Trumper, Victor, 146
Tunnicliffe, Gilbert, 80
Tunnicliffe, John, 64, 68, 80. 86
Twining, R H, 253
Twiselton, Frank, 249, 250, 251, 252, 255, 256, 266
Tyler, Yvonne, 269

Valentine, Bryan, 137
Verity, Hedley, 134, 137, 148
Vizianagram, The Rajkumar of, 116
Voce, Bill, 100, 102, 105, 121, 130, 216, 217

Walford, M M, 265
Walker, Horace, 39
Wall, Tim, 129
Walter, Joe, 75
Walton, Jimmy, 76
Warner, Sir Pelham 'Plum', 6, 23, 33, 39, 41, 42, 49, 73, 100, 101, 108, 109, 115, 118, 126, 133, 135, 144, 156, 222, 225, 226, 228, 229, 236-8, 264, 266
Warr, J J, 224
Washbrook, Cyril, 52
Watson, Frank, 27, 33
Wedlock, Billy 'Fatty' 98
Wellard, Arthur, 29, 208
Wellings, E M, 9
West, Peter, 166, 246
White, J C, 12, 85, 123, 124
White, Luke, 262
Wicks, Ursula, 183, 184, 185, 195, 204, 205, 256
Wilkins, Richard, 239
Williams, Bert, 12-14, 22, 42, 69, 74-6, 174
Williams, Michael, 270
Wilson, Andrew, 74, 77
Wilson, Andy, 16, 102, 125, 132, 135, 138, 148, 161, 166, 207, 210, 232, 253
Wilson, Liz, 189, 253
Wilson, Woodrow, 44
Wiltshire, Graham, 211
Witchell, H G, 65
Woodcock, John, 260, 262
Woods, Sammy, 71
Wooller, Wilfred, 101
Wright, Doug, 126, 135, 137, 222
Wyatt, Molly, 109, 161
Wyatt, R E S, 26, 50, 86, 109-11, 116, 122, 129, 132-4, 137, 145, 161, 228, 265

Yardley, Norman, 215, 219-221